The Terrapins

Maryland Football

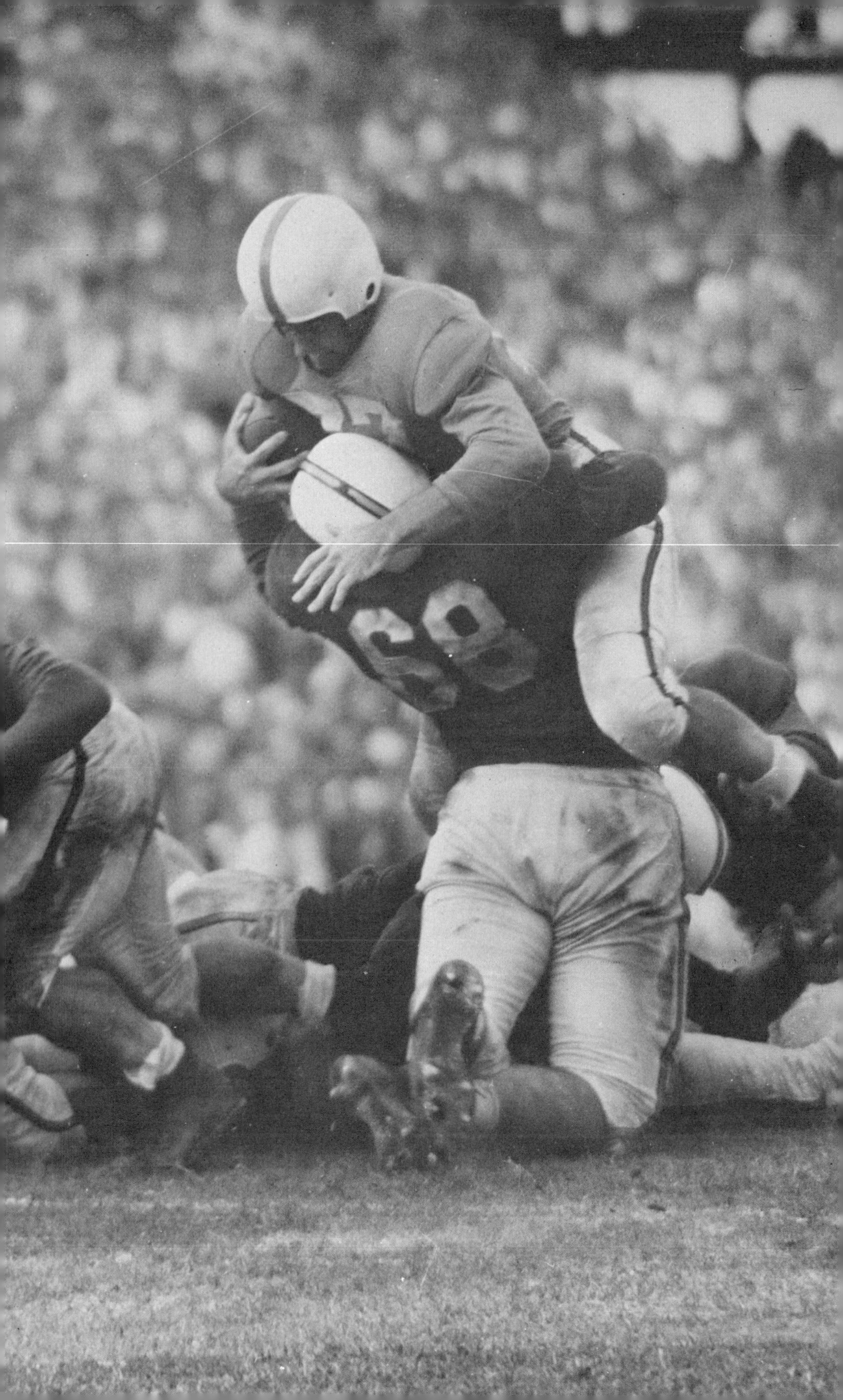

The Terrapins

Maryland Football

by
Paul Attner

THE STRODE PUBLISHERS
HUNTSVILLE, ALABAMA 35802

To My Wife, Mary Ellen,
Who Asked Why Not?

Library of Congress Number 75-012204
Standard Book Number 87397-066-7

Contents

Foreword

This book is not just the history of Maryland football but more the story of the individuals who contributed to building a tradition and to making this university the great institution it is today.

The book runs the gauntlet from the earliest struggles to championship teams and depicts the frustrations and jubilation that are so much a part of intercollegiate athletics.

As you become engrossed in this book you will recognize the names of many leaders in our community, state, and even nation. In reliving the stories of Maryland football these names will once again be an integral part of that tradition they helped build.

We are grateful to Paul Attner for the many, many hours he has devoted to this book. I am very proud that my years at Maryland can be included in the latter chapters.

Jerry Claiborne
Head Football Coach
University of Maryland

ACKNOWLEDGMENTS

To Al Heagy, a true gentleman, for his helping hand through the early years of Maryland football, for his views of the people and events he has witnessed, and for his patience;

To Jerry Claiborne, for his willingness to be interviewed countless times over the past three years;

To Therese Ryan, Steve Sigafoose, and Bruce Tanner of the Maryland sports information office, for their aid in my search for those sometimes elusive facts and vanishing scrapbooks;

To Betty Francis, Linda Kubany, and the rest of the wonderful women at Maryland who cooperated without hesitation when I needed help;

To Ray Murphy, for his hours devoted to reading proofs;

To Pam Igo, whose dedicated typing made all of this a reality;

To Pat and Mary Beyer, whose knowledge of the alphabet aided in organizing the list of all-time lettermen;

To David Strode Akens, for his vision in creating this sports series, and for his advice and guidance throughout the production of this book;

To Burt Shipley, Geary Eppley, Bosey Berger, Randy White, Jack Faber and all the other Maryland coaches and players—former and present—who contributed their knowledge and time to these pages;

And especially to three people—my mother and father, who gave themselves as selflessly to the production of this book as they have to my welfare all these years,

And Jack Zane, a friend, whose information, perspiration, humor, and trust made this project possible. Thank you, Jack.

Paul Attner

Saturday Ghost

On those crisp fall Saturday afternoons when the leaves are changing to bright reds and yellows and the sun engulfs the sky, a ghost haunts Byrd Stadium. He has both tormented and inspired those men who pace the sidelines and coach the University of Maryland football teams. He serves as the measure of success, the criterion of failure, the symbol of excellence, for all those who succeed him.

The ghost of Jim Tatum. He haunts Maryland football as perhaps no legend has haunted any other college sports team. Maryland football is Jim Tatum. Yet it is also more than Jim Tatum.

It is a rugged band of students growing long hair to protect their heads on tackles. The year is 1892.

It is a football captain so rugged he serves as a blocking dummy for the rest of the team. The year is 1896.

It is a 138-pound youth who looks so frail he is asked not to try out for the team, yet eventually winds up captain of the squad and president of the school. The year is 1905.

It is a quarterback lured back to the team by a plank steak to become a six-letter man in the sport. The year is 1912.

It is a sturdy fullback who knocks out four opponents on four straight plays and then becomes a professional on Sunday and runs for his life from angry townspeople. The year is 1920.

It is a Yale coach so confident of beating Maryland that he goes to Princeton on game day to scout, and winds up coaching his team on the phone. The year is 1923.

It is a long-legged end who is so sure he will not play that he does not bring hip pads along, yet scores two touchdowns to tie mighty Yale. The year is 1929.

It is an ex-Marine named Sarge who is so valuable that he sleeps on a feather bed. The year is 1931.

It is the son of acrobats, who never played football in high school, yet becomes perhaps Maryland's all-time player. The year is 1936.

It is a middle-aged coach who designed the T-formation but forgets how to handle his players. The year is 1942.

It is a young, hard-nosed ex-Alabama end who once played a game with a broken leg and is known simply as Bear. The year is 1945.

It is the Queen of England smiling as happy players carry their coach to her feet. The year is 1957.

It is a sophomore quarterback in his first start throwing enough touchdown passes to beat mighty Penn State. The year is 1961.

It is a pro coach walking away from two straight league championships for the good life of college. The year is 1966.

It is a quiet hulk of a player who can run faster than most backs and is stronger than most anyone and wins a trophy as the nation's best lineman. The year is 1974.

And it is the return to the glories of the Tatum years since the hiring of Jerry Claiborne, who showed Maryland could win in football without the sunny man from South Carolina stalking the sidelines waving his 10-gallon hat.

Maryland football is Curley Byrd, the only football player to move from football coach to president of the same major university. From 1905, when he first came to Maryland, to 1954, when he retired to run for governor, Byrd was Mr. Maryland. The football team and the school were molded in his image and grew in the direction he engineered.

This is Curley Byrd's story too.

It is also Bob Ward's. And Jack Scarbath's. And Bob Pellegrini's. And the Modzelewskis'. And Bill Guckeyson's. And Bosey Berger's. And Snitz Snyder's. And Leroy Mackert's. And Untz Brewer's. And Burt Shipley's. And all the other marvelous athletes who have played for Maryland since 1892.

It is a history filled with laughter and defeat, with national championships and All-Americans, with winless seasons and discouragements, with glowing records and heroics.

It is the story of the football team that struggled for years with a college still trying to find an identity. It is the story of a football team that picked on Yale, that won under Bryant, that flourished under Tatum, that returned under Claiborne.

It is the story of many games, of one game. It is the story of a Saturday afternoon in September of 1974 when 54,412 people jammed into Byrd Stadium to witness the return of Maryland football to the big time. The opponent was Alabama. The opposing coach was Bear Bryant, now a legend in his own time. A record crowd was lured to a stadium where, just four years before, a game could attract only 12,000 hardy souls.

It is the story of a fine October morning in 1892 when a crowd of a few hundred witnessed the start of this football madness at Maryland.

Here is the story of Maryland football.

A Fine October Morning

A surprisingly large crowd had gathered by the time Maryland Agricultural College's first official football game began on a fine October morning in 1892. But anticipation had not drawn the spectators to St. John's field in Annapolis. They merely were wandering by, killing time until the afternoon, when their beloved Navy team would oppose Princeton.

What they saw transpire that morning did little to whet their appetite for more football. St. John's, which already had been playing the game for almost a decade, toyed with the boys from the farmers' school, winning 50-0.

The Maryland players had not expected a better fate. But the game at least finally gained campus-wide recognition for the team that manager Sothoron Key and 13 players had labored so hard to organize. It gave the 90 or so students at what was once described as "the little battered college on the hill" something to identify with in a time when little else was going right for them or M.A.C.

Maryland Agricultural College long had had an identity problem. The difficulty began with the name. Meant to be a compliment by its founders, the word "agriculture" had become an embarrassment. Three pages of the school's initial eight-page catalogue were used to explain away the term. And there was this trouble with presidents. The school could not seem to keep one around for long. In the 27 years since the Civil War had ended, nine presidents had quit, enrollment had dropped, and money was scarce.

By 1892 another president, the school's 14th since classes began in 1859, had been hired to head a faculty of 12 and administer a budget of $50,000. The new head man, Capt. R. W. Silvester, was to bring stability to this tiny, privately run military school in the next 20 years. He also did not stand in the way of formal athletics.

Instead an athletic association was formed in his first year, and each of the students was assessed a $10 athletic fee to sponsor a football and baseball team. For the aspiring football players, it was a welcome event.

For two years they had been trying to get a team underway. In 1890, a year after a sophomore named George Hoblitzell had begun talking up the sport, 13 students challenged two high schools, Sandy Spring and Laurel, to games. They lost both. In 1891 another informal team lost to Hyattsville High and Gallaudet College but beat Sandy Spring 10-0.

The player-coach of that team, George Brooks, was not around in 1892, nor were many of the other pioneers on those first two teams: Pete Perry, Lawrence Towers, Dan Annan, George Calvert, Steve Gambrill (later a congressman), Hezekiah Best, J. B. Latimer, Mason Childs, Percy Seibert, Hazel Cashell, John Grove, E. D. Johnson, Chester Kemp, Charles C. Manning, or F. W. Besley.

College officials tried to help. They asked Howard Strickler, a graduate of Randolph Macon and professor of physical education, to coach. But Strickler chose to be a player and it fell to a student, W. W. Skinner, the team captain, to do the coaching. Until 1902, when student pressure forced the hiring of a full-time coach, squad captains inherited Skinner's duties.

Skinner had quite a conglomeration to direct. Most of the players were new to this rough-and-tumble sport, and even the presence of faculty members Strickler and Roland Harrison in the lineup did not help. Indeed the boys were outfitted much better than they played, what with their white uniforms adorned with capital letters "M.A.C.," complete with the periods, and their high-piled hair that served as natural helmets.

The season got worse following the St. John's loss. Johns Hopkins was next, and this time the defeat was even more decisive: 62-0. "By overwhelmingly defeating the Maryland Agricultural College at Clifton Park," said the *Baltimore American*,

Maryland's first official football team, 1892. Front row, left to right: Samuel Harding, Dick Pue, William A. Wooters, James W. Lawson. Center: W. W. Skinner. Second row: Barnes Compton, Gustavius Z. Graff, W. T. Rollins, A. B. Worthington, Pearse Prough, J. G. Bannon, Sothoron Key, manager. Top row: Clifton Fuller, Parker Mitchell, Clay Weimer.

"the football team of Johns Hopkins University showed what good material for athletics there is at the University, and what good management and training has done. Hopkins' first touchdown was made in 40 seconds. Strickler, Rollins, Worthington, and Pugh played best for Maryland."

The third and final loss was most embarrassing. Episcopal High held Maryland scoreless again 16-0. Pearse (Shorty) Prough made the defeat even more significant with his version of a wrong-way run.

Prough later recalled that the play started with him positioned on the left flank in the team's V-formation. Suddenly the ball popped his way, he picked it up and started running – toward his own goal. By the time he reached his own 20, his teammates had gotten his attention. He turned around and got back to the Episcopal 15, a net gain of 35 yards, before being tackled.

"Maryland showed an unaccreditable ignorance of football," is how the *Episcopal High Monthly Chronicle* put it.

It was not surprising. The founders of the school had not included sports in their dreams when they established an institution to elevate the ordinary farmer to prosperity and cultural refinement. The second agricultural college in the western hemisphere, it was built with state sanction on 420 acres of land belonging to a founding father, Charles B. Calvert. By 1892 a town known as College Park had sprung up near the school and a train station was established three-quarters of a mile from campus.

Campus life was spartan. Reveille was at 6:30 a.m., inspection at 7:30. An hour of military drills followed four hours of classes. After an hour for lunch, classes commenced again for two more hours. Prep school enrollment started at age 10, college enrollment at 15.

Yet even in this atmosphere, the failures of 1892 inflamed, rather than doused, the athletic fire at Maryland Agricultural College. President Silvester talked Levin Lake, Sr., a member of the board of trustees, into giving a personal note of $5,000 to erect a gymnasium. Previously students had used a board shed with a sawdust floor. The football team expanded its schedule to six games, and emerged as the school's first successful sports enterprise by winning all six.

The team had more help the second time around. Fred Lull, a chemist at the school's experiment station who had played three years at Rutgers, was a guard. Fellow faculty members Gustavius Graff, a librarian, and Harrison, a mathematician and an outstanding back, along with Strickler, also were team members. Strickler, still supposedly in charge of the squad but really an unofficial athletic director, confined his duties to quarterback while captain Samuel (Pop) Harding coached. Barnes

Maryland's first undefeated football team, the squad of 1893, was captained by Samuel (Pop) Harding (holding football), and included four members of the faculty.

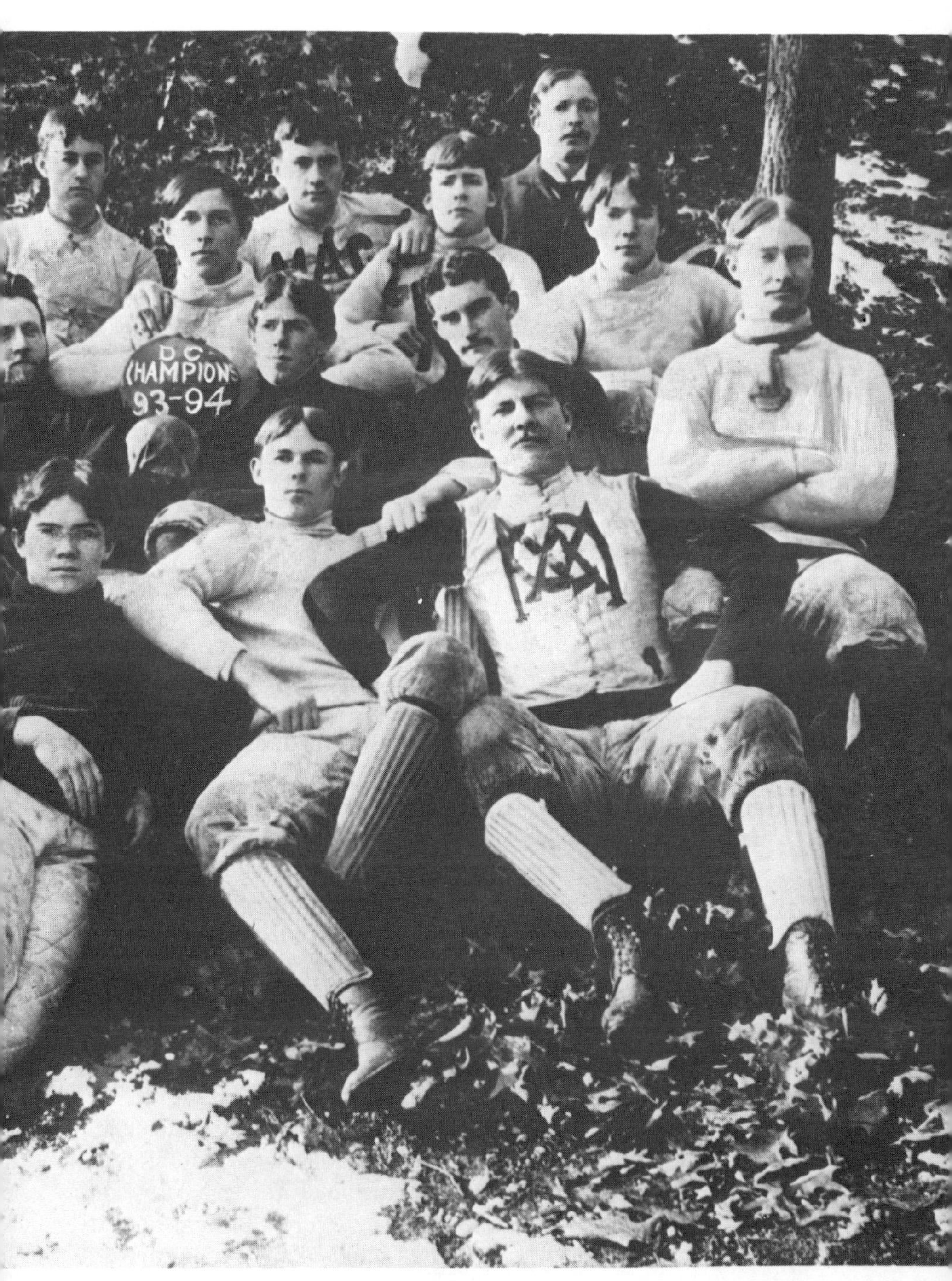
D.C.
CHAMPIONS
93-94

Compton, one of the best of the school's first players, was a halfback.

Eastern High in the District of Columbia was M.A.C.'s first official football victim, falling 36-0 as Sherman Rollins, Compton, Dick Pugh, and Strickler scored touchdowns. Central High was also shut out 10-0 and then Baltimore City College lost 18-0. But those were just preludes to the school's initial major conquest, a 6-0 drubbing of St. John's.

"By defeating St. John's today, M.A.C. won the collegiate championship of Maryland, having defeated Baltimore City College who has this season beaten both Western Maryland and Washington College," reported the *Washington Evening News*, which continued:

"The first half opened with St. John's in possession of the ball, but it was lost on the 25-yard line. M.A.C., after playing the wedge twice, sent Strickler around left end for a touchdown after a run of 79 yards. Compton kicked goal.

"When the second half began, M.A.C. had the ball. After playing 20 minutes St. John's claimed a false decision by the referee and left the field."

St. John's had a right to be upset over the officiating. As an unknown writer in an official Maryland publication confessed some 21 years later, the only touchdown came about "when M.A.C., aided by half the student body, shoved the ball over the goal line. St. John's left the field, and not without cause, as the finish of the game was, to say the least, unseemly."

But the writer could not resist one dig at the arch rival. The star of St. John's, he reported, was a professional wrestler.

That was not the end of M.A.C.'s problems. After beating Western Maryland 18-10, M.A.C. played the Orient Athletic Club from the District. The athletic club lost 16-6 but the captain told the *Washington Post* that its opponent "was the roughest he ever met. He says the Orients left the field because the college team refused to abide by the decision of the referee."

Complaints aside, the season had been a highly successful one and spurred formation of the Intercollegiate Football Association of Maryland, which also included Western Maryland, Johns Hopkins, Washington College, and Baltimore City College. The league was the brain child of W. W. Skinner, the

1892 quarterback and coach who now was the team manager. Skinner later was a member of the school's board of regents for 26 years and its chairman for five.

M.A.C.'s hopes of taking the initial conference title in 1894 collapsed against St. John's, which won 22-6 without any of the previous year's problems. "The game was a hard, well-fought contest throughout, marked by gentlemanly feeling which characterized the players on both sides," said the *Baltimore American.* "There was no wrangling amongst the players, nor with the umpires, no slugging."

But St. John's had pulled a fast one on its unsuspecting rival. Another school, Mt. St. Mary's, reported that St. John's "used two or three Lehigh players for the game with Maryland Agricultural to settle the State championship."

Under the direction of captain George Harris, M.A.C. wound up splitting six games, including a victory over Georgetown's second string. Hopkins was originally supposed to supply the competition but called the game off when its captain became ill. Georgetown included seven regulars in its lineup and then claimed a victory by forfeit when M.A.C., ahead 6-4, refused to play in the dark.

The star of that game was M.A.C.'s first football hero, a raw-boned ex-player from Washington's Business High, Grenville Lewis. He was to direct the school to its most prolific year in the wild, wonderful '90s.

The Lewis Way

"In 1894, Skinner and Harris called at my home in Washington and finally persuaded me to come to Maryland as fullback," Grenville Lewis wrote to Maryland sports historian Bill Hottel in 1953. "My major objective had been to get an education but the student body was interested in my playing fullback on the team."

So began the college career of this strong-willed athlete who even overcame the objections of the school's military commandant to keep a floundering football program going at the small agricultural school.

Before he graduated in 1897, Grenville Lewis was hailed by the M.A.C. yearbook as the greatest athlete developed at the school. Although a standout first baseman, his true love was football, which he played recklessly and without fear, in the spirit of the game before the turn of the century.

And how tough is tough? Teammates recalled years later at a reunion that he served as their human tackling dummy – and survived. Players of his stature had to be tough. A typical game was described in one paper: "When a man started to run he was tackled by the fullback, the halfback and the holdback. Then the whole team piled on top. It was an awful mixup. Arms, legs, and noseguards were all that could be distinguished."

Lewis had more problems off the field than on. After doing the bulk of the scoring for the 1894 team, he was elected captain for 1895. But the new Commandant of Cadets, Lt. Clough Overton, no lover of the rowdy sport, wanted no part of the team. Funds for equipment were cut off and he refused to delay supper formation so the squad could practice more than 45 minutes.

"There was such unanimous resentment that the boys themselves decided to not have a team," Lewis said.

Fortunately Lewis was able to smooth things out for the 1896 season. Again he was captain, and for the first time, he instituted training rules and a rugged preseason workout schedule.

"The team had little or no experience as players and I thought it necessary therefore, if we were to make any kind of a showing, that they must be sixty-minute men and depend upon superb physical condition," Lewis said. "To that end I persuaded President Silvester to give us a training table which he wholeheartedly did. Meals could be served after the regular evening meal; this permitted them to practice the full time and eat afterwards. Through the training table, I also controlled the food they could eat, therefore, discontinuing coffee and sweets from the bill of fare.

"The president generously arranged for us to get an unlimited supply of milk from the experiment station which was the only beverage served at the training table. All men on the training schedule increased their weight from twelve to eighteen pounds per man in spite of the strenuous routine I put them through."

Each morning the players took a 10-mile run. The practice field took care of any other soft spots. It was four-fifths gravel. Money and pants were scarce so when first stringers finished practice they gave their pants to reserves. Indeed, as the yearbook, *Reveille*, said, "Captain Lewis was not a man to do things by halves."

After all this, the season was almost anticlimactic, but in typical M.A.C. style, still controversial. The team played three practice games, losing two, but ended the regular season undefeated, winning five games and tying two.

Superstition helped in one contest. Lewis wore a bright and colorful sweater against Central High, and M.A.C. was losing at the end of the half. So his teammates made him put on his old, ragged jersey, and M.A.C. rallied to win 10-6 on a Lewis touchdown. Bethel Military Academy fell 20-10 although the

M.A.C. team spent half time jogging around the field to keep warm after discovering intermission accommodations were not available.

The Farmers, as M.A.C. was called, saved the best for last. Against what was then known as the University of Maryland in Baltimore, Lewis and Co. were down at the two yard line in the final quarter. Night had set in and the referees never noticed that the university team had slipped in three extra players. The Farmers did not score, the game ended in a 0-0 tie, but on Monday the university captain conceded the contest to Lewis.

One of the Farmers' tackles, Harry Howard, had difficulty stopping a far heavier opponent during the game. Finally, with his face bruised and bleeding, he asked to be removed. Lewis instead suggested he grab the man by his stomach and hold on. Howard did, and suddenly all types of running holes opened up.

Lewis had to overcome a major internal problem among the players to keep the season going. He caught halfback Charley Cabrera smoking and kicked him off the team. A group of "sideline quarterbacks," Lewis said, banded together to force his reinstatement. To accomplish this they resurrected an athletic committee of professors, which supposedly had been set up to run the team, but never interfered.

"I asked Gerry Schenck, then Battalion Major, to march the battalion into the assembly hall following supper that evening and issue my personal ultimatum: elect a new captain and coach or disband the Athletic Committee," Lewis said. "I left and they voted to keep me."

Lewis had durable players. Ben Watkins, one of the early fine running backs at the school, once ran head first into a goal post. Thinking it was a tackler, he backed off and rammed it again.

"The 1896 season," admitted the *Reveille*, "was a success beyond the fondest hopes of the management."

Lewis was gone in 1897 and there were still no full-time coaches among the now 19 faculty members at M.A.C. When the Farmers dropped to a 2-4 season, beating only two high schools, the sports editor of the *Reveille* had seen enough.

"We have no opportunity for the development of our teams except through knowledge transferred from one student

Grenville Lewis, holding the football as captain of the 1896 team, was so tough he served as the squad's tackling dummy.

to another and by observation," said the yearbook. "The only remedy is to procure the services of a competent coach who will originate and apply new ideas before they have gone down upon the innumerable pages of history. The expense would be little and the returns inestimable. As it is we have held our own among our contestants but by aid of such a movement we would ... far excel those who have been classed with us or have even defeated us."

The administration did not heed the call, at least not yet, but it did hasten the end of Strickler's overseer reign. He resigned in the spring of 1898 and was replaced by Dr. T. B. Spence, vice-president of the college.

Students, however, still coached the team. John Lillibridge guided the 1897 squad to its losing season and his replacement, Frank Kenly, had as much misfortune the next year. The Farmers again won only twice in seven games, but at least this time one victory was over a college, Rock Hill.

Sam Cooke, who had inherited Lewis' fullback spot the year before, had an especially rough time. Against Western Maryland he managed a wrong-way punt.

"Fullback Cooke of the visitors must have had eyes in the back of his head," wrote the *Western Maryland Journal.* "From midfield, he kicked the ball over his head and backward 25 yards, where it was recovered by Western Maryland. A touchdown soon resulted."

Nor was the Farmers' agricultural reputation enhanced a few games later in a 16-0 loss to Hopkins. "Our boys met M.A.C.," said the Hopkins paper, "and taught them a thing or two about football. We were very much surprised to find that the Farmers not only could not play football, but also seemed to be ignorant concerning the proper condition in which to keep an athletic field. Everyone thought the agriculturalists would surely know how to rake a field. Perhaps the professors hadn't taught them as yet." The game was played in a cow pasture.

The *Reveille* again was campaigning for a coach in the spring of 1900 after a third straight poor year, in which M.A.C. won only one game in five and just cancelled the rest of the contests. Cooke, the captain, started the downward trend by breaking an arm in the first contest. Nor did things get better in 1900, when the Farmers were 3-4-1 against an all-high school schedule. Finally, the bottom fell out in 1901. In nine games Maryland won just once, against a Marine team from the District. Even the Gallaudet reserves beat the Farmers.

The incensed *Reveille* finally was to have its way.

Finally, A Coach

In 1900 a scholarly native of Snow Hill, Maryland, was hired as an English professor at M.A.C. but he soon was organizing the speech department and chairing the Athletic Board. In that latter post, he made two of the most important decisions in the history of football at the college.

Charles Richardson, who would stay 40 years before retiring in 1939, was given the duty in 1902 of hiring a full-time football coach. The Farmers had struggled through five dismal losing seasons, and both the students and faculty had had enough. For a salary of $300 he employed D. John Markey, a businessman from Frederick, Maryland, who had played sandlot football for 12 years before attending Western Maryland, where he played and helped coach. Markey was to be the first of six hired coaches in 10 years before Richardson settled on a 23-year-old lad with curly hair, H.C. Byrd.

Markey, who later became a general of the Army, took over when Maryland Agricultural College was still very much in the small time of the football world. His first schedule had games against nine colleges, all local rivals except Delaware. Markey, despite his status as coach, decided he would continue to play – as a quarterback, halfback, and lineman.

Legend has it that college officials approved the decision after one of the players, halfback Ed Brown, had his life threatened by Georgetown fans and refused to play. Markey took his place. His presence did not help as the Hoyas won 27-0.

Nor did he help that much in any of the remaining games.

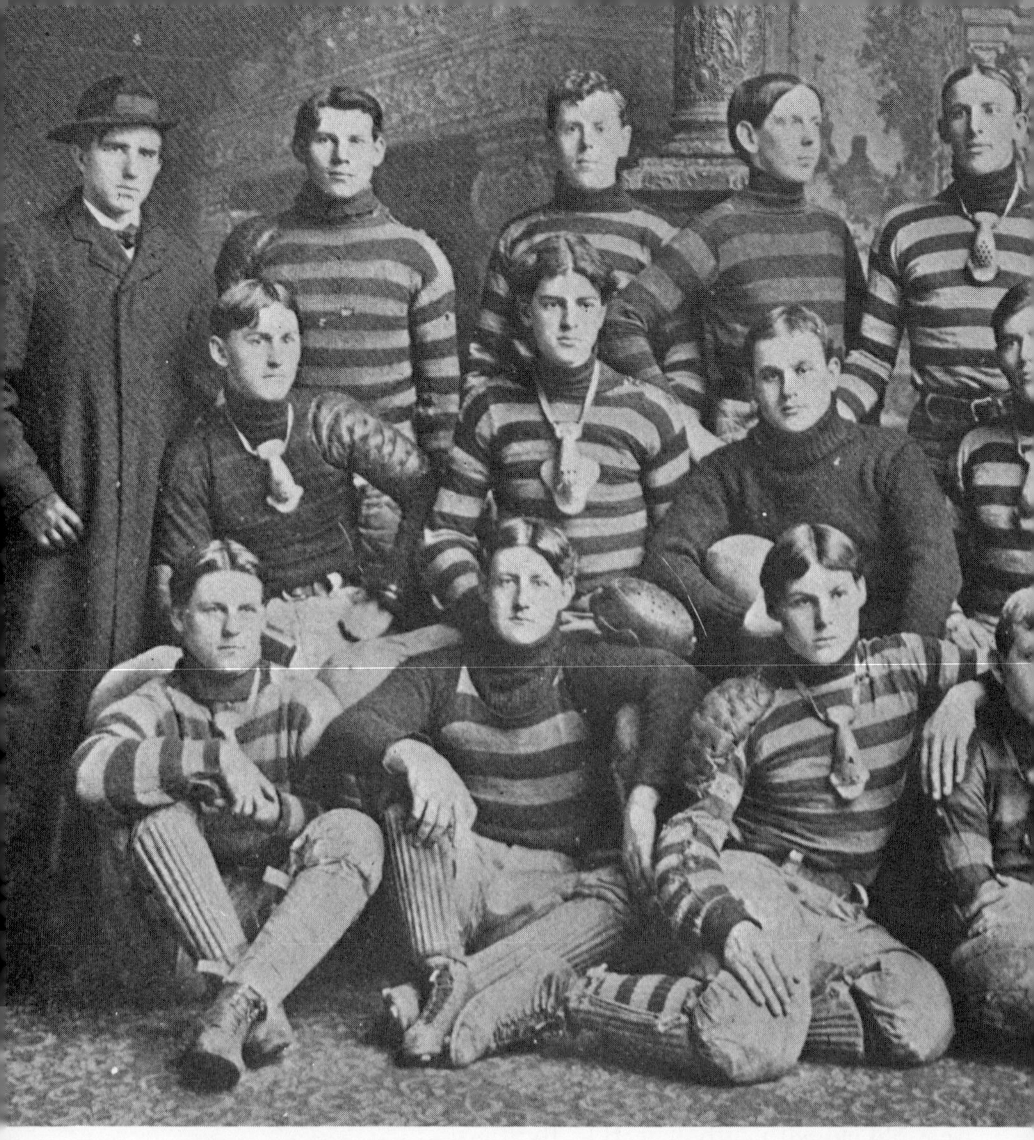

The Farmers won only two times, losing five, and tying two. The most spectacular victory came against Columbian (now George Washington) College. Just as Columbian was about to score a touchdown, the ball was fumbled and Harry (Big Easy) Watts picked it up and raced the length of the field for the winning touchdown in the 11-10 triumph.

Markey's past caught up with him in the finale against Delaware. M.A.C., according to the Delaware yearbook, padded its team with ringers.

"Our opponents were from Maryland Agricultural College, or, at least that was the name they had. It was learned that

D. John Markey (far left, in coat) ended the tradition of captains coaching the team when he was hired as coach in 1902. He had success at first, thanks to players like Harry (Big Easy) Watts (middle row, second from left), and Wilbur Stoll (first row, far right).

some of them had been down to College Park at sometime during their careers. The excuse given after the game by M.A.C. for padding their team was that they had no agreement with us to play bonafide students and that we had made no kick against padding." The game ended in a 0-0 tie.

Watts was Markey's captain in 1903, and led the Farmers to their most successful campaign since 1896. He had developed into a better-than-average kicker and runner, but he was outshone by another halfback, Wilbur Stoll.

Stoll scored 10 touchdowns during the 5-4-1 season and added two extra points. The *Reveille* noted he was best "at arguing," but most important, his highest ambition "was to play football."

"He made a record for himself as a ground gainer that was not exceeded by any player in the State," Markey said. "He proved himself about the best all-around player on the team."

Stoll was responsible for two of the wins. He scored four touchdowns against Washington College (28-0) and ran 85 yards against Maryland-Baltimore (11-0). But Markey's controversial playing status again dominated the campaign. In the Thanksgiving finale against Columbian, his presence was protested, but when Columbian was found to be using pros too, Markey played. He scored the game's only touchdown.

That proved to be the last great moment of his tenure at M.A.C. In 1904 he began coaching only two days a week, commuting from Frederick, while Buck Wharton, a chemistry professor and brother-in-law of Professor Richardson, coached the other four days. The result: a 2-4-2 season, with the only significant victory coming over Gallaudet, the school's first over the District university.

The low moment came against Mt. St. Mary's. Three times M.A.C. walked off the field when the Mount's coach yelled "Slug 'em boys" from the sidelines, only to be talked into returning by Markey.

But it was Markey's turn to leave M.A.C. before the start of the 1905 season. He was released by Richardson, who began searching for a replacement soon after the school had become somewhat of a maverick in the sport.

There was nothing soft about football in the early 1900s. Eligibility rules, or rules of any kind for that matter, were rare. Maryland Agricultural College decided, however, it would be different and released a written philosophy on football. Even the *Reveille* realized the new policy "was radical in the extreme."

M.A.C. declared that it would "henceforth foster clean athletics and would offer no inducements to any athlete, no matter if it lost every contest in which its team might take part." The *Reveille* applauded the action. "About all a man had to do to qualify for a college team if he was an athlete was to let his wants become known," the yearbook said. "They were never refused if he was a capable performer in any branch of

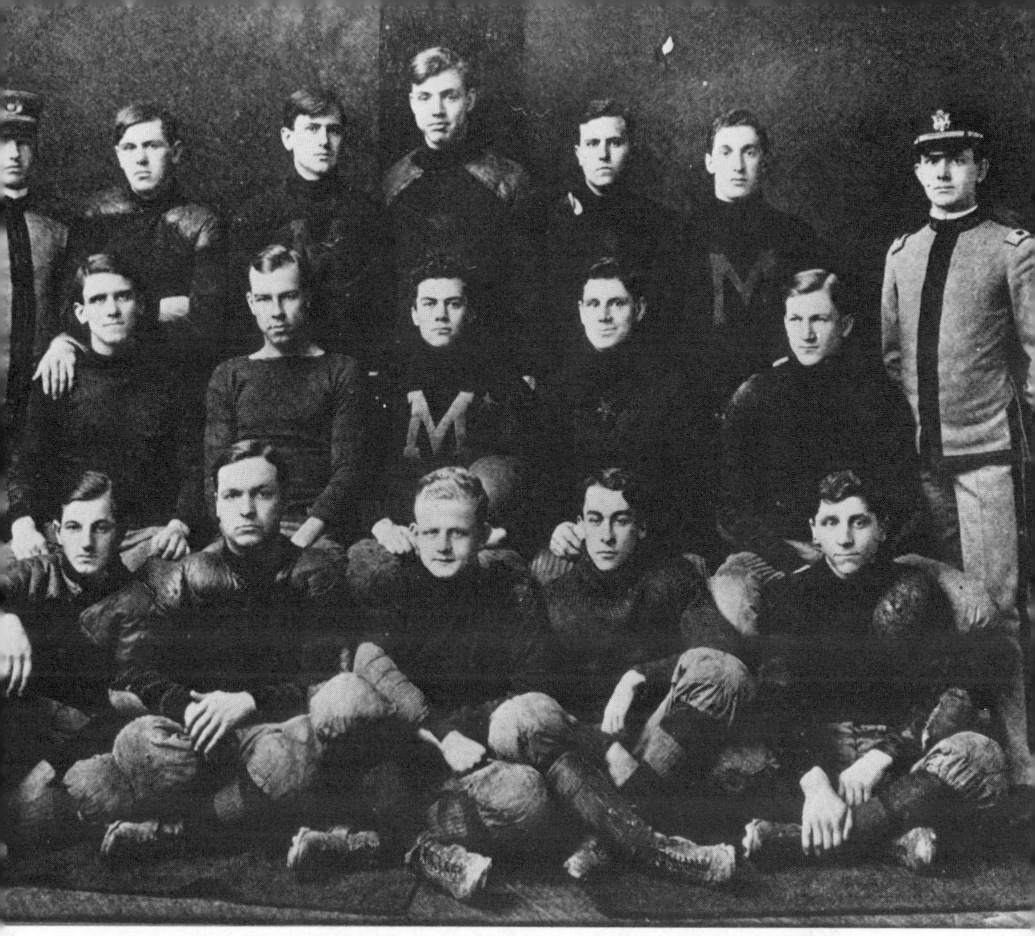

Curley Byrd (holding ball) was the captain and star player of the 1907 team but he still could not prevent a losing season. Barney Cooper (to right of Byrd) was the best running back.

sports."

M.A.C.'s decision came at a time when football manager Ferdinand Zerkel felt it necessary to explain in a letter to parents of the team's players why their boy "should play football."

Said Zerkel: "Your sons, Dear Mothers, will be happy in, and pleased with, their football work. They will enjoy every hour spent in practice, and every second spent in contest. They will learn to love their tasks upon the gridiron and they will take a deep and proper pride in their own prowess and power. They will learn to place confidence in themselves and appreciate rightfully their own abilities."

Into this milieu walked Fred K. Nielson, graduate of the University of Nebraska and lawyer at the State Department. Nielson was allowed to keep working at his regular job while supervising the football program at College Park. What he saw there did not please him.

"They must be running a kindergarten out here instead of a college," he said after surveying the squad in September. The team averaged 147 pounds. Three stars from 1904 were faculty members, and under the school's new policy, which barred anyone but "legitimate students" from playing, they could be only spectators. Two others, Stoll and center Jim Wharton, were kicked off the team. A third was not allowed to play by his mother, despite Zerkel's letter.

Somehow Nielson came up with a 6-4 record, even after trying to discourage a 138-pound youngster from playing. The player was H. C. (Curley) Byrd, who did not listen to his coach and finally wound up starting by the end of the season.

Nielson built his team around captain Barney Cooper, a solid halfback, and tackle Bill Bowland. The Farmers started quickly, beating Baltimore Poly and Gallaudet before losing to Western Maryland and then Navy. Byrd played his first game at end against the Midshipmen, was praised by the *Washington Post* for his defensive work and won a first-string position.

Nothing, however, topped a trip to William and Mary. Not only did M.A.C. win the game 17-0 but the *Reveille* reported that two tackles fell in love with two Williamsburg girls. Both the writer and the players wanted to return in 1906.

Nielson was most pleased with a 27-5 triumph over St. John's, M.A.C.'s first over its rival since 1893. Cooper scored twice and Alonzo McNutt added another on an 85-yard touchdown run. Byrd got the fifth score on a 35-yard end-around play.

Said the *Reveille*: "It was a team which shunned a mean action upon the football field more than it would have shunned the plague. A team that would have lost every game rather than take an unfair advantage of an opponent."

Nielson's honeymoon lasted one season. His 1906 squad produced five wins in eight games, a disappointment considering he had a horde of experienced players returning. Navy was held to a 12-0 victory and St. John's again was beaten 20-4 but the most significant game was the finale against Washington College. Curley Byrd was moved to quarterback and scored twice in the 35-0 victory.

The Farmers had a new coach in 1907. Nielson's bid for a raise was denied and he switched to George Washington University. M.A.C. turned to another former Nebraska player, Charles W. Melick, who was employed in the agricultural experiment station at College Park.

The magic of Byrd as captain and quarterback was not enough to prevent a reversal of the progress in the program since 1903. In losing six of nine games, the Farmers were plagued by a poor offense. Against St. John's, they were inside the five yard line four times and could not score. Against Gallaudet, Byrd raced more than 80 yards to the one, and again M.A.C. could not score.

Byrd graduated that spring, "his paths astrewn with broken hearts of guileless maidens whom he has 'loved to death', he-siren that he is, and never has our handsome Don Juan been found 'de trop' in feminine society or impromptu tete-a-tetes." But he would be back in a few years.

"We're Going To Surprise Them"

The script was familiar. Another season was almost over and Maryland Agricultural College was winning infrequently. Ever since Fred Nielson resigned as coach, the Farmers had been losing ground. M.A.C. had tried five coaches since 1906, including former star Barney Cooper, who shared the duties with E. P. Larkin in 1909. And now in 1911, No. 6, Charles Donnelly, who coached in a derby hat, was having his problems.

In the first six games M.A.C. had won just one. Included in the six losses was a crushing 27-0 drubbing by St. John's, but equally damaging was a 14-0 practice game loss to Central High. Professor Richardson had seen enough. He was aware that Curley Byrd was coaching Western High School in the District and had scrimmaged the Farmers, successfully, during the season.

"Richardson called me in on a Sunday and told me he could get Byrd as coach and what did I think," recalled Burton Shipley, the team's quarterback. "I told him if he thought he could, go ahead and do it, and he did.

"What Byrd did was so smart. He didn't touch Donnelly's offense and for a whole week, he watched the team play and did nothing. On Monday he took (Bill) Kemp, who was 195 and a powerful fella. He knew nothing about dodging but was strong and Byrd took him off end and put him into the backfield.

"He told the team he could build a defense to stop Western Maryland, even though they were undefeated and had this big fella, who weighed about 210 pounds, playing fullback."

Bill Hottel, who was to become Maryland's first sports

publicist, ran into Byrd a few days before the game. "If you don't have anything to do Saturday, come out to College Park and see us play," Byrd told him. "They are supposed to lick the pants off of us, but I think we're going to surprise them."

So Hottel and Byrd rode the streetcar from Washington to College Park. On their way to the game they stopped to buy a couple of chocolate bars to munch on, as a prelude to what Hottel thought would be a dull affair.

He admitted years later it was probably the last time he doubted Curley Byrd, who was then only 22.

Before the game, Byrd told Shipley not to "throw a forward pass in your own territory or you'll end up going the other way." But Shipley conveniently forgot the instructions. From his own 15 he completed a pass to Frank Hoffecker and then two more to get to the Western Maryland 20. "If one of those balls had gone bad, Dr. Byrd would have yanked me," said Shipley.

Kemp, the converted runner, ran two times and got to the 10. On the next play Shipley saw the defensive end "playing almost like a guard, he was leaning toward the middle to stop Kemp." So Shipley improvised. He gave Kemp the ball, drew it back, pulled it into his belly, counted three, and walked around the surprised end into the end zone.

"Byrd asked me where I got that play from," said Shipley. "I told him and he put it in the next week for good."

Western Maryland recovered a fumble on the M.A.C. 25 in the fourth period and moved to the five, but they fumbled the ball back, Shipley punted out of danger, and M.A.C. won 6-0. Byrd was kept for the season finale, which the Farmers also captured 6-2 over Gallaudet after Shipley drove the team from the 40 late in the fourth period, with Hoffecker scoring on a three-yard plunge.

The victory over Gallaudet, Shipley said, "was just icing on the cake. Beating Western Maryland was the key. That convinced Professor Richardson that Dr. Byrd was the man for the job."

It took Richardson, who had taught Byrd in college, until the summer to convince the college to hire such a young man as coach and English instructor. Just before he retired, President Silvester finally agreed, and Byrd became a full-time member of the college faculty at $1,200 a year.

He was to stay around for the next 41 years.

Maryland Man...For Life

He first came to Maryland when Grenville Lewis was the resident football hero. He did not leave for good until 65 years later, when he retired to his small farm in Laurel, Maryland.

Not even Curley Byrd, who was three in 1892 when Burton Shipley first saw the school, witnessed as much change at Maryland. At six, Shipley was a waterboy on Lewis' 1896 team. His father was foreman at the farm that raised produce for the school's dining hall and Shipley spent his early years watching the college lads play football. He grew up to become the university's only six-letter man in one sport—football.

Along with Byrd, he started what was to become a tradition at Maryland. For years, only alumni were hired as coaches for varsity sports. The school perhaps had the greatest inbred coaching staff of any college in the nation. They would come to Maryland, play football and usually a couple other sports, perhaps leave for a few years, and then return to teach and coach. Byrd did not believe in coaches just coaching. He did believe in loyalty, and these Maryland men had that in abundance – to Byrd and to the school.

Shipley was the prime example. He was head basketball coach for 24 years, head baseball coach for 37. He also helped out at times with football, served briefly as athletic director, taped ankles, and even mowed fields. He did anything Byrd wanted.

In the last baseball game he coached, he was thrown out for the only time in his career, protesting two "atrocious calls" by the umpires. He would not leave the field, which had been

Burt Shipley's father raised food for Maryland's dining hall. His son became the only six-letter man in football in the school's history.

named after him, and they did not force him to go.

Shipley enrolled in M.A.C.'s prep school in 1908 at age 17. "I was a day student, and we were called day dodgers and rats," he said. "There were only about 250 students and we wore uniforms like VMI. I would stop by and watch them practice football and this guy Cory came over and said, 'Rat, do you want to play football?' And I said, 'I'm too light.' He said, 'you're as heavy as I am, and I play.'

"So I went down the next day and got a uniform, just an old jersey, didn't even have one sleeve in it. In those days they didn't have pads like they have now. They had a pad sewed on the jersey. They had a scrimmage that day and had only 21 other people, so I played.

"This fella kicked the ball and I went down and this fella held up his hand and I said this is my meat and I let him have it. He jumped up and hit me on the chin. He was a senior, see. So I started off the field. The coach ran over and grabbed me and he said, 'Where are you going?' I said, 'I'm quitting. Any time your teammate hits you on the chin, you leave.' He said, 'I'll make that fella apologize to you. That was a fair catch. Don't you know you weren't supposed to interfere with him?'"

Shipley did not know the rule, but stayed after the offended player apologized. "The coach (William Lang) brought me to his room that night, gave me the plays and numbers and took me to Richmond the next game," said Shipley. "He said he had to play anybody who could hit that hard."

He lettered as a substitute end in 1908, and then switched to quarterback midway through the 1909 season. M.A.C. won two straight games after the move, before an outbreak of scarlet fever cancelled the rest of the schedule. But he recalls at least one triumph, over Rock Hill, should not have counted.

"I caught a punt and the fella was ready to tackle me and I saw Jimmy Burns out there and I passed the ball to him," he said. "You can't pass a forward pass when you catch a punt but the referee didn't know anything so they let it go."

He beat George Washington in 1910 by scoring a touchdown in the dark. "They figured I would drop kick the ball, but I faked to the back and whirled around end and scored. They never touched me. They couldn't see me. But that's the trouble with pro football today. I believe they could run from kick formation more than they do. It's just fourth down with a foot to go and they go back and kick."

The *Reveille* called him a "born leader, exceedingly aggressive and absolutely fearless." He was a pepper pot, always yelling, loving what he was doing. "I wanted to play 60 minutes every game or not play at all," he said. "There was no fun sitting on the bench."

He had a unique training method to prepare for his iron-man stints. He would eat "pie and stuff" on weekends, and get back in shape on Mondays. "I trained too much, I used to go stale," he said. "We played St. John's one day and I'm the safety man, and the fella went by me for a touchdown and I couldn't make my mind move over and catch him. I was stale. So I said the heck with training on the weekends."

Shipley did not think he was a smart player. He said Curley Byrd confirmed that one day. "These two professors were standing on the sidelines and they asked him, 'My God, how do you get along with that fella Shipley, dumb as he is?' Well, Curley told them, 'I don't care how dumb he is, his mechanics are good.'

"Well, I thought that was a pretty good answer."

The Devil Hath Great Power

The *Reveille* had to turn to Shakespeare to find an appropriate quote to describe Harry Clifton Byrd.

"The devil hath power to assume a pleasing shape," it said about Maryland Agricultural School's star quarterback in 1907. Even then, Byrd was the king of the college, a dashing lad who charmed the ladies, befriended the men, and emerged as the school's No. 1 sports figure and No. 2 scholar in his class. Legend has it that even then, Curley Byrd knew he would eventually wind up president of Maryland, and if he had really announced his intentions, probably no one that heard them would have doubted him.

Perhaps no athletic figure has ever dominated an American college in quite the manner that Curley Byrd dominated Maryland before retiring in 1954 from his president's position to run for governor of the state. The Rocknes, the Camps, the Warners, the Leahys, the Bryants, the Royals of football have confined their impact to the immediate radius of the sports world. Byrd used sports as a stepping-stone to greater heights. Maryland claims he is the only football coach to advance to the presidency of a major college. Yet he was more than just president. What Maryland is today, at least in terms of physical shape and size, is due to Byrd.

In his 18 years as president, he ran the school with an iron hand and with such power that his great antagonist, the *Baltimore Sun,* raised constant cries of anguish over most of his doings. The *Sun* claimed he directed the school like he would run a football team; Byrd really never disagreed.

And just as the story of the University of Maryland, the school, is not complete without the story of Byrd, so is the story of Maryland football incomplete without Byrd. Even in later years when a large, energetic man from South Carolina, Jim Tatum, built Maryland into a national football power, Byrd remained the dominant figure on campus in the eyes of the college family.

Byrd's peers readily admit that Curley's ambitions off the football field probably prevented Maryland from assuming a place among the football powers long before the arrival of Tatum. But they do not criticize him. "He was trying to do too much," is how they put it. "He had a school to worry about too. He couldn't devote as much time to football as he wanted to. But he had things in proper priority."

From 1912, when Professor Richardson succeeded in having him approved as football coach, until 1935, when he released his hold on the sport after two years of coaching behind the scenes so as not to arouse the board of regents, Byrd shaped and formed Maryland football while at the same time climbing through the ranks of the college administration. From coach to athletic director to assistant to the president to vice-president to acting president, and finally, in 1936, to president, he had a hand in most of the major events during the years Maryland was struggling for an identity – and at one point, its very life.

Byrd most definitely was a product of his times, and he changed as they changed. From a sports renegade in his early years to a free-wheeling, liberal-thinking administrator during the New Deal, he kept in the middle of life's flow. He was self-confident, oozing with pride, but he was convinced that history would vindicate his actions.

He was born in 1889 in Crisfield, Maryland, a small fishing village on the state's eastern shore. His family had been oystermen since the 17th century, but his father chose to sell, rather than harvest, oysters. He also mixed in some politics, and was ultimately elected to the state general assembly.

Curley was known as Clifton to his family, the nickname coming when he got into sports. He played football on a team sponsored by an Episcopal rector and arrived at M.A.C. in 1905

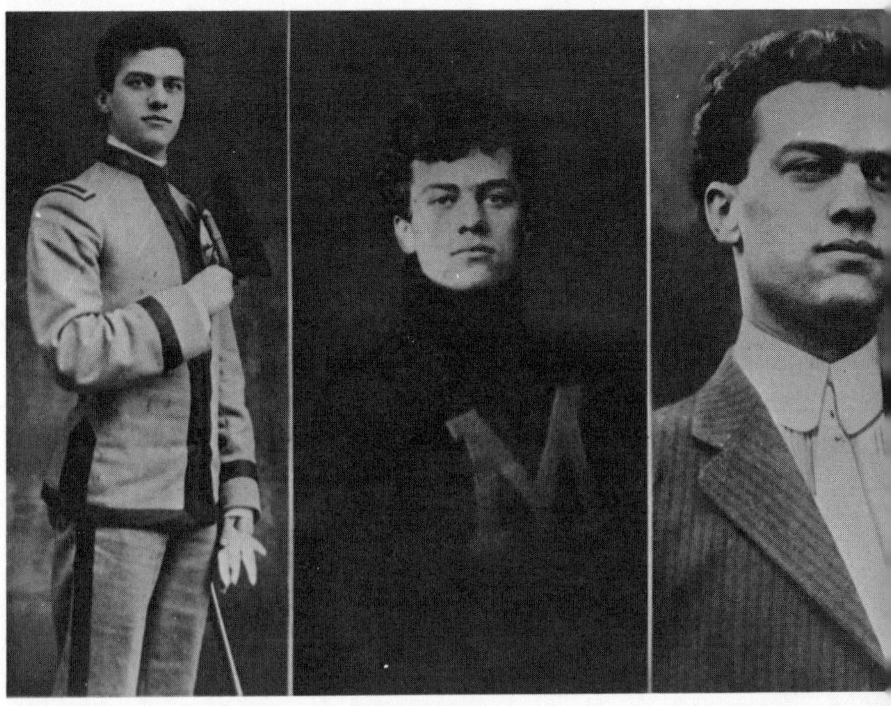

at age 16, seeking a degree in engineering and a spot on the Farmers' squad. But Fred Nielson, the coach, refused to let him play, saying he was too light at 138 pounds. Undaunted, Byrd returned the next day in a homemade uniform, complete with women's stockings. Nielson allowed him to remain.

On the strength of his personality alone, Byrd is always named among Maryland's all-time great players. He was a fine athlete but no All-American, at least not in football. He had good quickness and had a penchant for wide-open plays. The teams he played on were not outstanding, and he was easily a stickout.

He was probably a better baseball pitcher and sprinter in track. He shared the school 50-yard dash record (5.2) and set four other school track marks: 100 (10.0), 220 (22.3), 440 (52.0), and standing broad jump (9 feet, 4 inches).

He graduated in 1908, completing a four-year course in three, and according to the *Reveille* was the idol of the student body.

The stages of Curley Byrd's career at the University of Maryland: as a student in 1906, as football captain in 1907, as a rookie head coach in 1912, as assistant to the president in 1928 and as president in 1938.

Byrd was a dark, handsome youth, his face dominated by his curly locks and a marvelous smile. The *Reveille* took note of that smile during athletic combat:

"Did you ever enjoy the thrilling sensation of seeing Curley pull himself out of a hole in the pitcher's box? No? Then look with me. With three men on base, three balls, none out, and the opposition rooters wild with excitement, Curley is in his element. Caressingly, he pets the dusty sphere, shows his teeth to the spectators, grins amiably at his victim and 'batter out' sings the umpire. The grin widens, the frenzied rooters cool down, and then with feline grace, Curley puts on the finishing touches, while his opponents wake up to the fact that he has been playing with them again.

"So when Curley grins, watch out. Something is sure to break."

The grin carried Byrd beyond Maryland. When he graduated, there were no rules governing eligibility. He wanted to continue studying and did, playing football at the same time.

The first stop was George Washington University. He took law courses and was quarterback on the football team in 1908. In 1909 he did the same at Georgetown under his old coach, Nielson, before he was ruled off the team after a protest over his eligibility by Virginia. It was while he played with the Hoyas that one of the most durable of the Byrd legends had its birth.

With Byrd at quarterback, an underdog Georgetown played Fordham to a scoreless tie in the Polo Grounds. During the game Byrd completed two passes, one of which almost scored a touchdown. Years later author Morris Bealle, who wrote about football at both Maryland and Georgetown, claimed that Byrd, not Knute Rockne and Gus Dorias, first demonstrated the importance of the pass in football.

In time the story developed so much that Byrd was being credited with inventing the forward pass. He did not.

From Georgetown, Byrd went to Western Maryland and ran track. He also was playing semi-pro baseball in Hagerstown and Cambridge and was signed by the San Francisco Seals in 1910. In San Francisco fight promoter Tex Rickard, of all people, changed his life.

Byrd, 20 years old and earning $300 a month, was called aside by Rickard one day. "He talked out of the side of his mouth and used atrocious English," remembered Byrd. "And he told me, 'Youse is a fool.'

"I asked him what he meant. He told me, 'Get wise and quit dis racket.' He went on to tell me how I'd be a bum in 10 years or less if I stayed in it; that if I had any brains I'd go back East and use my education to get started on something solid."

While Byrd thought over Rickard's words – and the fact that the Chicago White Sox had purchased his contract and were ready to give him a trial – he had a run-in with a teammate and wound up being fined. He paid the penalty and left for home.

By the time M.A.C. tried him as coach in the final games of 1911, Byrd already had been employed as an assistant coach at Eastern College in Manassas, Virginia, head coach of the Western High team, playground director in the District, and sportswriter for the *Washington Star*, a job he kept until 1932. He became perhaps the only football coach writing for public consumption about himself and his team throughout his coaching career.

The young man the board of regents hired had a glamorous appearance and magnetic personality. He did not smoke, drink or swear, collected and studied Bibles, and prided himself on being able to quote appropriate Biblical phrases. He was enthusiastic, ambitious, and overwhelmingly alive. He bubbled over with ideas and dreams, most of which did not concern football, even then.

An old classmate, Dr. Levin Broughton, ran across Curley one day, before he had taken the coaching job, sitting on a hill on campus. He asked Byrd what he was doing.

"I'm drawing a sketch of M.A.C. as it will be someday," Curley replied. Dr. Broughton maintained that the campus essentially emerged along the lines of Byrd's sketches.

Plank Steaks And Victories

The 1912 season had not even started yet and already the rookie coach had a problem. His star quarterback was quitting.

"I had left school, didn't want any more of it," said the player in question, Burt Shipley. "I met Dr. Byrd out at old Griffith Stadium one day. Just happened to bump into him. He said to me, 'How about going downtown and have supper with me?' He asked me if I was quitting and I told him I had enough military, and didn't want any more of it.

"He asked me what I would do if he fixed it up so I wouldn't have to drill any more, would I go back? I still didn't know but he ordered me a plank steak, first time I ever had one, and that sold me. I went back and played for him for two years."

Ironically, Shipley was hurt the first game against Richmond and missed most of the season. But Byrd's charm was just starting to work. Before he was finished, Maryland Agricultural College had its best year since 1896.

The fifth game of his college coaching career, and third of the 1912 season, was the turning point. After nine straight losses to Johns Hopkins, the elite of Maryland's colleges, the Farmers finally beat the Blue Jays.

The final score was 13-0. It was the first of what was to become a Byrd habit during his coaching career: upsets over highly favored teams. He never coached a nationally ranked team or an undefeated squad. His rewards came from upsets, doing the unexpected against a stronger opponent.

A hint of what was to come in the Hopkins game appeared

in the season opener against Richmond. "The work of the Maryland team was far and above better than any showing by the school since it has been appearing against Richmond," said the *Washington Post*. "The backfield and the line were both much stronger and generally played superior."

The Farmers won 46-0. Lynn Loomis, on his first carry in his first varsity game, ran 80 yards for a touchdown. He had replaced a newcomer from McKinley High, William (Country) Morris, who was destined to become an all-time great at the school. Morris, duly inspired, registered two touchdowns of his own in the second half.

After shutting out Maryland-Baltimore, the Farmers traveled to Hopkins' Homewood Field. "Playing a style of football, the likes of which has never been seen on Homewood Field in many a year, the eleven for Maryland Agricultural College beat Johns Hopkins for the first time today," reported the *Washington Post*.

"The score," the *Post* said, "does not really show the superiority Maryland evidenced over Hopkins."

Byrd's team wasted no time in getting ahead. Morris went around right end for 60 yards and a touchdown soon after the opening kickoff. Then fellow halfback Frank Hoffecker sprinted 50 yards to the Hopkins' two, where Morris carried it in. He added the conversion and M.A.C. took a 13-0 lead into the second half.

Hopkins made one bid to score in the third period. Taking the kickoff, the Blue Jays got to the Farmers' three. But M.A.C. held. No gain, loss of four, no gain. "It was a brilliant piece of defensive work," said the *Post*. "The formation used was especially effective."

It was the first time Byrd's defensive genius was praised in print. His ability to solve opponents' offenses soon proved his strongest point as a coach.

"He wouldn't set up a defense until maybe Friday before a game," said Jack Faber, who played and coached under Byrd and later was Maryland head coach. "He really wouldn't spend that much time on defense. I remember we almost missed a train to Yale one time because he hadn't finished coaching the defense in practice yet.

"He'd tell the players, if you do what I tell you with this

defense, you'll stop the other guy. He was great on making sideline adjustments. He never had spotters or any help. But after a few plays, he would move a guy over just a little, or make some slight changes and that would take care of it.

"He had this linebacker, Julie Radice, who couldn't run. He'd say, Julie, do this and that and he would be responsible just for this area. He made it simple and gave Julie just what he could handle. And Julie did a heck of a job."

Byrd devised a 7-2-2 defense formation in the early 1920s, and then a 6-3-2 setup in the late '20s that were copied by other coaches. Both led to more big upsets for Maryland.

A third Byrd coaching characteristic also had its beginning in 1912. No sooner had the Farmers shocked everyone by upsetting Hopkins, then they turned around and lost 27-0 to St. John's. Year after year, Maryland would win games it should have lost, then lose ones it should have won, preventing a truly superior season.

Still, 1912 proved a very good year, climaxed by a 17-7 victory over Western Maryland, which had not lost at home in eight years. Shipley, returning from his ankle injury, opened the scoring with a field goal and then Bill Huntemann, a tackle, caught a touchdown pass after a double lateral in the backfield. Country Morris added the last touchdown for a 17-0 lead and, according to one newspaper account, he also "put on one of the greatest defensive displays ever seen on the local field."

A final game tie with Penn Military left the Farmers with a 5-1-1 record. The *Reveille* printed a cartoon of a football player with long fangs, and ran a caption under it: "We are beginning to show our teeth."

By 1913 Byrd again was the No. 1 figure on campus. His second season was almost as successful as his first. The Farmers beat Hopkins 26-0 and Western Maryland 46-0, and then added St. John's to the list 13-0, marking the first time they had defeated all the state schools in the same season.

A trouncing by Navy 76-0 was overlooked. The Midshipmen, everyone realized, were out of M.A.C.'s class. Even season-ending defeats by Gallaudet and Penn Military were forgotten. A 6-3 record was better than the students were used to and, besides, the team had Byrd and a horde of star players: Morris, Seymour Ruff, Hoffecker, Ken Knode, and Shipley, finishing

Coach Curley Byrd's first team in 1912 lost only one game. Country Morris (third from left, back row) and Burt Shipley (not in picture) were two of the standouts.

off his sixth and final season.

"May M.A.C. long continue to have Curley Byrd as coach," gushed the *Reveille*, "and her athletics will prosper. He has absolutely refined the idea that an athlete must necessarily be something of a tough for the school does not have on its entire staff a more refined, courteous, and genial gentleman."

Byrd already had developed an approach to coaching that would not vary for the next 22 years. "He never yelled in practice or a game," said Geary Eppley, who played under Byrd and later was track coach, athletic director, and dean of men at the school. "He never bawled out people. He pointed out mistakes and explained what you did wrong. He took a calm approach.

"The strongest thing he'd say was 'for cripes sake.' But he'd tell you what you were doing wrong in no uncertain terms. If he had time to spell things out, like at half time, he'd usually help you. That's why his teams always played better in the second half."

University of Maryland historian George Callicutt wrote that Byrd "loved people so sincerely that even hostile critics, if they dared talk with him, came away strangely charmed. He did not toady to views of others, did not catch them up in a great cause and did not overwhelm or dominate; but somehow he was so warm, so disarmingly frank and so righteously for anything that was right that almost no one could withstand his personality."

Byrd's philosophy was simple. "If you can't lead 'em, lick 'em. If you can't lick 'em, join 'em, and if you can't join 'em, seduce 'em." His charms worked even on crusty H. L. Mencken, who was assigned by the *Baltimore Sun* to do a series on Byrd. Mencken concluded that "the thing to do with a man of such talents is not to cuss him for doing his job so well; it is far wiser so long as hanging him is unlawful, to give him a bigger and better one."

His players were easy prey to his charms. There were a few that resisted him, but the majority worshipped him. They spoke of him with awe, never questioning what he did, only approving completely of his actions. Their loyalty to him even today remains spellbinding.

Byrd talked their language, even when he rose to heights as an administrator. His admiration for football never faltered from the time that he wrote a defense of the game in the 1908 *Reveille*:

"I believe that nowhere is there a greater opportunity afforded for the development of one's character than on the gridiron. There is no finer discipline in the world than that which is received on the football field. The lessons which are learned there are varied and many. Patience, persistency, quickness of perception are taught all together and in absorbing these lessons one learns to appreciate his own ability and to have confidence in himself."

Byrd, Burt Shipley believes, "had the ability to get inside players. He'd dress in the same room with them even 20 years after he was coach. He could think up more things in the football room than anywhere else. He didn't leave anything unturned."

His acts of generosity are legion. During the 1920s a poor

farm boy who worked as football manager to pay for his college board shared a room with the coach on a football trip. Byrd was appalled at the condition of his underwear. A week later the boy discovered a new bundle of underwear in his locker, and later, a $20 bill at Christmas. The beneficiary later became a prominent member of the university staff.

At times he almost seemed as generous to his opponents. He did not believe in recruiting, and while other schools he played long had been helping their athletes, he refused. And recruiting was vital to Maryland's football survival. Outside of Baltimore, only two high schools in the state played football. This situation did not improve until after World War II.

"We always used to schedule four or five schools every year we had no right beating," said Faber. "He liked the challenge. We were usually outnumbered. Few high schools in Maryland played football and most of his athletes had no previous experience when they came to College Park."

Indeed, Eppley remembers a favorite Byrd saying: "I'll make a football player out of him or I'll die trying."

"We used to tell him, 'yeah, and you'll kill us in the process,'" said Eppley.

Said Faber: "He would take those big farmers and make players out of them. His rivals would take players who were already good. It always made his job more difficult."

One recruit who knew how to play before coming to College Park was Morris, who is considered one of Maryland's all-time best defensive backs. He played only two years, yet left a bunch of Morris tales behind, all extolling his brains and quickness.

"He could do it all, change direction, run, tackle, hit people," said Shipley, who was a teammate both years. "He's the best halfback this school has ever had, I think. Smart. I wasn't smart, but he was. Always knew where to play, where to go."

Shipley remembered one game in which he had a bruised shoulder and Morris kept going over to his side and making all the tackles. "Hey, there's nothing wrong with me," Shipley told him. "They are going to go around your end and beat you."

"I know," said Morris, "but I've seen this team before and I know every play they are going to run. I'll be okay."

Morris was a four-letter man, also playing baseball, basketball, and running track. He played some minor league baseball and then managed, including a stint in the old Blue Ridge League where Shipley was his shortstop.

"He was witty, really quick," said Shipley. "At night we'd be walking up and down the street and he would say 'Let's go down to so and so and turn around and come back.' And we'd turn around and go back the other way, and someone would ask us, 'What did you do, change your mind?' And he'd say, 'No, just direction.'"

Shipley, however, is most proud of the time he outwitted Morris. Shipley called for a dropkick on third down against Western Maryland and Morris yelled at him that M.A.C. still had one more down to go.

"You're damn right I know we've got another down," replied Shipley. "But I don't want those guards charging through on me. Give me a chance. I think I can kick the ball through." Shipley was right. The ball came back to him and "I kicked it through and sure enough, no one bothered me and I had plenty of time."

Morris was so good that he even received credit for scoring touchdowns in a game against Johns Hopkins that he missed with injuries. Ruff was the correct pointmaker and had spent the night bragging to his friends in Baltimore about his feats. When the paper reported that Morris instead was the hero, Ruff's pals had a field day.

"We all knew that Country Morris could play," proclaimed the *Reveille*. "But no one dreamed that he would develop into the whirlwind of a halfback that he has."

Morris later became a coach of a boys' academy in Albany, New York, where he stayed for 34 years. When he retired, Byrd spoke at his testimonial dinner.

"I followed Byrd out to Maryland from McKinley High because I liked the way he coached," Morris said. "He used a soft approach and it appealed to me."

Morris, however, hardly used the soft approach to playing.

Country Morris is considered one of the best defensive backs in the early years of Maryland football. But he always thought of himself as a better offensive back.

In one game he was carrying the ball around end and tried to avoid a tackler by ducking under him. Instead, the two hit head-on and knocked each other out.

Morris had come from the Virginia countryside and when he moved into the District and playmates asked him where he hailed from, he said "the country."

"I didn't know there was any more than one country," he laughed. Morris had learned his football on a vacant lot across from his home. He told some older boys that he did not know the rules but they said they would teach him. "They said I should hit 'em hard and hit 'em low. They beat it into my head. It wasn't long before I was the first one chosen in the games.

"I got a reputation as a defensive player but I thought I was better on offense. I think Curley did too."

Morris never forgot how to hit hard and hit low. He played like that and coached like that and he still thinks he could play even in today's more advanced game. "I'm not as fast or as big as a lot of these people today," he said, "but I'd give 'em a hell of a run to make the team."

A Step Up

Vic Pennington was the type of player Curley Byrd loved. Years after Pennington had left Maryland, Byrd referred to him regularly in speeches. To Byrd, Pennington symbolized better than anyone the values of football.

Pennington came to M.A.C. in 1911 and went out for the football team. He did not make it. Again in 1912 he tried out, and again he did not make it. In 1913 Byrd kept him around, and he was used on the scrub team during the week. He played in one game.

But in 1914 Pennington got his reward. "Three years Victor Pennington had all kinds of adversities," Byrd would say. "Three years he had been battered on the scrubs that a good varsity might be developed; three years he had worked like a tiger with little recognition and no reward except the feeling that he had done his best; but in the fourth year he came into his own, won his position, and established the remarkable record of playing every minute of every game of the season.

"He took care of right end on an eleven which won the state championship and he was one of the best ends in the state. Inherent qualities of determination, capabilities developed by dint of perseverance under, at times, disadvantageous conditions, gave Pennington what he had worked for all that time. No man ever did more for his position on a football team than Pennington, but he has since said that the final achievement was worth the effort he had put forth, was the greatest personal satisfaction of his life."

Byrd preached the Pennington lesson to his players. Stay with something long enough and the rewards will come, he would say. For Pennington, the reward came his senior year against hated St. John's. He took a 30-yard pass from Horace Derrick and scored the only touchdown of the contest.

The same Derrick, in his first year out of Business High in the District, scored two touchdowns to help M.A.C. beat Hopkins for the third straight year, all on shutouts.

That streak came to an end in 1915, when the Blue Jays won 3-0 on a field goal by Bobby Hoffman after a blocked punt. It was Hoffman's 10th try of the day.

By then Byrd was in the midst of providing the school with nine straight winning years, a streak that would not end until 1921. Just as important to the students, he was faring well against the likes of Hopkins, Western Maryland, and St. John's, the school's three biggest rivals. The rest of the schedule was still an assortment of small and medium-sized schools, most of which were hardly football powers. But the team was not yet ready for the big time.

In 1915, Byrd began a school building campaign, which would soon become routine for the future university president who specialized in raising money and constructing buildings. This time Byrd, now also athletic director, started small, wanting only $12,000 to erect a new football field and training quarters that would be used "to provide boarding facilities for all men out for athletics and a home for the alumni when they come back for games."

This forerunner of modern athletic dorms was badly needed at M.A.C. The athletic teams dressed in Morrill Hall, one of four buildings on campus, and shared a single shower. The playing field was not any better. "They marked the field off and put a wooden fence around it and put canvas on the fence," said Geary Eppley. "We beat Virginia in Charlottesville one year and the students celebrated at Maryland by having a bonfire – with the wooden stands."

Ironically, Byrd's first money campaign was a flop. Insufficient funds were raised for the building and the school did not get a quality playing field until 1923.

The team, however, continued to win. In 1916, when the state took over control of the school and changed its name to Maryland State College, Byrd produced the best squad of his five-year employment. The Farmers lost only to Navy and

Haverford in eight games – and 10 more points would have won both of those contests.

The Maryland line was especially impressive. Tackles Lyman Oberlin, Ralph Into, or Walter Posey, guards Bill Kishpaugh and Clyde Tarbutton, and center Avey Williams formed a durable combination. Oberlin and Into were considered by Byrd two of the best ever at Maryland, although Into played only one year before going into the service. He later was an All-American at Yale.

Benefiting most from the line's blocking was a raw recruit with blazing speed, Edward Brooks (Untz) Brewer, who played high school football in the District and had run a 9.8 100 before coming to College Park.

Brewer still is considered the greatest kicker to ever play for Maryland. Byrd went as far as to call him the greatest all-around kicker in the history of American football. He was the epitome of the era's drop kicker, an artist at maneuvering the blunt-ended ball into coffin corners and over goal posts from seemingly impossible angles.

He had an unusual career at Maryland. He went into the service after the 1917 season and did not reappear until 1920, but in the meantime had already recruited another Maryland great, Leroy Mackert, for the team.

Brewer, who weighed 145 pounds, made seven field goals in 1916, four of which were at least 40 yards long. He alone won three games with his kicking, and his punting was consistently sensational all season.

It took two games for the team to develop, since Byrd started Brewer and two other freshmen, Ray Michael and Andy Fletcher, and a sophomore, Jamie Smith, in the backfield. After losing to Dickinson 6-0, the Farmers fell to Navy 14-7 in their best showing yet against a major college. It was a heartbreaking defeat.

"On straight football and defensively and offensively, in the line, Navy was outplayed," reported the *Washington Post*. "Navy's football team was outrushed and outhustled. Brewer punted superbly."

Navy found a way over the line, however. They passed for two touchdowns in the game's first 15 minutes. The first was set up by a Maryland fumble on its own 30. Maryland went 62 yards to score in the third period after Brewer ran to within a few feet of the end zone on a fake punt. The Farmers threatened again in the fourth period when Smith followed a Brewer block to go 45 yards to the Navy eight. But the Midshipmen held on downs.

Untz Brewer was one of the fastest backs of his day, but his real strength at Maryland was his amazing accuracy with dropkicks.

Brewer's kicking brought Maryland its first victory. Virginia Military had a 9-3 lead before a 20-yard Brewer field goal and a touchdown by Michaels put Maryland ahead 12-9. Brewer then wrapped it up with another field goal. Earlier he had a 93-yard punt.

Ironically, he missed a conversion against Haverford the next game to cost Maryland a 7-7 tie. But the Farmers bounced back to win their last four games.

The first was over St. John's 31-6, in which Fletcher had four touchdowns and St. John's could get inside the 30 just once. The second was over Catholic 13-9 in which Brewer kicked goals of 15 and 40 yards, and added a conversion. The third was over New York University 10-7. Brewer fumbled and NYU picked up the ball and ran for a touchdown to tie it up, but Untz then won the game with a 45-yard field goal.

The fourth was the sweetest, a 54-0 rout of Hopkins, Maryland's greatest victory yet in the series. "The College Park aggregation had everything," said the *Baltimore Sun*. "Hopkins had nothing. With as fine a quartet of slashing, plunging backs as ever has been seen on a state gridiron, and a line that charged like the Black Watch, the College Park eleven uncovered an attack that swept Hopkins to all corners of the field."

Brewer had run back the opening kickoff for a touchdown and added 46 and 45-yard field goals.

"State exhibited an unhaltable offense and a stonewall defense," reported the *Reveille*. "Poor old Johns Hopkins was made to look like an aggregation of chess champions."

The student paper, the *Maryland State Weekly*, was sure the victory was Maryland's greatest. "We congratulate ourselves upon being fortunate enough to be students at a college where such a team exists. Yes, Maryland State could have made no better investment than was made in producing a champion team. It means prestige, a larger student body next year."

After 25 years of football, Maryland was finally on the way to the big time.

"The successes of the team resulted in obtaining games with Princeton and Penn State," the *Reveille* said. "Particularly worth noting in this connection is that the State players earned for themselves a reputation for fairness and straight forward play that was commented on far and near."

Another Bronko Nagurski

It was halftime of the seventh game of the season and Curley Byrd had an idea. Why not switch that big tackle to fullback? Four plays into the third quarter against Catholic University, he knew he had made the right move.

"By the fourth play, he had run over four Catholic players and they had to leave the game," remembers Geary Eppley about Leroy Mackert's running debut in 1919. "He wasn't even breathing hard. He was some kind of tough person."

Mackert had met Untz Brewer in the service and had been talked into coming to Maryland. Brewer, however, did not receive his discharge before the 1919 season began, so Mackert was on his own. By the time he finished his two-year stint in 1920, he had become a legend at the school.

Maryland needed a Mackert. Progress in football had been curtailed by World War I. A depleted squad had managed winning seasons in 1917 (4-3-1) and 1918 (4-1-1), playing curtailed schedules with only a few good players. Others like Brewer, Eppley, and Walter Posey, a five-year letterman who was captain of the 1917 team before being called away, were serving in the war.

The standout player in those war years was quarterback Bobby Knode. His brother Ken had been quarterback from 1911-1915. Both later were major league baseball players. Bobby played four years with Cleveland and finished with a .266 lifetime average. Ken stayed a season with the St. Louis Cards, hitting .231 before going on to medical school.

Byrd also had not been idle. He was made assistant to the president in 1918 while retaining his jobs as football coach and athletic director. He also was active in behind-the-scenes politics as he began developing friends and contacts in high positions who later would serve him well.

His team had confronted one major power, Penn State, in 1917, and had been embarrassed, 57-0. Navy had not been any kinder, winning 62-0. In 1919 Maryland tried again, this time against Yale and West Virginia.

Yale was coming off two years of inactivity due to the war and had one of its poorest teams in its already long football history. But it was still far too much for Maryland to handle, winning 31-0. Maryland, now known as the Old Liners (after a nickname picked up by Maryland troops during a battle in the Revolutionary War), did not threaten once and picked up only three first downs. Only Mackert on defense played well.

The game had more significance, however, for the future. Yale decided to keep playing Maryland – it was a good tuneup for more important contests – and Byrd turned the series into

Leroy Mackert ran with such power that he once knocked four opponents from a game on four straight plays. He also was a quality tackle.

his own particular battleground. His teams, it seems, always played over their heads against the Bulldogs.

Mackert was still a tackle then, and doing it as well, Byrd said later, as anyone he had coached. But he moved him to fullback against Catholic two games later during a four-game winning streak in which Maryland did not allow a point.

At 6-2 and 193 pounds, Mackert was both strong and durable. He became, at least in the minds of Maryland people, so good that only the immortal Bronko Nagurski was as efficient at playing fullback one way and defensive tackle the other.

Mackert's legend started against Catholic. In the first half, Maryland lost five players to injury. At half time Mackert was prepared for destruction.

"They taped Roy from wrists to shoulders with old fashioned bicycle tire tape," a close friend, Bill Bowie, recalled years later. "The average man wouldn't have been able to comb his hair but Mackert went out, played tackle on defense and fullback on offense and without doing anything out of the ordinary, he made it pretty tough on the CU boys. They either ran into those tire-taped arms or got hit by them when Roy crashed the line. In either case they were stopped – cold."

Four line smashes by Mackert and four CU players left the game. He also found time to throw a pass to Bobby Knode for Maryland's first touchdown in the 13-0 victory. He outdid even that performance in the finale against Hopkins, passing for one touchdown and scoring the other himself in the 14-0 triumph. Knode, who caught the pass, finished with 39 points for the year.

Mackert had played for Lebanon Valley College for two years before the war and was 25 by the time he came to Maryland. On Sundays he would play pro football, a common occurrence in his time.

"Mackert and others like him – George Halas, Curley Lambeau, and a few others – paved the way for pro football," wrote Francis Stan, columnist for the *Washington Evening Star*. "They had to run through irate crowds to the bus depots of some of the small Pennsylvania mining towns to escape harm when they upset the local teams. The Mackerts and the others played under assumed names and received little glory and practically no gold."

Maryland stops Johns Hopkins' Turkey Jones during the 1919 game. Maryland won 14-0 behind the play of Leroy Mackert.

Mackert was no dumb strongman. He edited the weekly student paper during his school days and then received a master's degree from Columbia after graduation. He later completed most of the work toward a Ph.D. at the same school before returning to Maryland in 1931 to head up the new physical education department. In that position he developed an intramural program and began varsity wrestling and golf programs. He also served as an assistant coach and chief scout under Byrd.

"To hear him talk, you'd think he was rough and tough," said one of Mackert's teammates. "He had a deep voice, but he had a heart of gold. But he'd punish you if you tried to tackle him. He was a big plow horse."

Mackert tried his best to control his strength. He went to a dance in the District one night and stood in the stag line where a police officer kept pushing everyone back, especially Mackert. The third time he pushed him, Mackert picked him up by the collar and slugged him.

A warrant was served on him and he went to court. A witness was asked if he had hit the officer. "If he had," came the reply, "the officer wouldn't be here to testify today."

Spreading The Word

It was a momentous year for the little school in College Park, still attended by less than 6,000 students. The floundering professional school complex in Baltimore and Maryland State merged, resulting in a two-campus setup and a new name – the University of Maryland. And the football team registered its first major upset over out-of-state competition, a 10-7 triumph over Syracuse.

That versatile man, H. C. Byrd, was responsible for both.

Historian Callicutt says that Byrd was perhaps "the only man who caught visions of the possibilities created by the merger of the university and the agricultural school."

Byrd encouraged State's president, Dr. Albert Woods, and the school's board of trustees to listen to the overtures from the university, which was desperately in need of new funding. He lobbied in the legislature for the bill which created the merger. Critics complained that he was "building a university his teams could be proud of."

Just four years before, Byrd was involved in the movement to have the state acquire complete control of Maryland Agricultural College and turn it into a state college. "He was especially effective with his alumni contacts and his political acumen," said Callicutt. "Sometimes as errand boy for the president and sometimes on his own, he went about attracting prospective students, buttonholing legislators, speaking to every civic group that would give him a hearing and charming everyone within earshot."

The merger gave Maryland State new life. For the first time, the school could obtain the funding needed to expand its facilities and grow away from its still lingering image as a "cow college." The football team was helping. An improved schedule was spreading its name beyond the state's borders. The first such expansion came on a November Saturday in 1920.

Syracuse had lost only once in seven games before meeting Maryland, and was among the nation's best teams, a distinction it had held for years. It was playing Maryland only as a breather before a season-ending confrontation with Colgate.

Maryland shocked both the Orangemen and the football world with a 10-7 victory. "A big surprise was handed the Syracuse football team and 3,000 who braved the icy blasts when the Maryland University eleven, ably coached by Curley Byrd, and a powerful backfield of Brewer, Mackert, Groves, and Plassnig defeated the Syracuse football machine," reported the *Washington Post*. "It was a well deserved victory for the Southerners," the *Post* writer said. "For they played football every minute."

Maryland jumped to an early lead when Syracuse fumbled and Dutch Plassnig grabbed the ball and ran 30 yards to score. Syracuse came back to tie it up later in the first quarter but did not threaten again until the last period.

Brewer, finally back at Maryland from his war service, missed a 40-yard dropkick on the next series. But Syracuse fumbled again and Brewer had a second chance, this time from the 36. Despite a difficult angle, he converted.

That was not the end of Brewer's heroics. He punted seven times, averaging more than 60 yards. One traveled 72 yards and another 65, the latter, Mackert explained, coming under most difficult circumstances:

"I failed to block out my man and I was sure I was going to be guilty of allowing the punt to be blocked. But Brewer calmly stepped to one side, kicked the ball underneath my arm 65 yards down the field over the safety man's head."

Syracuse, which had beaten Hopkins 47-0 and outweighed the Old Liners 15 pounds per man, drove to the Maryland eight in the fourth period, only to be stopped on downs and insure the Old Liners' most notable victory to date. Syracuse had gained 18 first downs, Maryland five. "The heroes of the game were Brewer and Mackert," reported the *Reveille*. "They proved powerful on both offense and defense."

Mackert was called on repeatedly to run by quarterback Johnny Groves. Finally Mackert told him in the huddle: "Listen, Boothead, if you want to know the numbers of the other players, I'll give them to you." Groves carried around the new nickname for the rest of his life.

As soon as the students back in College Park heard the news of the victory, they built a giant bonfire. At the height of the flames, they tossed in a few cans of gasoline. The blaze could be seen for miles. The students had a snake dance around the fire and sang college songs long into the evening. A few of the more lively types piled into a truck and drove to Washington, where they went up and down streets yelling out the score and cheering.

"They were one of the top teams in the country," said Eppley. "Nobody, including us, expected us to win as we did. Brewer did the trick. They'd drive and we'd finally hold them somehow. Untz would get off one of those long punts and then they'd have to drive back. I mean that was our strategy too. I broke my nose in the game. Had it splattered all over my face."

The victory over Syracuse was the fifth straight for Maryland, which added a sixth in a finale against Hopkins 24-7. During that stretch the Old Liners allowed only two touchdowns, and in eight games gave up only three. In the ninth, however, they surrendered five – to Princeton.

The Tigers, who wound up winning six games and tying Yale that season to rank among the nation's strongest, demolished Maryland 35-0. Byrd's defense managed to shut out its foe for most of the first half before All-American Don Lourie broke loose for a 60-yard touchdown. It was a very rough game.

"I remember that Andy Nisbet got kicked under the heart," said Eppley. "A Princeton tackle was playing with copper covering his toe and somehow Andy got kicked and he was crazy as a loon. He was pretty near out of his mind. Then Brewer broke his collarbone and Romeo Pagannucci got hurt and Mackert took a slug at somebody in the third period and was thrown out. We didn't have any subs left. When the game was over, I took Andy to the dressing room and we heard this noise and he said, 'we must have scored.'"

That defeat had come on the heels of the school's only other loss, a 6-0 shutout by Rutgers. Otherwise, Byrd constructed his best unit to date, built around Mackert and Brewer and supported by Eppley at end, Nisbet at tackle, John (Piggy) Moore at guard, and Zeke Bailey, one of Maryland's best ever, at center. Mackert scored eight touchdowns, including three against Washington College and also punted until Brewer recovered from his Princeton injury.

Hopkins wanted no part of Mackert, protesting that his two-year career at Lebanon Valley made him ineligible. He finally was allowed to play and Maryland won.

That ended his career but Byrd's upset heroics had just begun.

Speed Of A Thunderbolt

There really was not any reason for University of Maryland fans to expect what happened to its football team in 1923. No reason at all.

The previous two years had been the first failures in Curley Byrd's reign. Untz Brewer, playing without his pal Leroy Mackert, salvaged two wins and a tie in 1921 with his kicking. But all Maryland could wind up with was a 3-5-1 record after joining the huge Southern Conference as a charter member. Brewer had a 40-yard dropkick to beat Rutgers 3-0, and a 32-yarder to upset Virginia Tech 10-7. Playing in mud and rain in Baltimore, he had 26 and 40-yard successes to tie North Carolina State 6-6.

Otherwise Syracuse (42-0), Yale (28-0), and Carnegie Tech (21-0) had walloped the Old Liners. Princeton (26-0) and Yale (45-3) did the same in 1922, while Penn had a little more difficulty getting a 12-0 triumph. It still added up to a 4-5-1 season.

But Byrd was encouraged by the last three games, victories over Hopkins 3-0 on a field goal by Groves; 54-0 over Catholic as newcomer Kirk Besley, in his first year of football anywhere, had three touchdowns; and 7-6 over N.C. State on a 60-yard interception return by Groves and a conversion by Nisbet.

Sixteen of the top 22 players from that 1922 team were back in 1923, including a fine backfield of Besley, Groves, Cecil (Tubby) Branner, and a tough fullback named Jack McQuade. The line had a powerful tackle in Joe Burger, two quality guards in Tony Hough, and a sophomore, Irving (Bottle) Hall, and an experienced center, Rosy Pollock. Another sophomore, Bill

Supplee, had impressive talents at end.

The team had another plus. The athletic facilities and staff were finally beginning to develop. Byrd hired Country Morris and Burt Shipley as assistants, with Shipley also put in charge of basketball. A new gymnasium and, finally, a new stadium were being completed.

The stadium, the one Byrd had wanted in 1916, cost $60,000 and was built across the street from the main campus. It had a capacity of 5,000 with room for expansion to 15,000. And it had the first real locker room facilities in Maryland's history. In challenging alumni to provide funds for the complex in 1919, Byrd revealed that he had passed up an offer to move elsewhere "at great personal financial sacrifice" on the belief they would support his teams.

"Our squads have with heroic fortitude overcome almost unsurmountable handicaps in past years," he wrote, "but we have reached a point where we shall be outdistanced unless we can continue to advance."

Students and alumni responded in 1923 by petitioning to have the stadium named after Byrd. Their wish was granted and at age 34, Byrd, the irrepressible football coach so full of energy and ideas, achieved an honor usually reserved for those already dead.

Ironically, the 1923 team developed into one of the three greatest in the pre-World War II era at Maryland – and one of Byrd's two best – by playing its finest games on the road, away from its new facility.

The season itself began handsomely. Playing Randolph Macon in the yet undedicated stadium which was built by a company owned by former Maryland player Harry Watts, the Old Liners won handily 53-0. McQuade and Branner each scored three touchdowns, and Ed Pugh two. McQuade added four conversions.

Randolph Macon, however, was no Penn. Winners of two national championships, one of the founding football schools, Penn had scheduled Maryland as a prelude to its Ivy League season. But for the last time that season, Byrd had a completely healthy team as he traveled by train to Franklin Field. It was a sturdy group he fielded that day: Supplee and another sophomore, Ralph Lanigan at the ends, Walter Bromley and Burger, both veterans, at tackle, Hough and Hall at the guards, Pollock at center, Besley and Groves at quarterback, and Pugh, Branner and McQuade at the running positions.

It was also a good enough team, that day, to beat Penn 3-0 before 40,000 stunned fans. "For so early in the season," Penn coach Louis Alonzo Young said later, "it was remarkable that it did not make a single mistake. It is a well-coached, experienced, great team."

The victory brought Maryland its first national headlines. "Maryland's Eleven Wins Glory By Defeating Penn," said an eight-column banner headline in the *Washington Post* sports section. "In the fury of a final attack launched with the speed of a thunderbolt and savage in its impetuosity, the sons of Maryland yesterday sent Penn down in defeat," began the story.

Groves had been the carrier of lightning. With a few minutes left in the game, he had kicked a 24-yard field goal to win it, but the *Post* was confident that "three meager points do not by any manner of means represent the margin that existed between the victor and the conquered."

Twice Penn had made saving tackles to prevent touchdowns. The second came in the fourth period after Maryland blocked a punt and Groves replaced Besley to try a dropkick. He missed. Maryland got the ball back and McQuade drove between right guard and center and broke into the open. The 180-pound Maryland fullback was stopped at the 10 by Penn's 134-pound back, John Flues. Both were injured on the play and had to leave.

Maryland, however, had a first down. It could not score and Groves dropped back to kick. "The youngster was as cool as a cake of ice," reported the *Post*. "He never cast his eyes away from the goal posts that loomed before him. Groves took the oval as the Penn forwards crashed through the line like juggernauts. Deftly he dropped the pigskin upon the turf and his toe met the oval and straight between the posts soared the pigskin."

Penn tried desperately to rally. The Quakers tossed a pass downfield but George Heine, who had replaced the injured McQuade, jumped up and intercepted it. He then punted 65 yards on third down to get Maryland out of trouble. "I can still see the ball going," he said years later.

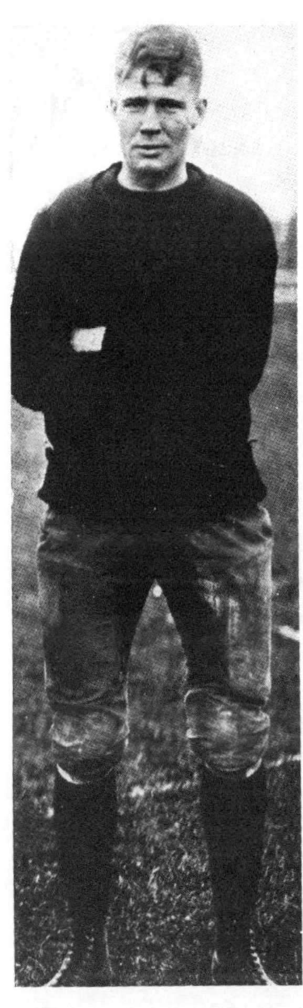

Johnny (Boots) Groves, "cool as a cake of ice," booted the field goal that beat Pennsylvania in 1923 and brought Maryland its first football fame.

Bottle Hall remembers the game with the special pride of an overlooked lineman. "The Philly papers said that Penn had six men in their backfield, unfortunately two of them, Hough and me, were from Maryland. It was the only compliment I ever got as a guard. But they were the easiest line to get through I've ever seen."

The victory brought notoriety to a number of Maryland players. Besley, the papers said, ran the team like Napoleon in moleskin. He was known as Nappy from then on. McQuade was a "Hercules, slashing the line and tearing apart the forwards of Penn with amazing skill and power. He was battered into a crippled pulp by his sustained slashes at the line."

The most honored, however, was Supplee, the 6-3 lithe end who parlayed talented basketball hands into an ability to catch passes. From this one game, plus a fine showing later against Yale, he made some All-American teams, although he was left off Walter Camp's official unit. He was the first Maryland player to receive this sort of national publicity.

Supplee, who later joined the school's faculty, was praised lavishly by Penn's coach after the game: "I have seldom seen an end who could catch forward passes with the uncanny manner that Supplee did. Not once did he miss a pigskin near him. Seven times he succeeded in gaining ground, the longest being for 17 yards. Not only did he make remarkable catches, but he was hard to stop when he caught them. Frequently he carried the tackler along with him and not once was he stopped as he caught the ball."

Hall described a special play designed to spring Supplee. "Zeke would block a man, hesitate, and then turn right and jump up for a pass from McQuade. You had to be five yards behind the line to throw and Supplee would be open just like the backs coming out of the backfield are today." Supplee was named the greatest end to play in Franklin Field that season. His style was compared to an "Oriole flitting hither and yon to keep his rendezvous with the ball."

His passing mate, McQuade, was cut from a different mold. He was a driving ball carrier, a scintillating blocker, and devastating on defense. He once knocked out two tacklers during a run against North Carolina.

"He wasn't a great big guy, must have weighed 180 pounds, but not really much more than bones," said Hall. "He'd back up the line, and he'd go into them head first with his arms out and something had to give when he hit. He was a better blocker, I think, than runner, but he was good for the short yards. He had good leg drive."

McQuade, who came from the District's Eastern High, was basically an even-tempered sort. But Hall remembered he got upset once. "I roomed with him for a semester. That was when we had our first coeds. He used to just jump out of bed, throw on a bathrobe and go to class. With the girls around, he had to get dressed. That really upset him."

McQuade kept his hot hand the next week against Richmond, scoring a touchdown, kicking a field goal, and tossing a pass to Besley for another score in the 23-0 victory, the team's third straight shutout. But then Virginia Tech upset the Old Liners in Griffith Stadium 16-9, and Byrd's men came in for some pointed criticism.

"The mighty Byrd team which conquered Penn two weeks ago was not the same in any way, shape or form," said the *Washington Post*. "They were outplayed and outgeneraled in practically every department." At least in the first half. That is when Tech's Don Rutherford made field goals of 33, 43, and 32 yards – and missed two others – to put his team ahead 9-0.

The second half saw a different Maryland. The Old Liners took the opening kickoff and marched in for a touchdown, with Groves, who came in for an injured Besley, catching a pass from McQuade for the score. But Rutherford insured the victory with a 10-yard touchdown pass after faking yet another dropkick.

Hough broke an ankle in the defeat, a staggering loss, although Maryland went on to beat North Carolina 14-0 behind a touchdown by McQuade, and St. John's 26-0 behind long scoring runs by McQuade and Pugh. But the team lost its other starting guard, Hall, with a broken elbow. And with Yale next, the Old Liners had to patch together a new line.

In three previous meetings, Maryland had managed only a field goal against Yale. So coach Tad Jones was hardly concerned about losing to these upstarts, even considering they had defeated Penn. He was in the midst of one of his school's great seasons, which would result in another national championship for the Bulldogs. After beating Army and Georgia, and with Princeton and Harvard coming up, it was logical to not worry about Maryland.

Jones decided to go to Princeton and leave the game to his assistants and players, who included such notables as Memphis Bill Mallory, Greasy Neale, and Ducky Pond.

The coach's scouting mission lasted until he received a score from Yale Bowl: Maryland 14, Yale 0. He scrambled to a telephone, called the Yale dressing room, and coached the rest of the afternoon over the phone lines. The 20,000 spectators in Yale Bowl were just as stunned. "They couldn't believe that a bunch of southerners were kicking around their precious team," said Hall.

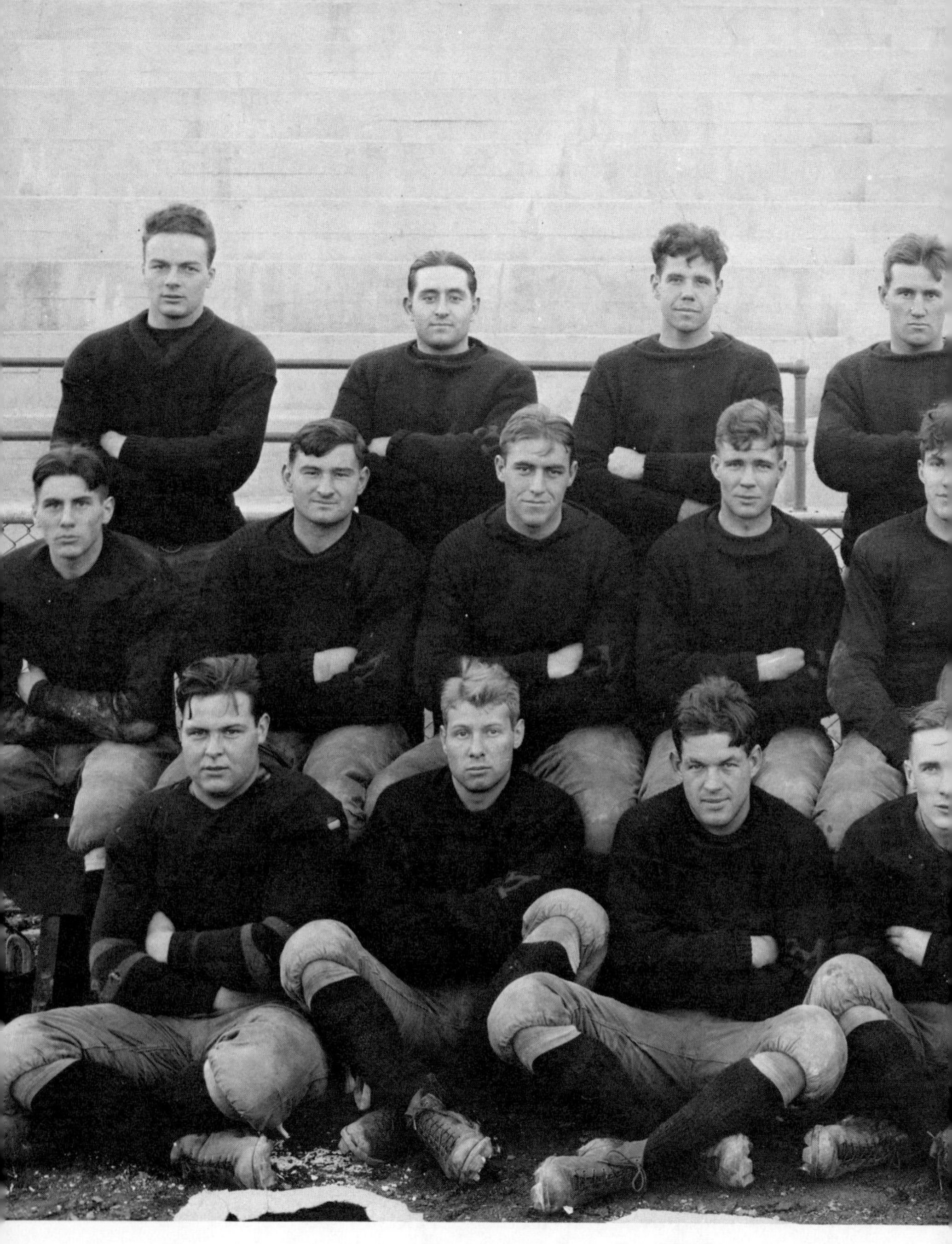

The 1923 Maryland team that beat Penn and almost upset Yale. Front row, left to right: Fred Herzog, Skeets Parker, W. D. Bartlett, Aubrey Wardwell, Jess Gundry, Ector Latham, Gomer Lewis. Middle row: Kirk Besley, Walter Bromley, Joe Burger,

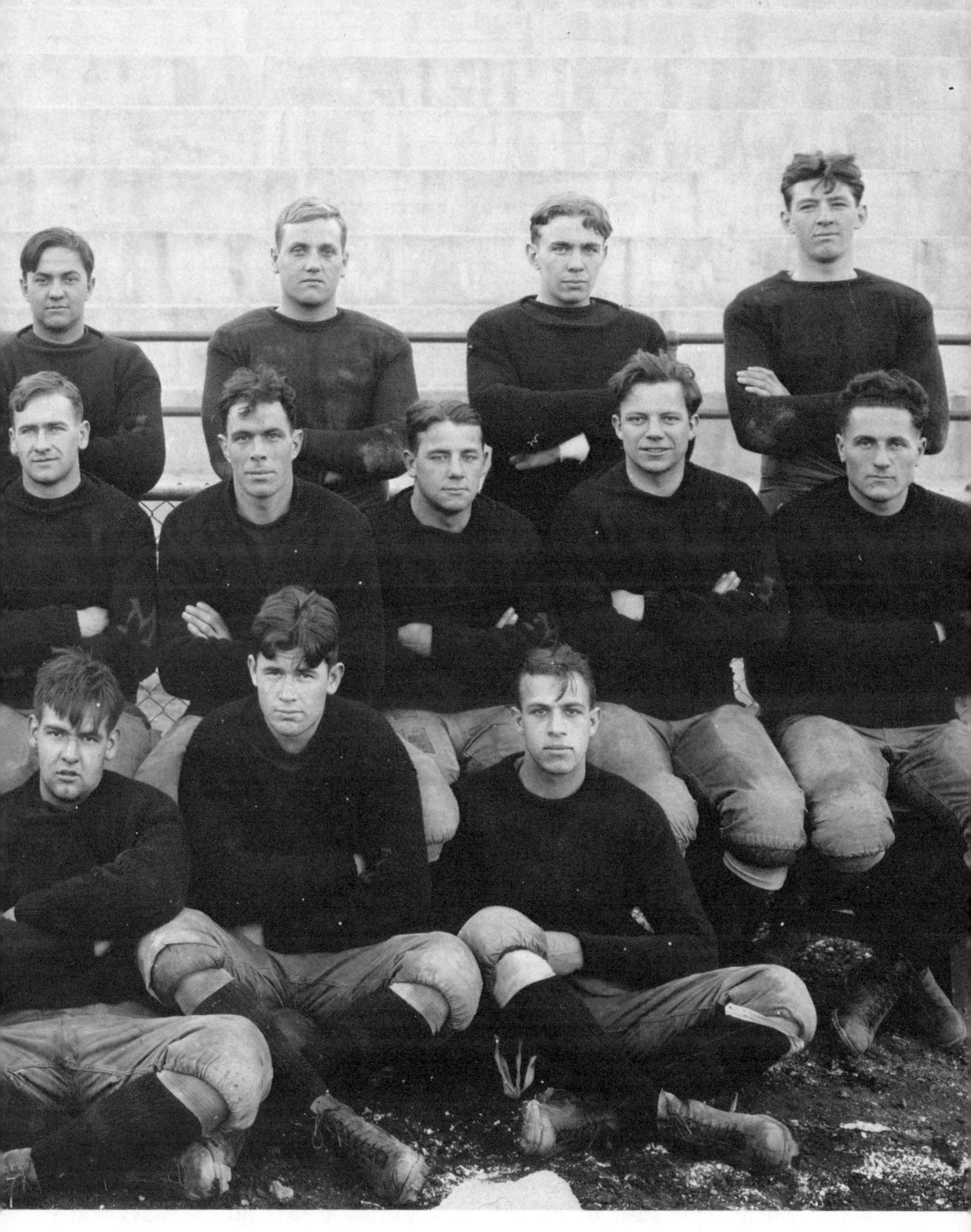

John Groves, Jack McQuade, Rosy Pollock, Mac Brewer, Tubby Branner, Downey Osborn, George Heine. Back row: Walter Young, Tony Hough, John Waters, Ed Pugh, Irving Hall, Arthur Bonnett, Pat Lanigan, Bill Supplee.

Neither could the Maryland players. The two new guards, Mack Brewer and Harold Bonnett, were inexperienced, and Burger had a bad knee at tackle. And Branner had been left at home after missing a Friday practice in order to watch a high school game. Downey Osborn, his replacement, was a sophomore.

Yet on its first possession, Maryland went 85 yards to score. "It was one of the most brilliant drives ever seen in the Yale Bowl," reported the *Washington Post*. McQuade, Pugh, and Osborn took turns slashing through the Yale line, then a pass from McQuade to Supplee and another to Groves moved the ball to the Yale 24. Groves then took another McQuade pass for a touchdown.

Yale and its fans had hardly recovered when Maryland again went 85 yards for another first-quarter score. McQuade connected with first Groves, then Burger, who had shifted out to an end. Finally Groves pulled in yet another McQuade pass of four yards for his second touchdown and a 14-0 lead.

"Maryland performed a feat in the opening period not accomplished by Princeton or Harvard in modern football," one newspaper wrote. "It prevented the Elis from registering one first down."

Yale regrouped in the second quarter. Osborn fumbled on the Elis 35 to stop a third scoring drive and Neale immediately ran to the Maryland 22. Pond ultimately plunged for the touchdown. Mallory later added a 33-yard field goal to cut the deficit to 14-10 at the half.

A punt by Yale's Mal Stevens in the third period sailed over Pugh's head and was downed on the Maryland two. The Old Liners punted out to Stevens on the 40, and he returned it to the two, where Mallory scored for a 16-14 lead.

The game ended that way, with the statistics just as close. Yale had 227 total yards, Maryland 223. Maryland 16 first downs, Yale 13. Maryland completed 10 of 14 passes for 208 yards, Yale rushed for 185. But Curley Byrd and the Maryland players never thought they lost the game.

"We were robbed," said Heine. His complaint was over a fourth-period field goal try by Groves, the hero of the Penn win. Maryland had driven to the Yale 25, and Groves dropped back to try a 38-yard kick. "It didn't miss," said Heine, who had replaced the injured McQuade in the third period. "It was eight feet inside the post but the referee wouldn't call it good."

Byrd maintained it was good "by a country mile." But it did not count, and when another Maryland fumble in Yale territory—its fifth of the game—stopped the Old Liners' final scoring threat, Yale had survived what the *Post* called "the greatest surprise the bowl has seen since it opened in 1914."

The game ranks as one of Maryland's greatest, even in defeat. Byrd said it was the most glorious effort by any team he had coached.

Maryland went on to beat North Carolina State 26-12 with McQuade scoring twice and Besley returning an interception 41 yards, and Catholic 40-6 in the stadium dedication game, before finishing with a disappointing season-ending tie with Hopkins 6-6. The *Post* compared Hopkins to David knocking off Goliath, but only a missed conversion by Groves deprived the Old Liners of their eighth victory.

From this 1923 team came four players Byrd picked on his all-time squad: McQuade, the bull-like fullback; Supplee, the flitting end; Burger, the tall husky, intelligent tackle; and Hough, the tough guard who was so cocky he would challenge his opponents to outfight him.

Byrd drilled the team by scrimmaging it every week against either the Third Army Corps or the Quantico Marines. A fellow by the name of Eisenhower coached the Army team.

"They were the dirtiest guys I've ever seen," said Hall. "First day I played them, I had every tooth loosened. You'd tape hard pieces of leather across the back of your hands in those days. It was a wicked tool."

Heine and Hall recalled the day when Lanigan was manhandling a much larger Army player. Eisenhower got angrier and angrier and finally yelled at his man, "How can you let him do that?" Lanigan glanced up and yelled back, "Why don't you come down here and show him?"

Lanigan, Pugh, McQuade, Burger, and Hough later all joined the Marines and made the rank of colonel. "Lanigan said he lived in fear that Eisenhower would be his commander and remember who he was," said Hall.

Hough, Pugh, and Burger, along with Heine, also all came from the same high school, McKinley Tech in the District. Years later, Burger, stationed in Shanghai, was picked to referee the area's yearly football game. The game's organizer asked him if he knew anything about the umpire, a Lt. John Hough.

"Yes, he used to play right guard next to me during my years at Maryland," replied Burger.

And how about a Lt. Pat Lanigan, who will be the linesman?

"Sure," said Burger, "he played right end."

"Goodbye," said the organizer. "I'll call you tomorrow when you are sober."

Instead Of Washing Dishes

If he had wanted to wash dishes, Maryland would never have heard of Gerald (Snitz) Snyder. But the fun-loving Snitz was not going to wash dishes, even for a scholarship at a Pennsylvania prep school, and that decision initiated a series of events that brought him to College Park.

Both parties benefited from the result. Maryland got one of its all-time great runners. Snyder got an education, and loads of enjoyment, out of his college career, despite constant run-ins with the not-always open-minded Curley Byrd.

Snyder made famous a Byrd offensive innovation, the spinner or fake reverse. The widely-respected former columnist of the *Washington Post*, Shirley Povich, gave Byrd credit for creating the play, although legend laid its hands on Michigan's great coach, Fritz Crisler.

"The play was made to order for Snyder," said Louis (Bosey) Berger, who was a freshman during Snyder's senior year. "He had all the right tools." Those gifts included a quick start and power.

"No one ran the play afterwards with the ability of Snyder," wrote Povich. "When he carried the ball, he was the personification of leg-drive through the middle."

Snyder came to Maryland as a freshman in 1925 during a second straight disappointing season for Byrd's players. Following the ecstasy of 1923, the 1924 team – despite the presence of such stars as Supplee, Burger, Hough, Lanigan, Besley, Osborn, Pugh, and Hall from the year before – was struck by injuries and fell to a 3-3-3 record, including scoreless ties with Catholic, North Carolina State, and Hopkins. The 1925 team dropped even more, to a 2-5-1. Yale had administered back-to-back wallopings of 47-0 and 43-14.

Fortunately for Byrd, who still disdained recruiting, players like Snyder occasionally wandered into the football program.

"I was at Bellefonte Academy outside Altoona, Pennsylvania, after I got out of Windber High," Snyder said, "I had a partial scholarship but I didn't realize that meant washing dishes. I did it for two weeks and that was enough. I went home."

Snyder had intended to wind up at the University of Pittsburgh. But now, at age 20, two years out of high school and not about to mine coal, he went with a friend, Jack Keenan, to Maryland, a school he had heard of only after that 16-14 loss to Yale in 1923.

"We had a hard time finding Maryland, we came to Washington and asked where the University of Maryland was," Snyder said. "They said Maryland Agricultural? I said no, the University. Finally we got someone to tell us to take the street car and we did and told them they had a couple of players."

Snyder had been a center, guard, and tackle in high school where he was toughened up by playing on rock-hard fields. On Thanksgiving Day his team traditionally competed in snow and the officials used coal dust to mark off the field.

He was not a serious student at first. "I figured I'd hang around a semester and then leave, but it was so much fun playing football, I decided to stay."

The fun began in his freshman year. Grades were a problem, and against Navy he was ineligible to play. In the second half, with a substitute freshman coach looking the other way, he put on another player's uniform. "I played as Rosie Fredenwald and they never knew," he laughed.

His antics continued throughout his career. At least twice Byrd caught him after he had been out "having a few kicks" on road trips. Once he was allowed to play, but against Florida in 1927 he was suspended. Then came a controversy over captains in 1928, a dispute Snyder says Byrd started because of him.

"There weren't that many seniors on the 1928 team and I

was pretty sure to be captain," Snyder said. Byrd maintained he went to strictly game captains to cut out what had become heated competition between fraternities to elect a year-long leader.

"I played my senior year but I really didn't have my heart in it," Snyder said. "I was bitter as hell at Curley. I wound up lacking two units to get my degree, so I came back in 1931 and got them. I don't think he ever thought I could get a degree."

The relationship deteriorated so much that Snyder refused to pick up his weekly scholarship stipend from Byrd until his senior year. By then he owed money to both his fraternity and the athletic department and had to go to Byrd to get $150. It was so easy, he said, "I did it again. But that was all."

Snyder—he was called "Snitz" after a family tradition—was converted into a running back by another Pennsylvania native, Leroy Mackert. The rest came as a result of the fake reverse.

"It was the way we did it," said Snyder. "They'd see me run it a couple of times and give up the ball, then I'd have the ball. You had to cut sharp, the ends would block in and all you would have to do is cut. Once past the line, all I had to beat was the safety."

Byrd employed a double wing, with the fullback getting the snap from center in the middle of the backfield. The fake reverse keyed off cross blocks, the guard blocking the tackle and the tackle blocking the guard, or the end would block the tackle and the tackle the end.

"Sometimes you find players perfectly suited to a play and this was the time," said end Al Heagy, who played with Snyder in 1927 and 1928. "He was built like a brick wall, so big chested. He wasn't speedy but he could cover ground and he could get through that reverse hole very fast. He'd get into the clear and then just overpower the safety.

"He'd go right off my tail at end and next to either Ham Adams or Fred Ribnitzky at tackle. It was made to order to beat a seven-man line."

Ray Poppelman, who later would also make good use of the fake reverse, called it "a very quick opening play, a lot like the draw play in today's football. It would look like a reverse but you'd fake to the wing coming around and then hide the ball on your hip. If the fake was good and you hid it right, you could turn and go right through the hole created by the cross block."

Like Mackert before him, Snyder went on to pro football. He played with the New York football Giants in 1929 and had Steve Owens and Jack Haggerty as teammates. Anytime owner Tim Mara wanted to win a game, he would offer an extra $50 per man.

"It would work," said Snyder, "but we were getting only $2,500 or $3,000 to play and it wasn't much. You were still a bum if you played pro football in those days. I decided after playing one more year in Stapleton, New York, that I should quit and get a respectable job."

So he started working for the government and did not stop until he retired 21 years later. But that was long after he had done a respectable job of upgrading football at the University of Maryland.

Picking On Yale

A near-victory over Yale had brought Maryland into big-time football in 1923. Now, two victories over that same football bully would revive a struggling program.

The first, in 1926, was a momentous occasion. It came in Yale Bowl and again, like 1923, was most unexpected. Maryland had lost three of its first six games and had been trounced by a strong University of Chicago squad 21-0. Snyder, on a 60-yard scoring run and a short touchdown pass reception, had been able to give the team a respectable victory, 14-6, over North Carolina.

Yale was in the midst of a poor season and would finish with a 4-4 record. Still it always expected to beat Maryland, which now had lost six straight times to the Bulldogs. The seventh time was different.

"Chalk up another first for Curley Byrd and the University of Maryland," trumpeted the *Baltimore Sun*. "There is nothing in the history of strictly home-bred Maryland football to equal or even approach what the Old Liners did at New Haven. It was the old story of good, sound football plus inspiration."

Yale was never a factor in the 15-0 triumph. Maryland, which outweighed the Bulldogs, outplayed them from the opening moments. Captain Mike Stevens got things started by picking up a Yale fumble and sprinting 65 yards for a touchdown. In the second quarter, end Ham Adams blocked a punt and carried to the Yale 15. Stevens then made a 20-yard field goal.

In the third quarter, Stevens recovered a Yale fumble on the Eli 20. The Old Liners drove to the one, where Lewis (Knocky) Thomas scored.

Yale never threatened. "Yale didn't derive much pleasure from her attempts to gain through the Maryland line," said the *Washington Post*. Indeed, such players as Earl Zulick (198 pounds), Adams (180), Gus Crothers (188), Art Wondrack (192), and Gil Dent (172), dominated the line of scrimmage.

"Through a dismal and at times discouraging October journey, Byrd and his assistants brought along a team that hit New Haven like a raging Florida hurricane. It was a team at the top of its form," said the *Baltimore Sun*, which added a poem:

When the boys are in a panic,
Dreading foes that loom titantic,
Note the man who grows satanic,
  Shouts "absurd."
This gent loves to find 'em burley,
Brainy, brawny, sour and surly,
You can't reckon with Curley;
He's a Byrd.

But even beating Yale—and having the goal posts torn down by happy Maryland rooters afterwards—could not sustain the Old Liners through their last three games.

They tied Virginia on a 63-yard run by Stevens. Washington & Lee won in the final minutes 3-0, on a field goal by Ty Rauber after Maryland could threaten only twice.

To salvage a winning (5-4-1) season, Stevens had to kick a 17-yard field goal to beat Hopkins 17-14, after Maryland trailed 14-0 at the half. Byrd achieved the turnabout with an un-Rockne like half-time talk. "Can you and will you go out and get 14 points against Hopkins and show that you really are football players?" he asked.

Stevens, who did not play until the second period, helped set up both touchdowns with his running and passing skills before Thomas ran over for the scores. Then a final drive of 52

Captain Mike Stevens scored a touchdown, kicked a field goal, and recovered a fumble that led to another touchdown in Maryland's first victory over Yale 15-0 in 1926.

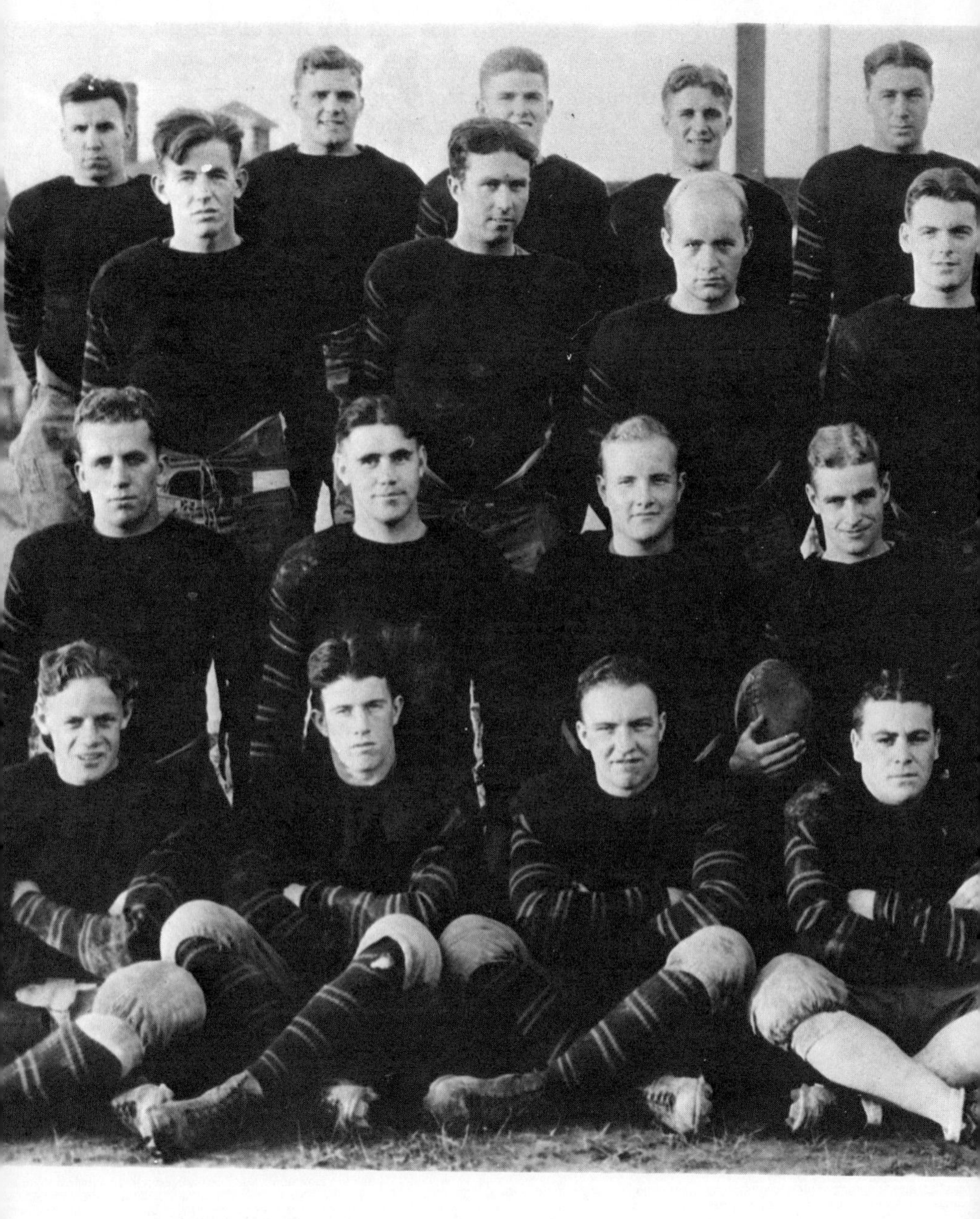

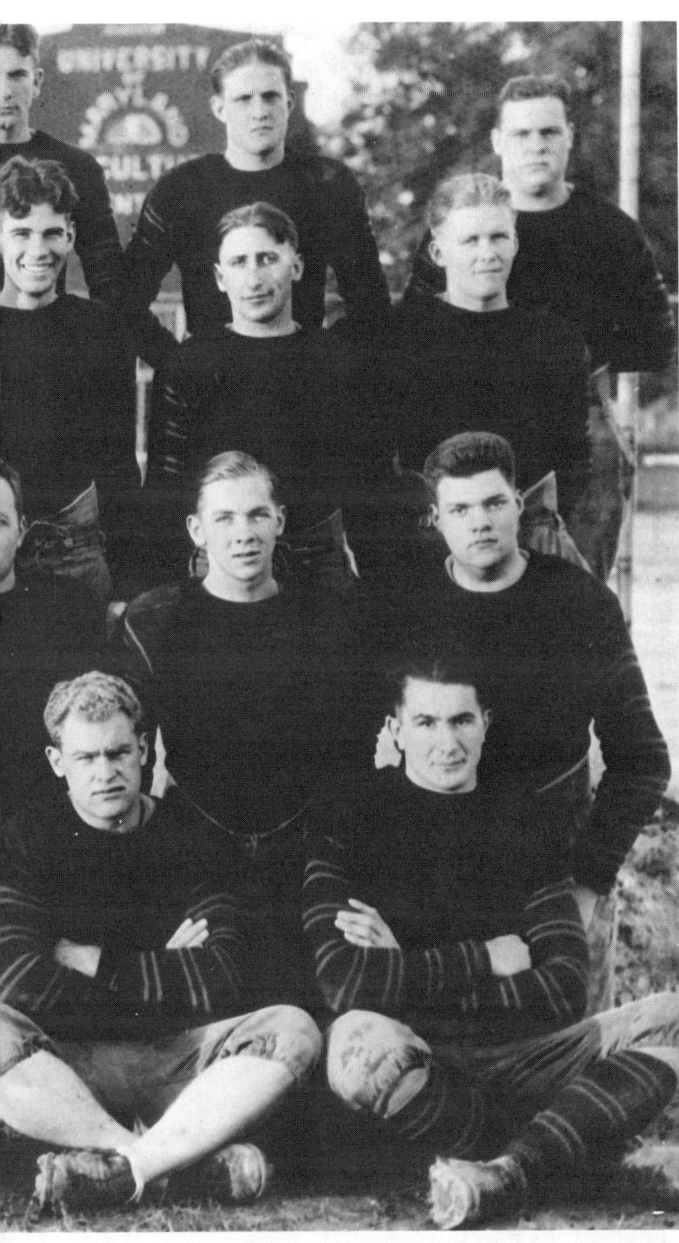

The 1926 Maryland team that gave the school its first victory over Yale: "There is nothing in the history of strictly homebred Maryland football to equal or approach what the Old Liners did...."

yards led to the winning field goal. Stevens was carried to the dressing room by the Maryland rooters.

The next season, however, was a horrible flop: four wins in 11 games, although Maryland outscored Washington College 80-0. Yale got revenge 30-6, Vanderbilt some glory 39-20, and Hopkins, well, the Blue Jays got sweet satisfaction. After not beating Maryland since 1915, they survived a 14-13 triumph when they blocked an Old Liners' conversion.

Byrd had been most charitable to his old rivals. He started his second team and fell behind 14-0 before inserting the regulars. Writing in the *Washington Star*, he said that "many newspaper stories..... are exceedingly charitable toward the Maryland coach. To tell the unvarnished truth, if the coach had elected to spend the afternoon duck hunting or reading a good book or magazine instead of attending the game, Maryland probably would have won without much difficulty. Actually Maryland was about three touchdowns stronger and would have won by about that margin if it had started and played the game as it ordinarily would have played against some of the other elevens it meets."

Snyder had been spectacular at times during the season. He ran 91 yards with a kickoff against Yale and 77 yards from scrimmage against Vanderbilt.

Byrd was just as harsh with himself in the early part of the 1928 season, which was shaping up as yet another dismal one for the Old Liners. Through their first six games they had won two, lost three, and tied one, a disappointment to both the coach and his talented squad.

"We knew we had the good players but we just couldn't seem to pull off the big play when we needed to," said Snyder, then in his senior year. Byrd had a veteran team. Heagy was a standout end, one of the best Byrd had produced, and end Charlie Dodson made some all-star teams. Tackles John McDonald and Herman Lombard were both rugged blockers, Julie Radice a fine linebacker, Augie Roberts a quality punter, and Bill Evans a dangerous passer.

And the Old Liners had two of their all-time greats, Snyder

Snitz Snyder liked to run with the football and have fun. "He was the personification of leg drive through the middle."

and guard Omar (Gus) Crothers, a 195-pound senior from Elkton who had never played football before entering Maryland. Crothers, Byrd said, "was a bearcat in leading interference and almost immovable on defense."

It took Yale, again, to bring out the best in Maryland. The Bulldogs had a 4-1 record, losing only to Army, before entertaining Maryland. "The proportion of the Elis' triumph had been regarded as the only doubtful point in the clash," said one paper afterwards.

Instead, Yale wound up losing 6-0, to the shock of 35,000 fans in Yale Bowl. "Maryland outplayed Yale throughout the game," reported the *Washington Post*. "It outpassed and outhustled its favored opponent. Maryland lit on Yale like a

The 1928 Maryland team that beat Yale 6-0 included Snitz Snyder (middle row, fifth from left), Bill Evans (top row, third from left), Charlie Dodson (bottom row, third from right), Al Heagy (bottom row, second from left), and Gus Crothers (bottom row, fifth from left).

swarm of hornets and obviously stung the Eli players with surprise with their quick changes in tactics from passing to punting."

Maryland took the opening kickoff and got to the Yale 30 before Roberts had to punt. But the drive quickly established Maryland's domination.

The *Post* called that first march "a vicious assault" but the Old Liners could not benefit completely from it until the middle of the third quarter. Snyder and Evans had been combining on passes successfully for much of the afternoon and Snyder thought he had located a weakness.

"I went up to (quarterback) Moon Evans and told him I could beat this guy on a pass," he said. His chance came when

Yale fumbled a punt by Roberts, who had kicked brilliantly the entire contest, and Dodson and center George Madigan fell on the ball at the Eli 20. Two running plays moved the ball to the seven and then Roberts faked a kick and passed to Snyder for the touchdown.

"We were trying our darndest to win the game," said Snyder, who gained 137 yards in the contest. "No one thought we would. Yale was supposed to be super. They had beaten Georgia and Brown and Dartmouth."

Yale coach Mal Stevens had helped to arouse the Old Liners. "Before the game we were trying to decide on the time of the quarters," said Snyder. "He wanted it one way, we wanted it another and finally he went to Curley and demanded it be 30-minute quarters. They finally settled on 15. But we were pretty disturbed by the whole affair."

The Bulldogs made one last bid to win. They blocked a Roberts' punt in the last four minutes and returned the loose ball to the Maryland six. Three plays gained three yards, and then Evans knocked down a fourth-down pass.

Yale's passing problems ultimately cost it the game. The Bulldogs completed just three of 17 tries while Maryland was 9 for 18. Evans and Roberts picked up 115 yards on passing alone.

The victory ignited the Old Liners. They won their last three games, beating Virginia 18-2 after the Cavaliers had grabbed a 2-0 lead; Washington & Lee 6-0 in Griffith Stadium, as Snyder gained 145 yards, and Johns Hopkins 26-6 on Thanksgiving Day as Snyder added 180 yards.

"It wound up a lot better than anyone could have hoped before we played Yale," said Snyder, who had outgained Yale on the ground and wound up with 1,255 yards rushing for the season. He became only the second Maryland player to be mentioned on some All-American teams.

Unknown, Unhonored, Unsung

Louis (Bosey) Berger had come along on the trip to Yale on this November Saturday in 1929 to sightsee. He never expected to play. Indeed, in the first seven games he had only been in once, as an end, and had been hurt on a block. Now as a halfback he was third string and did not even know the plays.

But at half time Curley Byrd approached him. "Berger, you're playing in the second half."

"Where?" the surprised Berger replied.

Maryland was behind 13-0, and halfbacks Augie Roberts and Buck Miller were injured by midway through the third quarter. That left Berger, who had stayed on the field for most of intermission and ran around, trying to stay warm.

"I didn't have my knee pads or my hip pads on," said Berger. "I figured I'd never need them."

Berger's debut was hardly auspicious at first. He twice lined up offsides and Maryland was penalized. Then quarterback Moon Evans took over. "I'll tell you what to do and you do it exactly," he told Berger.

"A couple of times we told him to get the hell down the field and out of the way," said George (Shorty) Chalmers, then a young sophomore halfback. "It was a complicated offense and if someone didn't know what he was doing, he could get hurt."

Yet Berger could still do two things: run fast and catch almost anything thrown his way. And before he was finished that afternoon, Yale found out how well he could do both.

Yale again was heavily favored to win. The Bulldogs had

lost only to Georgia in five games, and just two weeks before had come from behind to beat Army 21-13 after trailing 13-0. The hero of that victory was sophomore Allie (Little Boy Blue) Booth, the 5-foot-6, 144-pound mighty mite who came off the bench in the second quarter and gained 223 yards and scored two touchdowns and then returned a punt 70 yards for the winning score.

Booth played enough against Maryland to stake Yale to its lead, although he did not see action in the first quarter and was removed midway through the third. Yale jumped ahead 7-0 on a one-yard run by Booth after Maryland fumbled on its own 34. The Bulldogs took the opening kickoff in the second half and marched 70 yards to add another touchdown, but Chalmers blocked Booth's conversion.

His leg hurting, Booth was then pulled from the game, only a few minutes before the unknown Berger was to make an appearance.

Bosey's chance came when Roberts was roughed up on a tackle and removed from the contest. Yale was penalized for the play and Maryland had the ball on the Bulldogs' 30. Evans, who was to outgain Booth for the day, faked a pass and ran to the 14.

Evans called for a pass from Chalmers to Radice. "I never considered throwing to Berger," said Chalmers. "He wasn't in the play." But Berger, going where Evans told him, was open over the middle in the end zone. Chalmers threw to him and Berger looked up and saw the ball. "I just caught it, it was that simple," he said.

Yale then blocked John McDonald's conversion try to keep a 13-6 lead. It stood up until midway through the fourth period when Maryland took over on its own 15 after a fine Bulldog punt.

A series of short passes mixed with runs by Evans moved the ball to the Yale 47. The Bulldog secondary was pulled in, anticipating more of the same passing game, but Evans sent out the speedy Berger for a long throw from Chalmers.

"I just ran as fast as I could and he threw me the ball," said Berger. "When I caught it, I just kept going and then got out of bounds before one of those big Yale guys hit me." He was downed at the Yale four.

Evans then called a triple pass, Evans to Chalmers to Berger. "I usually lined up on the right wing, but this time I lined up on the left and Shorty got on the right," said Berger. "Evans took the snap, gave it to Chalmers, who pitched it to me. Everyone thought Evans had the ball, and I was so open no one was within 15 yards of me."

Berger had almost messed up the scoring play, however. "He started running too soon and was too far away for a handoff, which is what it was supposed to be," said Chalmers. "I had to lateral to him 20 or 30 feet away." McDonald made the conversion this time to insure the 13-13 tie.

"Human machines and individuals have at times seemed to rise above themselves and attain heights undreamed, and so today a group of men from Maryland, calling themselves a football team, rose to stun into silence one side of the great bowl," wrote Curley Byrd in the *Washington Evening Star*.

Byrd claimed that "no football team that ever came from the South to invade a Northern gridiron accomplished more within a given time and with the odds vastly against it then did that which today represented the Old Line State and while every man who stepped out on the field did well, it was a substitute back, unknown, unhonored and unsung, who stretched his slender legs into long strides that ended in two touchdowns."

Yet the coach himself had done almost as much to gain the tie as Berger. The Yale game marked the first success of Byrd's 6-3-2 defense, a significant change from the 7-2-2 formation used by most teams. "Maryland knew that extreme measures would be required to prevent Booth from breaking into the clear in the secondary defense and then causing all sorts of trouble," wrote the *Baltimore Sun*.

So Byrd put three linebackers behind a six-man line and gave Booth two lines to run through. With Radice sparkling at linebacker, Booth got off only one sizeable run and Maryland contained Yale's famed off-tackle power plays.

Evans wound up gaining 84 yards to Booth's 55, and Maryland finished with 15 first downs to 13 for Yale.

The tie unraveled the team's talent. It beat Virginia Tech 24-0 the next week, then demolished Hopkins 39-6. Berger, called Bad News by one paper, scored three times against the

Blue Jays, including twice on that triple reverse-pass that worked against Yale.

The season finale was against undefeated Western Maryland, a power under future Harvard coach Dick Harlow. The Green Terrors, as Harlow's men were called, shut off Chalmers' passing, limiting Maryland to four completions in 10 attempts for 37 yards. They also cut off Maryland from scoring and registered a 12-0 victory.

The Old Liners had moved to Western Maryland's four in the second quarter on a pass from Chalmers to Heagy and a six-yard run by Berger. But a Chalmers pass fell incomplete in the end zone and Maryland lost its only scoring opportunity.

"Once upon a time, down in Crisfield, there was a little boy who believed in Santa Claus until he reached the age of Ferris waists and short haircuts," wrote the *Baltimore Sun*. "The little boy's name was Curley Byrd and he grew up to be coach of the University of Maryland football team.

"Yesterday, it seemed for a moment that Curley's faith in St. Nicholas would be renewed for the good saint slid down the flagpole, carrying a big round touchdown for Curley's team. But they were careless little boys and lost the right to score, so St. Nick gave two touchdowns to the good boys from Western Maryland College. Twenty thousand persons watched him do it."

Bosey, Shorty, Sarge, And Punchy

They were to form one of Maryland's all-time productive backfields. Bosey Berger, the receiver who hated to block and tackle. Shorty Chalmers, the standout passer and fine kicker. Al Woods, a tough, ex-Marine who played so fiercely he occasionally would knock himself out. Ray Poppelman, another ex-Marine and a scintillating runner who would break Snitz Snyder's rushing records.

The four teamed up initially in 1930, but Curley Byrd had an inexperienced line. Maryland could manage just a 7-5 record despite beating all four Virginia schools for the first time. The youthfulness of the team, which had only three seniors, showed in the close defeats, three of which came by a touchdown or less.

Berger led the state in scoring with 12 touchdowns, and Chalmers made 22 of 26 extra points. Poppelman, who, along with Woods, was in his first season, got off to a slow start before sparkling.

Albie Booth enabled Yale to revenge the 13-13 tie by scoring two touchdowns and passing for two more despite once again not entering the contest until the second period. A one-yard plunge by Chalmers had tied the game at seven all in the first quarter before Booth came in. His first play was a touchdown pass; his second was his own 33-yard run for a score. Maryland managed another touchdown on a 60-yard pass-run from Evans to Berger in the second period, but two more touchdowns by Booth in the fourth gave Yale a 40-13 triumph.

North Carolina won 28-21 the next week on a 94-yard fourth-quarter punt return. Maryland then went on a five-game winning streak, beating St. John's, Virginia Military, Virginia, Washington & Lee, and Virginia Tech, before running into Navy.

The Midshipmen scored just once, on the game's second play when Bullet Joe Kirn went 65 yards for a touchdown, running over Berger en route to the end zone. Berger knocked him down, but Kirn got up and continued. The touchdown held up despite three Maryland penetrations inside the Navy 10 which came up empty handed.

That was the first of three games Maryland had to play in a week. On Thanksgiving Day the Old Liners topped Hopkins 21-0, even though Byrd started his second team and Maryland did not score until the third period. Then on Saturday, Maryland played Vanderbilt in Nashville, losing 22-7.

"We hopped a train and rode all night after the Hopkins game," said Berger. "We were bushed. And Vandy was quick. I said to one of the guys, 'Do you think our long stockings are slowing us up?' It seemed that way, the way they were catching us from behind."

Western Maryland, undefeated again but tied once, ended its season with a 7-0 victory over Maryland. The only touchdown was scored by fullback Harold Koppe, who could not get into Maryland two years before.

It was obvious to Byrd at the end of the 1930 season that one of his best teams would be returning in 1931. It had an experienced line, and it had those four backs.

Berger was the best all-around athlete of the four. Byrd once said he would like to have worked with him in track for two months. "I could have him running 49-second quarter miles by the time I'm through," he said.

But Berger was too busy playing baseball, which he did after starring in basketball, which came right after his football heroics. Berger was one of the greatest athletes to ever play for Maryland. He was its first All-American basketball player, beating Kentucky and Adolph Rupp for the Southern Conference title one year on two last-minute baskets. He was so good in baseball that he wound up playing six seasons in the major leagues after at one time being called the minor leagues' best

Bosey Berger was Maryland's first All-American basketball player and a big league baseball player. He was also good enough catching a football to make him a feared receiver.

prospect.

He never played football at McKinley Tech in the District. "I was too busy with baseball and basketball," he said. "I wanted to go to Duke and play there but I didn't get a scholarship. Charlie Dodson, who was an end for Maryland, was working at the phone company with me and he arranged for me to talk to Faber and Shipley about coming to Maryland."

Berger scraped up enough money to go to Maryland, where he slept in Shipley's house for two months. He loved to eat, and when Faber told him he would get a free late meal if he played football, he came out for the team.

"I had kicked and thrown a ball around a lot when I was a kid so I figured why not," he said. "In those days, it was hard to pass up a free meal." Berger could not make the first freshman unit and even with his touchdowns against Yale, did not letter his sophomore year. And that still gnaws at him. "They stopped giving out letter sweaters after the sophomore year," he laughed.

Before he graduated, however, he was to team with Chalmers in what became one of Maryland's all-time passing combinations. The forward pass was still not a respected weapon in those years, and it was thought that Byrd was somewhat daring letting Chalmers and Berger do so much running and catching. "I can see how much more we could have done if we had been as sophisticated as they are today with the pass," said Berger.

The two never had practiced together before the Yale game in 1929, although they were in the same fraternity and had played on the same freshman basketball and baseball teams. Soon they were forming a mutual admiration society.

"Bosey had the hands, the quickness to get to and catch a ball," said Chalmers.

"He could do it all," said Berger of Chalmers. "He could block much better than me. He'd get on me when I'd miss a block. He could kick, he could tackle. He was maybe a better baseball player than football player too. And a good basketball player."

It is surprising that the two were as successful as they proved. The double wing Byrd used was not conducive to passing. Chalmers had to come from a wing to get the ball and Berger, at the other wing, often had to fight his way into the secondary.

When he was not throwing touchdown passes to Bosey Berger, Shorty Chalmers was raising pigeons in his dresser drawer.

But Chalmers was a sweet passer. He had been throwing since he played single wing in high school in Newark, Delaware, and then at Tome Prep School in Maryland. "It was natural for me to pass," he said.

Chalmers was one of the first football players at Maryland to receive scholarship help. He was not actually recruited but visited the school himself to make sure aid was waiting when he showed up in the fall. "I got room, board, books and tuition," he said. "Some prominent alumni would give you a suit or some money. That happened until the middle of my senior year when the depression dried it up."

The man they called Shorty–"I got the nickname in high school, I was 5-8 and my brother was called Slim, he was 6-3, 240"–liked to keep to himself. "I don't think he went to a dance at school," said Berger. "The only time he wore a tie was on road trips." Instead, Chalmers liked to trap muskrats, chew tobacco, and raise pigeons. "I remember one time he came to school with one suitcase and it had two white shirts and a musk-rat trap," said Berger.

A friend at Maryland got Chalmers interested in the pigeons. He used to keep them in his top bureau drawer at school. "I had to exercise a few of them in front of a mirror every morning," he said. The hobby intrigued his teammates so much that they would locate birds for him and help him catch them. He is still at it–racing pigeons every weekend now. "I have about 110 in all," he said.

Poppelman was Chalmers' roommate one semester. "He slept in a feather bed and I slept on a mattress," said Chalmers. "He said it was the only way he could get to sleep."

The bed is perhaps the university's most famous. It was the final bargaining point Byrd agreed to in order to satisfy Poppelman, who had decided that he did not like the "lousy beds they had at the school." So he went to a furniture store, bought some items for both Chalmers and himself and told the man to go see Curley about paying the bill.

"It shocked Curley but he paid it," said Poppelman. "It

Ray Poppelman, who broke Maryland's season rushing record, was considered so valuable by Curley Byrd that he slept on a feather bed.

was a nice bed—but it wasn't a feather bed. I had to get something other than bunks. Chalmers slept in the upper bunk and he'd chew tobacco and spit it down behind the radiator, which was behind the bed. I wanted Shorty on the same level with me."

Poppelman could afford to be a bit brazen. He and Woods played for the All-Marine team at the nearby Quantico, Virginia, base and they were both older and better players than most of their college teammates. Quantico had a crack team comprised of mostly outstanding former college players and both had their choice of schools to attend. Byrd landed them with what Faber said were "the first real complete scholarships Curley ever gave out."

Poppelman had attended San Fernando, California, High School and had been recruited by most of the big west coast schools. But he wanted to go to the Naval Academy and got an appointment from a local congressman, only to lose it when the congressman and his father became entangled in a business dispute. The Marines told him that he could get an appointment if he obtained the rank of corporal. He joined up, played football in San Diego where he met Woods, served in China for awhile, and then was shipped to Quantico. By then the Marines had talked him into attending a regular college.

He had been a sergeant and drill instructor in the Marines—his Maryland teammates called him Sarge—and when he came to Maryland, he thought he was "pretty hot stuff." Yet he also was suffering from an inferiority complex. Byrd brought him out of it be letting him call signals his last two years. "It gave me more confidence," he said. "Curley was quite the psychologist. He knew how to handle me, and keep me from getting moody."

Poppelman ran most of the plays that had made Snitz Snyder so good. But he was a different type of runner. "He was shifty and he changed directions well," said Heagy. "Snitz was more of a power runner."

His Marine sidekick, Woods, hardly ran at all. He was strictly a blocking back, although in the Marines, he, not Poppelman, had a far better reputation as a rusher. "I was known as the Red Grange of the Marine Corps," said Woods. "But when I got to Maryland, they needed a blocking back and I could block and Poppelman couldn't. So I wound up blocking and Ray

Al Woods was known as "the Red Grange of the Marine Corps," but he was strictly a blocking back at Maryland, where he later coached.

wound up running."

Woods got out of high school in 1924 in Columbia, Missouri. His father had died when he was six, and he did not have money to go to college. He joined the Marines and finally transferred to Quantico where he, Poppelman, and the rest of the Marine team would scrimmage Maryland occasionally. Byrd recruited them after seeing them play in these workouts, although he needed political help from Maryland's governor and a senator to get Poppelman out a year early.

"Al was tough, so tough," said Faber. "In his freshman year, we went to VMI for a game. You knew you would get bad officiating when you went off campus and we did. Woods got so mad he chased the ref into the stands and I had to pull him off. I thought he'd kill him."

Woods was a defensive halfback for a while his freshman year until one game when he got so disgusted with the way a teammate was tackling he pushed him aside, moved into his linebacker spot, and made three of the next four tackles. Faber told Byrd and Woods became a linebacker.

He was relentless on defense. He would hit people straight on with his head and would occasionally black out doing it. "We called him 'Punchy,'" said Berger. "He'd hit with his head so much that after a game we'd be ready to go to a dance and he'd be looking for the game."

Woods remembered one game against Virginia in which he got banged on the head and staggered off the field afterwards with a teammate. He turned and said they had better get back on the field. The teammate told him the game was over. "Who won?" Woods asked.

A Team Of All Stars

An examination of Curley Byrd's all-time team chosen from players he coached pinpoints how good his 1931 Maryland squad was.

He picked 22 players. Of those 22, seven were on the 1931 squad, including Woods, Berger, and Chalmers. End John Norris was a first-unit selection and end Al Pease was on the second team. Guard Jess Krajcovic was on the first team along with Woods, while tackle Ernie Carliss was on the second with Berger and Chalmers.

Byrd had brought those players and the rest of the squad along patiently. Krajcovic and Pease started all three years at Maryland and Carliss and Norris for two. Two other members of the front line—Courtney Hayden at guard and Skip Faber at center—also were two-year starters, leaving tackle Charles Keenan the only inexperienced player.

"We really weren't that big," said Berger, "but we were tall and rangy and we had good quickness." Indeed, the line was not big. Krajcovic was 6-1, 183; Hayden 5-11, 181; Faber 5-8, 162; Carliss 6-1, 194; and Keenan 6-0, 188. John Mitchell, who also played center, was 5-11 and 160.

Byrd worked the team as hard as any he had coached. During the first week of two-a-day drills, the players lost so much weight he had to ease up on the workouts. Perhaps he was motivated by the fact that this was his 20th team at Maryland. It was also to be his last great team—the best he ever had.

Its final record was 8-1-1. Only once in the entire season

Seven of the 22 players on Curley Byrd's all-time Maryland team played on the 1931 squad, which was his best in his 23 years as coach. Those players included John Norris (top row, sixth from left), Jesse Krajcovic (third row from bottom, third from left), Al Pease (bottom row, fifth from left), and Ernie Carliss (bottom row, second from right).

were the Old Liners outplayed, and that was at Vanderbilt. Offsetting that loss was their first victory over Navy, a surprising tie with Kentucky, and a rout of still-powerful Western Maryland. Byrd considered only his 1923 team, the one that almost beat Yale, as talented.

The opener against Washington College hardly gave an inkling as to what lay ahead. The visitors, usually a pushover for Byrd, took advantage of nine Maryland fumbles to stay close despite 110 rushing yards by Poppelman. Woods, who would ask Byrd each year if he could carry the ball more, only to be rejected, got off the best run of his career, going 80 yards up the middle for the Old Liners' first touchdown. Chalmers added the second in the fourth quarter for a 13-0 victory.

"He'd tell me, 'Al, I'll put you at back next year,' until finally I had to tell him it was my senior year," said Woods. "He just told me, 'Woods, you're my blocking back.' That's why the run against Washington College was so satisfying."

Next was Virginia, a 7-6 victim. The Cavaliers led until the

fourth quarter on the strength of a second-period touchdown pass set up by a Berger fumble. Poppelman fumbled so much Byrd finally replaced him with Charlie May, who scored the tying touchdown to end a 60-yard drive in the final five minutes. Chalmers then booted the winning conversion.

Maryland had not played Navy from 1917 until the rivalry was renewed in 1930 with yet another Navy victory. "To the country at large, a meeting between Maryland and Navy may not be of great importance but to the athletes of both institutions, every game, no matter what sport, has in it much the same spirit you'll find in the various neighborhood battles of your own home town," said Navy coach Rip Miller before the 1931 game.

For the first time in its football history, Maryland entered a contest against a big-time team conceded at least an even chance of winning. With 10 starters back from the 1930 team that lost to Navy 6-0, the Old Liners were more experienced and, with its passing attack keyed by Chalmers, more explosive.

Yet through the first two games, they had scored only 20 points.

Miller feared Maryland's passing attack and his worry proved justified. The Old Liners scored just once, on a pass from Chalmers to Pease in the third period. But it was enough for a 6-0 victory before 20,000 fans in Griffith Stadium, Navy's first Washington appearance since 1922.

The winning score came after Hayden recovered a fumble at midfield. On the first play from scrimmage Maryland executed a triple pass behind the line of scrimmage, with Chalmers winding up with the ball at his own 35. He then tossed a 40-yard pass to Pease, who had gotten behind Navy's Joe Tschirgi. Pease caught the ball on the 25, evaded Tschirgi's tackle, and scored. Chalmers' conversion was blocked.

Navy, which was hindered by an ankle injury to Kirn, whose run had beaten Maryland in 1930, was contained offensively by the play of Pease and Krajcovic until the fourth quarter. A Chalmers field goal attempt was blocked, and Navy recovered on the Old Liners' 35. The Middies got to the nine but lost the ball on downs, then got it back on the 20 after a bad punt, only to be stopped again.

The Midshipmen lost two fumbles and tossed four interceptions but still outgained Maryland 159-147. "Outside of Navy's big drives, it rarely gave its ball carriers good starts," said one paper. "That was due mainly to fierce charging done by the Marylanders."

"That Maryland team is better than people realize," said Miller. "They are high class."

The Old Liners' next opponent was high class too. Kentucky, along with Maryland and Vanderbilt, was considered a major contender for the Southern Conference title. It had two fine backs, Shipwreck Kelly and Cecil Urbanik. "This is the first season Maryland has been a title threat," said one paper. "If Maryland wins, it can look ahead with some confidence to its game against Vanderbilt."

Kentucky outweighed Maryland 15 pounds per man along the line and physically whipped the Old Liners all afternoon. The Wildcats had more first downs 17-6, and more yards 263-157, but Maryland managed a 6-6 tie—one paper called it a "moral victory"—after leading 6-0 at the end of the first half.

"The Old Line stalwarts took the pounding of their brave young lives from the biggest football team to invade metropolitan Washington in a decade but left the field richly compensated with a 6-point deadlock," reported the *Washington Post*.

Kentucky had been victimized by that old Maryland standby, the triple pass. Following a poor punt by Kelly, May, who had replaced Poppelman, took the snap, faked a run around his right end and tossed a back pass to Chalmers, who was headed in the opposite direction. Chalmers spotted Norris free and hit him on the 15. Norris ran the rest of the way into the end zone to complete the 45-yard touchdown. Chalmers' conversion try missed.

Kelly atoned for his punt by breaking off a 48-yard run in the third quarter. He was pushed out on the Maryland seven but Urbanik scored on the next play for the touchdown. Both teams later had chances to add to their totals but fumbles and interceptions spoiled the opportunities. Maryland lost Woods with an injured knee and Keenan with a broken nose, and only the punting of Chalmers kept Kentucky off balance.

"They had five guys coming at you all the time," Chalmers said of Kentucky. "Our traps wouldn't work. We had to outrun them. But we still should have won. I didn't miss that extra point. The ball went through and then curved off. The ref took a long time, he was waiting for the umpire to make the decision.

"I had been a dropkicker in high school, but as soon as I arrived at Maryland, they changed me to a place-kicker. They said it was more accurate. I liked to drop-kick for distance but place-kicking was better on a rough or wet field."

That ended phase one of the season, which had produced three victories and a tie, but little offense. Then, against VMI, the dormant Maryland attack exploded for a 41-20 triumph. The blast took a while coming. VMI led 20-13 at the half after two Berger touchdowns had gotten Maryland the jump. But Poppelman, shrugging off early season fumbling problems, helped the Old Liners get untracked in the third period.

First he returned a punt 40 yards to the VMI 40. Another triple pass, this one to Berger, placed the ball on the one, where Poppelman scored to tie it. Poppelman returned another punt 20 yards and, with the help of a Berger reception, again scored from the one. His running set up a third touchdown, which

Berger scored from the four. Poppelman, who gained 41 yards in that quarter, finished the scoring in the fourth period with a five-yard plunge.

He had 140 yards in all and one writer said that "had the All-America board witnessed his third-period play the backfield ace of the Old Liners would have been unanimously chosen for the 11. He gave the spark to the Maryland team which turned it into a furious violent attacking unit."

Poppelman topped even that performance against Virginia Tech. He had 156 yards and two touchdowns in a 20-0 victory in which Berger had his fourth score of the year. The triumph set off the first bowl talk in Maryland history, which was quickly doused in two ways–by a student newspaper editorial

Ray Poppelman drives around the end for some of his 156 yards against Virginia Tech in 1931.

and by Vanderbilt.

The newspaper said that Maryland "has a definite policy against the playing of games after the regular listed schedule. There is such a thing as tradition and an athletic policy which is not jelly-like in substance. Football at Maryland never has entered the commercial world. It shall never enter the lists in the future for the game will never deteriorate into a sheer money-making spectacle." Vanderbilt was much more direct. It ended the Old Liners' hopes of an undefeated season with a 39-12 triumph.

Vanderbilt had not lived up to its early season hopes, and had lost two of its last three games, to Tulane and Georgia. Maryland was undefeated and its passing combination of Chalmers and Berger was starting to concern Deep South football experts. "The Old Liners are great showmen," reported a Nashville paper. "No other folks in Dixie combine the razzle dazzle and hokus pokus which Maryland displays. They run a guessing contest behind the line. They practice fraud on their enemies by shuffling the football around via double and triple passes. And George Chalmers is credited with being the surest forward passer in the conference."

The Maryland offense managed to stay close for a half. The Old Liners scored on four runs by Poppelman from the 15 after a long triple pass to Berger. They went ahead 12-7 on a 38-yard pass to Pease from Chalmers after an interception by Poppelman.

Vanderbilt scored at the end of the half to lead 13-12 at intermission, and then the lighter Maryland line, which was outweighed by 15 pounds per man again, gave way in the third quarter. The Commodores scored twice at the beginning of the period, one on a 61-yard run, and led 39-12 entering the final stanza. They outgained Maryland 499-184 on the ground, but Chalmers completed seven passes for 144 yards.

Its hopes of a Southern Conference title shattered, Maryland still managed to beat Washington & Lee 13-7 on two touchdowns by Poppelman, the first set up by three Chalmers passes that gained 63 yards. Poppelman gained 175 yards behind the blocking of Woods, who had not played since the Kentucky game. Hopkins was even easier 35-14, as Byrd used mostly reserves at the game's start and then his regulars in the third quarter. Chalmers threw for three scores and Berger had three touchdowns. Poppelman gained 155 yards, all in the second half.

The season had been a success even before the finale against Western Maryland. But what Maryland did against the powerful players of Dick Harlow gave Curley Byrd perhaps the greatest triumph of his career. It was also the last significant victory in his coaching term at Maryland, which would end three years later.

Western Maryland had had its two and a half year unbeaten string snapped earlier in the season by Georgetown. Yet it was still a fine team, especially on defense and Maryland, which had lost heartbreakers to Harlow the last two years, was only a slight favorite. What happened shocked even Byrd.

From the time Maryland stopped Western Maryland's first drive on its 10 until the Green Terrors scored late in the game, the Old Liners were overwhelming. Their 41-6 triumph was the worst Harlow, the intellectual coach who loved to collect bird eggs, had suffered in his seven years at the school.

"It all came together that day," remembers Berger. "Anything we did went right." Poppelman scored three times, Berger twice, Chalmers once (plus five extra points), and Woods was devastating on defense. The Terrapins, as Maryland was now being called more frequently, were not penalized once during the game. "Behind the superb blocking of Krajcovic, Hayden, Carliss and Keenan, the Terrapin ball-toters shot through yawning gaps in the Terror forward wall, a formation Coach Harlow had tried to strengthen by sending eight men to the line of scrimmage. An attack such as Maryland let loose today hasn't been seen in this city in years and the Terrors stood up under the assault about as long as cornstalks might resist a Kansas cyclone," reported one paper.

Chalmers said that Maryland added a few extra plays for the game. "They started off like our regular ones but then went different. In my junior year, they read everything I was doing but they couldn't do it this time."

Poppelman had never played better. He rushed for 201 yards, a school record that stood until 1974 when Louis Carter broke it in the final regular season game. He had touchdown runs of 55, 47, and 30 yards and gained 114 yards on just six carries in the second quarter. On almost every one of his runs, he was helped with blocks from Woods.

Berger was almost as brilliant. He scored Maryland's first touchdown on a 40-yard pass from Chalmers. Then he returned the opening kickoff of the second half 86 yards for a touchdown, even without the benefit of the flying wedge, which both teams had agreed before the game not to use on kickoffs due to the injuries the formation had caused.

Maryland outgained Western Maryland 441-203 and outrushed the Terrors 360-93. Woods, the long-forgotten Red Grange of Marine football, even had 10 rushing attempts—and gained 72 yards. In the second period Maryland totaled 143 yards, Western Maryland 10. "Many people still consider it the most perfectly played game ever by a Maryland team," wrote Maryland sports historian Hottel. "It was totally unexpected."

For Berger and Chalmers, the contest marked the end of their careers. Berger added nine touchdowns to his 12 of the season before and Chalmers finished as the south's best-known passer. Poppelman, who gained 1,350 yards for the season to break Snyder's record of 1,255, and Woods would return for one more campaign. But with the loss of eight starters, including Norris, Pease, Hayden, Krajcovic, Faber, and Carliss, Byrd would never again see a repeat of the Western Maryland performance.

End Of An Era

By the 1934 season, practice sessions for the Maryland football team had become much more arduous than the games on Saturday. The Terrapins were working long into the night, waiting for Curley Byrd to walk down the hill from his office, take off his collar, put on an old sweatshirt and take up where his assistants had left off. "We had a great pass defense in '34 because we worked on it so long every practice, waiting for Curley," said Al Heagy, by then in the chemistry department and an assistant coach.

Byrd officially was no longer football coach. He had dropped the job, so the Board of Regents were to believe, after the 1932 season. Replacing him was a board of coaches led by Jack Faber, a self-described not-so-brilliant quarterback on the 1924 and 1925 teams who also was lacrosse coach. But Byrd was not ready to let go quite yet. "I was a front for Curley," said Faber, who also was in the biology department. "He was still in charge. He made all the decisions, he ran the team during the games. He just couldn't devote as much time to it as before. But he made most of the practices."

Events in Curley Byrd's life were drawing him further away from football every year. In 1932 he was appointed to the newly created post of university vice-president under President Raymond Pearson. He was still writing for the *Star*, and had interests in a bank, a real estate company, and a publishing company. He was by now a familiar figure at the legislature in Annapolis where he worked vigorously for financial support for the school.

Byrd had survived an effort in 1924 by Gov. Albert Ritchie to have him fired after making what Ritchie considered an uncomplimentary speech. The two were at odds again the next year when Byrd managed to get an $8 million appropriation approved, only to have Ritchie threaten to veto it—and the university—out of existence. Byrd fought off the veto and later coaxed another $20,000 out of Ritchie for a new field house, promising that the rest would be raised. It was not, and the state had to pick up the whole cost. Byrd wound up naming the building after the governor.

His hand was everywhere. He named the student newspaper the *Diamondback* in 1921 after a native Maryland turtle. In 1933 he officially adopted Terrapin—a fighting turtle—as the school's athletic nickname. Years later, according to historian Callicutt, when the new university chapel was being dedicated, and no hymn seemed suitably nondenominational, he promptly wrote the words for one himself.

Despite the fact the nation was in the midst of a depression, Byrd was doing well financially. In 1933 he was making $5,000 as vice-president, $4,000 as athletic director, and $2,500 as coach, plus he had additional income from his private jobs. In 1935 when he finally gave it all up to be president, he said that he would have been worth as much as $1.5 million within two more years.

Other than coaching, the job that appealed to him most was sportswriting. And it was from his job at the *Star* that emerged one of the most famous Curley Byrd stories. He had covered a game between Georgetown and Carlisle and returned to the office to write a flowing story that covered five columns in print. The next week he was called into the managing editor's office and was told what a fine story he wrote.

"Thank you," said Curley. "Don't you think, however," the M.E. said, "that in five whole columns of flapdoodle, you might have found room for just one little line telling who won?" He had left out the score.

Byrd's last football team, in 1934, almost became his best. After a 5-6 season in 1932 and a 3-7 record in 1933, his worst at Maryland, Byrd and Faber put together a 7-3 turnaround for his finale. The only blemishes were a 7-0 loss to Washington &

Lee, a 16-13 defeat by Navy in a highly disputed game, and a 17-14 failure against Indiana. Sixteen more points and Byrd would have had that elusive unbeaten season.

The campaign also marked the beginning of Bill Guckeyson's career at Maryland. Before he was finished in 1936, Byrd already was hailing him as the best football player in Maryland history. For his sophomore year, though, Guckeyson was overshadowed by speedster Norwood Sothoron, who had missed the 1933 season with an appendicitis operation, and George Sachs, who developed into a fine passer. In all, Byrd had at least eight decent backs, and was so deep that sprinter Earl Widmyer, who was the standout runner in the 1933 squad, was relegated to second string.

Maryland lost two of its first three games. The Washington & Lee contest cost the Terrapins the Southern Conference title as W & L wound up the only undefeated team in the league, one game ahead of Maryland. The Navy loss is still debated by the Terrapins, who claim game films showed that a touchdown by Guckeyson should have been allowed. Instead, the referee ruled he had stepped out of bounds.

"We saw the films the next week and it clearly showed that he never stepped out," said Ed Fletcher, a lineman on the team. Still, Navy was Guckeyson's first significant college performance. He caught two touchdown passes from another sophomore, Jack Stonebraker, to spearhead a fourth quarter rally.

The most significant victories were over Virginia (20-0) and Georgetown (6-0). It was Maryland's largest margin of victory to that date over the Cavaliers and its first meeting with Georgetown since 1907. The two schools would stage some marvelous games before the Hoyas de-emphasized the sport.

The Terrapins won six of their last seven behind the passing of Sachs, the running of Sothoron, the kicking of Guckeyson, and the all-around play of 6-5 sophomore end Vic Willis. Maryland finished with a 19-0 triumph over Hopkins in the final game between the two schools. Byrd used reserves throughout against the outclassed Blue Jays, who won 11 of the teams' 32 meetings.

Two significant events then took place. Female cheerleaders were introduced, and Byrd was appointed acting president of the university on July 1, 1935.

He was not much of a quarterback in his playing days, but Jack Faber became Curley Byrd's most trusted assistant and twice shared the head coaching job.

The responsibilities of his new position finally forced Byrd to give up football for good. "He always kind of remained unofficial coach," said Faber. "He loved to have long talks with Jim Tatum in the 1950s. Football was his love. He could never give it up completely."

Byrd needed a replacement. Faber was his righthand man, but his teaching duties and lacrosse responsibilities already gave him a heavy schedule. Yet Byrd was not yet willing to let someone run his football team without some control from the president's office. The solution: he hired veteran Frank Dobson and called him "field coach." Faber stayed on as "head coach," a glorified title for a liaison man between Byrd and Dobson. "I handled all university policy in regards to the football team," said Faber. "Dobson did the coaching. I was happy with the arrangement."

In Byrd's 23 years as head coach—plus those two games at the end of the 1911 season—he had won 118 games, lost 82, and tied 15. Recruiting infrequently and drawing from a state where few high schools played football, he had produced a number of standout players and standout teams. It was not until the 1940s that he decided to make football big time at the school. But in his tenure as coach, he had done much to lay the foundation for its future successes.

The first success was Bill Guckeyson.

The Immortal Guckeyson

His parents were circus performers. Acrobats. He inherited their coordination. "He was the most coordinated human being I have ever seen," said his friend and teammate, Ed Fletcher. "His talents were overwhelming. He could do anything he wanted in sports, with a minimum of practice. I don't think there was a sport in which he wouldn't have been outstanding."

Those who knew Bill Guckeyson and saw him perform his marvelous athletic achievements regard him even now with unwavering admiration and awe. He was to them Superman in jock duds, a legend even before he finished his career at Maryland. Guckeyson had not played football at Bethesda, Maryland, High, yet is considered among his college's finest players. Later, when he continued his education at West Point, he became a standout ice hockey player despite never having put on skates before. When a shoulder injury prevented him from participating in track his junior year at Maryland, he went out for baseball, hit .320, and was courted by the great Walter Johnson to take up the sport on a pro level.

"At a track meet one time, I was entered in the javelin and Guke the shot," said John Gormley, another teammate and friend. "For some reason, he couldn't throw the shot so I told him he should try the javelin. I showed him how to take the steps and how to throw and he wound up getting off a better throw than me."

He eventually became an accomplished javelin thrower, and just missed making the 1936 Olympic team in the event.

Bill Guckeyson, the son of acrobats, never played football before entering Maryland. He is considered by many to be the school's all-time player.

His best throw was 208-5. He put the shot 46-8½ and tossed the discus 135-11. In six dual meets his senior year, he scored 83 of a possible 90 points.

He lettered for two years in basketball, one in baseball, two in track and three in football. He was the first football player Maryland had pushed for All-American honors. He was twice named All-Southern Conference halfback and played so well against Indiana in 1935 that the Hoosiers named him the best back they had faced all year, despite the fact that they also had encountered Chicago's great Jay Berwanger.

Guckeyson flourished in the era of the triple threat football player. He punted with great accuracy and distance, he ran with a deceptive gait that Georgetown coach Jack Haggerty compared to Red Grange's, "only a helluva lot better." He was a fine passer, a sure-handed receiver, a sufficient blocker, and a demon defensive player.

"He had such natural talents," said Faber. "He could do anything. He was quick and fast. There was nobody close to him and he played in an era with many good backs. He just had it. No one taught him how to play. He was too good to coach."

He ran with what Heagy called "a wonderful pace" that allowed him to follow his blockers and then dart into the secondary. "He was electrifying," said Heagy. Ed Minion, who was a running or pulling guard during Guckeyson's career, marveled at the way he could set up a block. "I was able to get leverage blocks on defensive ends and halfbacks because of his moves," said Minion. "It made my Saturday afternoons easier."

Light-haired and quiet, he was the epitome of the All-American boy. His teammates can never remember him smoking, drinking, or swearing. "You had to like him," said Fletcher. "He never was critical. He was great to be around." He had been raised by his grandmother, a fiery type who followed him to all his games and even helped coach him in track. From her, his teammates say, he learned competitiveness and a gentlemanly behavior.

Yet there was another side to Guckeyson. He was a practical joker, "the sneaky type," as Minion puts it. This trait came out best through his ability to draw. "One time he drew a picture on the blackboard of his ROTC commander running to the bathroom with his pants down," remembered Fletcher. "It was hilarious. The only problem was that it never got erased and he got into trouble when the commander and the ROTC students saw it the next day."

Guckeyson was Maryland football in 1935 and 1936, during which the Terrapins managed 7-2-2 and 6-5 records. In 1935 his tale of heroics was something out of Hollywood:

He carried four times for 100 yards and one touchdown and kicked seven punts for an average of 57 yards before leaving in the second quarter of Maryland's 39-6 triumph over St. John's.

He scored the only touchdown on a 14-yard run and punted 13 times for a 47-yard average in a 7-0 victory over VPI. His first six punts averaged 49 yards and were not fielded by the safety man.

After losing to North Carolina 33-0, Maryland beat VMI 6-0 on a touchdown by Stonebraker. Guckeyson saved one touchdown with a tackle and set up Maryland's score with a 29-yard run.

His kicking led to a 20-6 triumph over Florida. His 75-yard quick kick forced Florida to punt from its three, and he

Bill Guckeyson takes off on a 66-yard touchdown run against Richmond in 1936. He earlier had a 66-yard punt return and an 80-yard punt. Such performances were commonplace during his career.

returned it 40 yards to the Gator one, where Charlie Ellinger scored. His quick kick in the second period was fumbled and recovered by Maryland on the Florida 21. After a three-yard gain, he passed 18 yards to Willis for the touchdown. An 85-yard punt in the third period forced Florida to kick again, and then he went 18 yards to set up Stonebraker's 16-yard scoring romp.

"Bill Guckeyson came to Florida with plenty of ballyhoo behind him," wrote a Gainesville paper. "And for once a widely heralded star came right up to the mark. Maryland swears that Guckeyson was a stranger to football when he went to school there. He had not played in high school. He's certainly a quick learner. He has one of the most deceptive loping strides with a change of pace that we've ever seen on a halfback."

He scored one touchdown against Virginia after passing to Willis to move near the goal, and gained most of the yardage before Ellinger's winning run in a 14-7 victory.

He passed 33 yards to Willis for a first down at the Indiana one, where Gormley scored. The Hoosiers, however, overcame a 7-6 deficit by scoring a touchdown in the final minutes for a 13-7 win.

By scoring two touchdowns in a 12-6 triumph over Georgetown, he sent writers scurrying for new adjectives. "Bill Guckeyson, an apparition cloaked in black and gold, beat Georgetown yesterday, not Maryland," said the *Washington Herald*. "Lanky Bill Guckeyson decided to make Georgetown's homecoming his own private goal-going party," said the *Washington Post.*

Guckeyson ran 50 yards for a touchdown on the game's third play, then took the opening kickoff in the third quarter and returned it 90 yards for his second tally. "With a pair of Georgetown runners bearing down on him, Bill darted to the right, then skimmed along the sideline. There were Hoyas all around him. How he remained within bounds will ever be a mystery. At times he was less than a foot away from the boundary as he sped toward the field's middle mark," reported the *Post* about the kickoff return.

He punted 13 times in the pouring rain to keep favored Syracuse locked in a 0-0 tie. One came after the snap bounced to him on his own one. He picked it up and kicked to the Syracuse 44.

In beating Western Maryland 22-7, he passed for one touchdown, set up another with an out-of-bounds punt at the Terror nine, and scored a third on a 60-yard run with an intercepted pass. He also tried eight punts, none of which were returned. In all he gained 66 yards rushing, passed for 56, caught one pass for 15 yards, and intercepted two others.

His 1936 performance was not quite as brilliant, mainly because he missed the opening three games with an injury. Yet he still had his sensational moments despite a somewhat disappointing season for the team.

His first appearance was against Virginia, and he promptly returned a punt 60 yards for a touchdown in the 21-0 victory. He passed for one score, ran for another, and punted a school-record 511 yards against Syracuse in a 20-0 triumph. He raced for a touchdown against Florida in a 7-6 loss after setting up the score with a 38-yard pass to Willis. He returned a punt 66 yards against Richmond in the first quarter, then ran 66 yards for another score in the third. He gained 119 yards in all in the 12-0 victory, and he booted an 80-yard punt. He registered Maryland's only touchdown in a 13-7 loss to VMI. He caught a 55-yard pass from Ellinger in the first period and gained 103 rushing yards but Georgetown won on a fourth-period touchdown 7-6. He intercepted a pass and started a play that resulted in three laterals and a first down on the Washington & Lee 35, setting up Maryland's first score in a 19-6 triumph. He gained 85 yards, punted six times, and ran for 20 yards on his last career carry, but Western Maryland won 12-0 in the season finale.

"His performances," said the *Baltimore Sun*, "do not show either his flaming defensive spirit, his ability to block for others or his uncanny punting."

Said Dobson: "During my four decades of coaching, from the University of Georgia to the University of Maryland, it has been my privilege to be associated with hundreds of fine young American boys, many of whom stood out above their teammates because of particular skills or qualities, but few had the inspirational leadership and the sterling character that made Bill Guckeyson the greatest athlete I have ever known."

Guckeyson wanted a career in the military and he got an

appointment to West Point, where he hoped to play more football. But in his sophomore season, it was ruled that athletes who used up three years of eligibility at another school could not participate in football at either West Point or Annapolis. So, in between struggles with math that forced him to repeat one semester, he starred in track, basketball, baseball, hockey, and soccer, his specialty in high school. According to Maryland sports historian Hottel, he was hailed as the greatest all-around athlete at West Point since Elmer Oliphant, generally considered the school's greatest.

He graduated from West Point in 1942 and became a pilot. "I saw him for the last time in Richmond just before he went overseas," said Fletcher. "He was married by then. She was a great girl, just like you would expect from Guke." Guckeyson was shot down and killed in Europe on May 21, 1944, while on a bomber mission.

The Roller Coaster Years

Frank Dobson represented a gamble by Curley Byrd, who had prided himself on having all Maryland alumni on his football staff. Dobson, who attended Princeton, was definitely an outsider in what was such a closed camp that Byrd, Faber, and Eppley, by now the athletic director, all lived within yelling distance of each other in College Park.

Dobson, however, also represented experience and success. He was head coach at Georgia in 1909, head coach at Clemson from 1910 to 1912, and then head coach at Richmond for 20 years, where he compiled a 105-55-16 record while also handling basketball, baseball, and track. He had been a pro in both basketball and baseball, playing one season with the Pittsburgh Pirates.

"He was a sweet, low-keyed person, a fine gentleman," said Ed Fletcher. "He never yelled or got very upset at anybody. He was a fine coach. He really knew his football."

Dobson had never graduated from Princeton. While playing football for the Tigers, he also was paid $3 for performing for the Dowington, New Jersey, professionals. The president of Princeton, Woodrow Wilson, heard of his two-timing and dropped him from the squad. Eventually, he even managed a minor league basketball team and was a professional singer on the side.

Byrd decided to let Dobson take full control of the football team in 1936 after a successful (7-2-2) campaign in 1935. Byrd himself had less time than ever to worry about football.

Frank Dobson had to try out as a field coach for a year before Curley Byrd would let him have full charge of the football team. Dobson did not find a lot to smile about later.

He had finally been appointed president of the school in 1936, with the "acting" title dropped. As usual where Byrd was concerned, the appointment did not come without controversy. Byrd, who did not have a Ph.D., lacked the educational background required of most college presidents and many considered him unfit for the job. A student petition with 1,700 signatures urged his permanent appointment and a large majority of the faculty supported the appointment. The Board of Regents approved it 7-2. Later he was to receive an honorary doctor's degree from Western Maryland.

Dobson produced a strange mixture of seasons at the school. He went from having an outstanding team in 1937 to producing two of the school's worst in 1938 and 1939. The second of those failures cost him his job.

Dobson disliked recruiting, which contributed heavily to his dismissal. He never sought talent and wound up trying to coach teams that lacked the quality of his opponents. "He would talk to a recruit as a student but not as a player," said one Maryland athlete. "He never emphasized football and it hurt him." As a coach, Dobson believed in a psychological approach. He would spend hours analyzing his players, trying to determine what positions they would best fill. "He probably has the most complete tabulating system in existence for analyzing players on a collegiate grid squad," said one paper.

"Dobson was mild-mannered, thoughtful and considerate," said Heagy, who worked under him as an assistant. "He really liked his players and tried to treat them well."

The players responded in 1937, a year which began with no one, writers or coaches, quite knowing what to expect from Maryland, now that Guckeyson was gone. They knew that Jim Meade, a halfback opposite Guckeyson the season before and a talented punter—perhaps better than even Guke himself—was returning, but even Meade could not replace a Guckeyson.

Yet Dobson and his players produced the third of the three outstanding pre-World War II Maryland teams. It was equalled only by the 1923 and 1931 showings and missed surpassing both those campaigns by 16 additional points.

The star of the team was Meade, who picked up the nickname "Jarring" from the way he smacked opponents on tackles. "He wasn't as fast as Guckeyson but he was stronger," said

Jim Meade was the type of player, his coach said, "that you would pick first if you were choosing sides."

Faber. "He was a punter, linebacker, ballcarrier, and a great lacrosse player. Guke was more versatile, but Jim was so tough. He was a big, strong guy, a paratrooper later in the service.

"He was the kind of guy that you would pick first if you were choosing sides. I'd want him on my side all the time, he was that tough."

Dobson used both a single and double wing, and in the single wing Meade was the tailback. But even more impressive than his running was his kicking. His strong leg enabled him to boom punts, and he later practiced his trade with the Washington Redskins in pro football.

"Meade was one of the best of that era," said Faber. "He would go into the line time and time again and just run people over. He wasn't pleasant to tackle."

Maryland opened the 1937 season by beating St. John's 25-0, in the final game between what used to be archrivals. The Terrapins wound up winning the series, 18 victories to 11. The next game also was the first loss of the year, a 28-21 heartbreaker to Penn in which Dobson's thin squad was eventually worn down by the Quakers.

For a while, however, the contest was all Maryland's. "From the time Meade punted the kickoff back to the startled Pennsylvanians until this last trick (an on-side kick) failed," reported the *Baltimore Sun*, "Maryland played smart football, capitalized upon opposing mistakes, and for much of the game, kept the Penn defense tipped far enough off balance to appear less robust than it really was. Except for a deficiency in both departments of passing, both on attack and defense, Maryland may well have left the field victorious."

Maryland had scored two minutes into the game on a pass from Charley Weidinger to Blair Smith. Penn came back to tie it up, but Maryland then drove 79 yards in 13 plays for a second quarter touchdown on a one-yard Meade plunge. The lead held up until Penn registered three third quarter touchdowns on pass plays. Meade scored in the fourth from six yards out with three minutes to go. Four Terrapins had played the entire game.

Against Western Maryland, Meade made a quick touchdown after a 65-yard drive to give Maryland a 6-0 lead. That is all the Terrapins got, as Western Maryland cut off Meade's power thrusts. It took fine defensive plays by Weidinger and

Frank DeArmey to preserve the shutout for Maryland.

Another shutout, the Terrapins' third of the season, followed against Virginia 3-0 on a field goal by sophomore Pershing Mondorff, who was strictly a soccer player in high school. The 44-yard boot came late in the fourth period after Virginia had fumbled on its own two.

The victory that made this team more than ordinary came in Byrd Stadium. Syracuse arrived undefeated and highly regarded, and left defeated—Maryland's fourth shutout victim in five games. Meade upstaged Syracuse's Marty Glickman, gaining 92 yards to Glickman's 25, and his total was only 25 less than Syracuse could gain in total on the ground. "They call him Jarring Jim at Maryland," said one paper, "and he lived up to that nickname so far as Syracuse was concerned. He jarred the big Orange team all afternoon."

Meade did not score either touchdown. The first was a 43-yard pass from Weidinger to John McCarthy in the second period. The second came late in the fourth when Frank Skotnicki intercepted a pass on the Syracuse 30 and went into the end zone to wrap up the 13-0 victory.

Florida finally registered a touchdown against the tough Maryland defense, which included sophomore tackle Ralph Albarano and guards Mike Surgent and Willie Wolfe. But Meade scored from the two after a Weidinger to Bill Bryant pass, and then a Weidinger to McCarthy pass, which McCarthy lateraled to Nick Budkoff who carried to the two, set up Weidinger's winning touchdown in the 13-7 triumph.

Mondorff accounted for Maryland's fifth straight victory with his second winning field goal of the season. This one came from 28 yards with one minute left for a 9-7 triumph over VMI. The kick offset a second period touchdown that put VMI up 7-6 after Weidinger had thrown 32 yards to Blair Smith for a score.

Even Mondorff could not help Maryland against Penn State, a 21-14 winner. The Nittany Lions got off to a quick 14-0 lead before Weidinger hit Meade for a 13-yard touchdown and Weidinger ran over from the two for another score. The Terrapins twice drove to the Penn State one, only to miss a run off a fake field goal the first time and have Mondorff miss a real field goal the second time. Then the Terrapins gambled on a

Pershing Mondorff (50, arrow), a soccer player in high school, boots a winning 44-yard field goal against Virginia in 1937.

fourth down on their own 35 late in the game and failed, and Penn State needed only two plays to win the contest.

Before 22,000 fans in Griffith Stadium, Maryland upended Georgetown 12-2. Weidinger and Meade again starred, with Meade scoring one touchdown from the two after Weidinger passes set up the six-pointer. Weidinger then threw to Smith for the second touchdown in the fourth period. Skotnicki, a standout all season in the secondary, intercepted two passes and knocked down four others.

The Terrapins ended the season by blanking Washington & Lee 8-0 for their fifth shutout of the year. Surgent blocked a punt out of the end zone for a safety, and Weidinger ran two yards for a touchdown to end an 11-play, 80-yard drive. By now Maryland was being called the Magicians for their tricky offense and ability to pull off late-game victories. They were also ironmen, as people like Weidinger, Surgent, Wolfe, and Albarano played every minute of every game.

Dobson had special love for his guards, Wolfe and Surgent, who opened wide holes for Meade all season. Weidinger had shown great improvement over the 1936 season, especially in

Frank Dobson had halfback Jim Meade on his 1937 team, but his real love was for guards Mike Surgent (below) and Willie Wolfe.

his role as tactician. And then there was the coach. "Frank Dobson rates a big hand," said the *Baltimore Sun*. "He placed a smartly coached team on the field. No coach can produce without good material, but many of them fail even with full sized squads. He knows his football. His teams are thoroughly schooled in fundamentals, and the leading coaches of the football world will tell you there is no substitute for that."

Within two years Dobson would be fired. He had back-to-back 2-7 years, the first coming after Meade and Weidinger were hurt. In the second, he lost his last seven games. "He didn't recruit and Curley had to fire him," said Faber.

Byrd's search for a new coach proved unsatisfactory, so he settled instead on what Faber called "the first three-headed coaching monster in the history of college football." He chose Faber, Al Woods, and Al Heagy to coach the team as a unit, although the other two agree that Faber made the final decisions.

Byrd had wanted Dick Harlow, now at Harvard after so much success at Western Maryland. But word got out to the newspapers and Harlow rejected the post because of the public pressure the stories created.

"Curley thought we had good seasoning in all those years we were assistants," said Heagy. "We really carried on much the same as before. I coached the line, Al the backs and Jack did the coordination."

Faber describes himself as "not much of a player." He saw some action in 1924 and 1925 but mainly was part of what he called "the scramblers, the ones who used to play the varsity on Wednesday. We used to get hurt by our own people more than by the varsity." Heagy and Woods both had been much better football performers.

The three got along splendidly, but with the limited material left by Dobson the program continued to have problems. The Terps were 2-6-1 in 1940 and 3-5-1 in 1941, even though they had a sophomore tailback named Tommy Mont in the latter year.

"I knew that Curley was looking for a big name coach," said Woods, "we all did. I told him he should give us some big time money to work with, if he wanted us competitive."

Maryland, the trio knew, was not competitive with big-

Jack Faber, Al Woods, and Al Heagy formed what Faber called the "first three-headed coaching monster in the history of college football" during the 1940 and 1941 seasons.

time schools. In 1941 it had lost to Duke 50-0, Penn 55-6, and Georgetown 26-0—the three best teams on its schedule. Byrd had said that if he could "develop a team compatible with our educational program that will win half its major games, we would be happy." But that was not happening, mainly because the school was not making the commitment to football of its rivals.

Unlike most other Southern Conference schools, the Terps still were recruiting infrequently and offering limited scholarship aid. Of the 42 top players on the 1940 squad, 31 were from Maryland and six were from the District. Faber and company changed that ratio a bit in 1942 when eight out-of-state sophomores (in a class of 17) joined the varsity.

By the early 1940s only 20 or so high school and prep schools in the state played football, and the caliber was not very good. Alumni began pushing to upgrade the program, especially in recruiting of athletes outside the state. Big name coaches, like Bob Neyland of Tennessee and Wallace Wade of Duke, were mentioned. And the school newspaper urged a new look in football:

"Frankly, we believe that the boys who play college football deserve financial aid where they need it. They work hard enough in the course of a season to qualify for pay on a fulltime job."

Byrd was staying low-key in his public comments, but the improving schedule and the fact he admitted the alumni association would be permitted to offer scholarships to out-of-state players revealed his real course. Finally, in 1942, he made a major commitment. He hired the famed Clark Shaughnessy away from Stanford with a five-year, $10,500 per year contract.

"We gladly gave up our jobs," said Faber. "Clark was a big name. Everyone was happy he was coming." The trio did not exactly fade away. Faber and Heagy continued to coach lacrosse and Heagy and Woods helped out with football. Faber still is the chairman of the school's athletic board. Woods and Heagy, who now works with Maryland's letterman association, both eventually retired after 41 years at the college.

Maryland's Model T

"We were in awe of him. He was so famous and we didn't really know what to expect. But we were anxious for the season to start. We wanted to show him we could play."

Tommy Mont still has a hint of awe in his voice when he speaks about Clark Shaughnessy. Of all the Maryland players, Mont got to know Shaughnessy the best since he was a quarterback, and Shaughnessy put in hours of extra work with all his quarterbacks. Yet no one really got to know Clark Shaughnessy that well.

"He was a completely dedicated football man," said Mont, "but he was so absorbed in what he was doing that I think his relationships with his players suffered. He thought the technical aspect took preference, I think. It just amazed me then and now seeing the great football mind he had at work."

Shaughnessy was the father of the modern T-formation, which really was one of the oldest alignments in football. "I just dusted it off and jazzed it up a bit," he said. He had coached the great Jay Berwanger at the University of Chicago while learning the intricacies of the T from George Halas and Ralph Jones. When Chicago gave up football in 1939, he was hired by Stanford and took a 1-7-1 team and turned it into an undefeated, Rose Bowl-winning aggregation the next season. He stunned critics with his success. He turned Frankie Albert into a dazzling T-quarterback and started a rush to the formation among his peers in the coaching profession.

After a 6-3 season in 1941, he came to Maryland with his

T and scrapped the school's single and double wing formations. "It was all so new to us," said Mont, "but we knew it had worked at other schools for him so we went at it enthusiastically." Mont was not the only one trying to pick it up. Notre Dame's Frank Leahy visited spring practice to learn the T from Shaughnessy and would spend his nights in Mont's room reviewing the steps and fakes of the quarterback.

Shaughnessy also brought Bears players to the camp to help. "Sid Luckman and the others came in and worked with us," said Mont. "We had some great instructors."

In Shaughnessy's T, Mont did very little running. He handed the ball off and passed, a change for him from his responsibilities in the single wing. But the concept of the T was different from anything the players knew. "Always in the past, the offense tried to coil up power in a ball, then explode it, splitting the defense. The effort was made to stretch the defense thin, then penetrate it," said Shaughnessy. "Our approach is different. We coil up the defense in as small an area as possible, then run around it or throw over it. We shuttle tackles and ends back and forth along the line laterally, shifting guards sometimes in an unbalanced line and sometimes in a balanced line. Shuttling tackles and ends, shifting guards, and setting a man in motion forces the defense out of a set position. It makes old set defenses obsolete."

The Shaughnessy T was complicated. "He made the lineman think in the huddle on every play," said Heagy, who became a full-time assistant for that one season. "The quarterback would give a play number and the number would be accompanied with a letter for the type of blocking, the hole it was going through and the back. He would sit up through all hours of the night drawing plays. He would draw a basic play and we would draw variations.

"He was all business. He didn't fly off the handle or get excited. He was very professional, very aloof. But I never saw a man work so hard to devise an offense."

His work paid off. The 1942 team was Maryland's most successful since 1937. It finished with a 7-2 record, losing only to Duke (42-0) and VMI (29-0). Shaughnessy's offense was 11th in the nation, gaining 2,759 yards, an average of 308 a game. The Terps averaged 156 yards rushing, and 152 passing, fifth best in the country. Mont was just as impressive. He completed 66 of 127 passes for 1,076 yards and 12 touchdowns. He was eighth nationally in completions and fifth in total offense.

Mont had come to Maryland from Cumberland, where he played at Alleghany High. He was a triple threat, a fine punter, passer, runner and place-kicker. "I especially took pride in my punting," he said. Shaughnessy discouraged comparisons of Mont with Albert. "I'll say that Mont has the potential to be a

Frank Leahy of Notre Dame (center) came to Maryland in 1942 to learn the T-formation from Clark Shaughnessy (right). Curley Byrd looks on.

great player," he said. "He fits into my conception of a T-quarterback perfectly."

The opening game of 1942 held two surprises for Maryland fans. One was the ease in which the Terps beat Connecticut 34-0 on three touchdown passes by Mont, who completed nine of 14 passes for 215 yards. The other was the team's new colors, red and white. They had been wearing black and gold, but Shaughnessy liked red. He had a red car and his Stanford teams wore red, so he changed the Maryland uniforms. His supporters said that was okay, since the state colors were cerise, black, silver, and gold.

Shaughnessy also disliked Terrapins as a nickname, figuring it gave out the wrong impression (slow and stolid) and he tried to revive Old Liners as a substitute.

He was a lot more successful winning games. Maryland next downed Lakehurst Naval Air Station, which had a mixture of pro and college players, 14-0. "In the first quarter I spotted a pass play I thought would work," said Mont. "It was in what Shaughnessy called the danger zone, so I told the team in the huddle that I may not be the quarterback any more." But the pass set up the first of the Maryland touchdowns. Mont was six for 13 for 170 yards.

After Maryland had beaten Rutgers 27-13, the College Park campus came alive. The students gave the team a loud sendoff at the railroad station for the trip to VMI, and everything was at a high pitch. Except the train never left the station. "There had been lots of rain that week and the river was high and we couldn't get across any bridges," said Mont. Shaughnessy wanted to call the game off, but VMI insisted that its homecoming contest be played.

So at 5:00 p.m. the 33-man team finally boarded a train, went up to Valley Forge where VMI met the players with open Army trucks. The convoy arrived in Lexington at 5:00 a.m. Nine hours later VMI, led by fullback Joe Muha, rolled to a 29-0 victory. The Terps had only one threat, which ended with a fumble on the VMI eight.

Maryland rebounded the next week against Western Maryland. Mont, who threw five interceptions against VMI, picked apart the Terrors for almost 200 yards, and fullback Jack Wright headed a proficient ground attack in the 51-0 victory.

Tommy Mont was going to Virginia Tech before being talked into attending Maryland. He broke all the passing records before he graduated. He later became head coach.

The Terps then upset Florida 13-0 as Mont passed 22 yards to Jack Mier for one touchdown, then intercepted a pass to set up the second score, a 24-yard heave to Bob James, who later was to become Atlantic Coast Conference commissioner.

Duke, which had gone to the Rose Bowl the year before after beating Maryland 50-0, shut out the Terps 42-0 this time. Maryland got into Duke territory only twice. Mont was more effective against Virginia, tossing two first-half touchdowns and setting up a second-half score with an interception. He was 11 of 19 for the game. Wright and Hubie Werner each scored twice in the 27-12 victory.

Shaughnessy ended his first season with a 32-28 victory over Washington & Lee. Mont, who now coaches at DePauw University, has used that contest as an example of "how not to let down in the second half." Maryland had a 26-7 lead entering the third quarter after Werner went 27 yards for one touchdown, Wright plunged one yard for another, Monk Mier scooted 27 yards for a third, and Mont passed 27 yards to Johnny Gilmore for a fourth.

"They said something to me at half about how I was near a national passing record," said Mont. "I don't think I completed a pass in the second half." He did, just enough to get Maryland another touchdown in the fourth period and hold off W & L's rally.

The season had been a delight for Maryland fans. Wright, who Shaughnessy called "the perfect fullback for a T-formation," scored eight touchdowns and Werner had seven. Mont was among the nation's best passers. Shaughnessy had emerged once again as a prominent coach.

Then, to the shock and dismay of the players, the rooters, and Byrd, Shaughnessy quit, jumping to the University of Pittsburgh. The move caught everyone by surprise but by then World War II was eating into the athletic ranks and most of Shaughnessy's players would not be returning next year. For his new coach, Byrd hired Dr. Clarence Spears away from Toledo. Spears, who had compiled a 138-61-13 career record over 25 years at Dartmouth, West Virginia, Wisconsin, Minnesota, Oregon, and Toledo—and had coached Bronko Nagurski—ran a strictly civilian-player program at the school. He did surprisingly well, considering he had to compete against much more experienced clubs. His squad of 17-year-olds, 4-F's and a few veterans won four of nine games in 1943 before falling to a 1-7-1 record in 1944. Spears then decided to enter private medical practice, leaving Byrd again without a coach.

With the war winding down, he could select from a larger field this time around. The man he settled on, a young former assistant and player at Alabama, would later become a legend among college coaches. His name: Paul (Bear) Bryant.

The Bear

On the day Gen. Douglas MacArthur raised the American flag over Tokyo, Paul Bryant was named head football coach at Maryland. It was his first college head coaching job, although he had been a successful assistant first at his alma mater, Alabama, and then at Vanderbilt. At 32 he was ambitious and tough, and a winner, something the Terp players discovered before the end of the 1945 season.

Byrd, who reviewed more than 100 candidates for the job, had made his decision after Bryant, then a lieutenant commander in the Navy, had been told that the Navy Preflight School team in Chapel Hill, North Carolina, which he was to have coached, would not field a squad anymore. It also helped that Bryant could bring a ready-made team with him.

"He called me into his office in Chapel Hill and asked me to meet with the preflight team," said Vic Turyn, Bryant's quarterback. "He said he could go to Georgia Tech or Alabama as an assistant or to Maryland as head coach, but he would go only where the players decided to go. We met and chose Maryland. There were 25 at first."

Fifteen wound up at College Park, including Dick Johnston and Bob Crosland, former Duke players; Harry Bonk, a fullback from Bucknell and Dartmouth; Gene Kinney, Dartmouth tackle; Leroy Morter, Dartmouth end; and John Schrecongost, Bethany center. Bryant mixed them with 15 lettermen from the 1944 team. "We've got what amounts to a pretty good group of freshmen," said Bryant. "The youngsters should develop as the

Paul (Bear) Bryant, flanked by assistants Carney Leslie (left) and Ken Whitlow, had not become a legend yet when he started his head coaching career at Maryland in 1945.

season progresses and by next year we ought to be able to play a better class of football."

Bryant had long sought a chance to prove his ability as head coach. "Maryland was a great opportunity," he said. "We were fortunate to get some more experienced players to come to the school, but I made some dumb mistakes. I was overanxious to prove how good I was and I overcoached. But it was still an exciting time."

It was also an exciting time for the players. Bryant was a different breed of coach. He was still young enough to get on the field and demonstrate, instead of talk about, how he wanted things done. "He taught hard-nosed football," said Turyn. "We'd really hit. It seemed like every day, he'd get upset and throw down his hat and say, 'let's hit.' I'd pair off with a fullback and we'd be bleeding by the time we stopped. He taught us to block and tackle face up. I know my face was raw flesh all season."

Bryant only asked his players to be as tough as he was in his collegiate days at Alabama, during which he once played a game with a broken leg. He was an end opposite the great Don Hutson, and his team went to the Rose Bowl in 1935 and beat Stanford. "He thought nothing of hitting along with us," said Turyn. "On this one play, Harry Bonk and I would double team the end and we were giving him an awful beating and Bryant was yelling at him. So we told Bryant to go over there and try to stop us. He tore us apart with his elbows. We'd try to work on him as hard as we could but he'd usually come up best."

Bryant enjoyed those early coaching days the best. "I like getting down on the field," he said, "and working. I could get to know the players so much better and I felt like I was doing more." Now, at Alabama, he spends most practices supervising affairs from a 20-foot tower.

The players responded to his aggressive ways with respect and performance. "He had us believing that regardless of our size we were so good we couldn't get beat," said Turyn. "The guys would do anything for him. He had a soft spot in his heart off the field. He would do anything for you."

Years later, when Turyn was working for the FBI, he was located in various cities throughout the country. Bryant would keep up with the moves, and everytime he was in a city along with Turyn, he would call his ex-player. "He preached loyalty and he gave loyalty back," said Turyn. "It wasn't hard then to see he would be a success. He was so intense. Football was his life, and he wanted to be the best there was."

Bryant refers to his early coaching career as "my upchucking days," for the way he would get sick before games, right along with his players. With the upset stomach, however, came victories that year at Maryland, six in nine games. "We would have been undefeated if it weren't for my bad coaching," said Bryant, using a line that became a common Bear remark during his fabulous career, which has included six national championships.

A delayed discharge from the Navy prevented Bryant from

17

getting to Maryland until late September. Heagy spent a weekend with Bryant in North Carolina going over plays, then ran the team until Bryant showed up.

Maryland's first game was eight days after Bryant took charge, but the Terps still handled Guilford College easily 60-6 with eight preflight players in the starting 11. Seven of the nine Maryland touchdowns were scored by preflight players.

Maryland received one Top 10 vote after beating Richmond 21-0, as halfback Dick Poling ran 67 yards for a touchdown and Bonk added two other scores. Poling hurt his leg and did not play against the Merchant Marine Academy, but Maryland won its third straight, 22-6, scoring on its first possession for the third game in a row. Bonk registered that touchdown, his fifth of the season, and reserve Bobby Piker added two more.

Talk of going to a New Year's Day bowl stopped the next week against Virginia Tech. The Gobblers upset Maryland 21-13. "I took them too lightly," said Bryant. "They had lost the week before (38-0 to William and Mary) and I thought we'd have an easy game." Instead, VPI picked up its first victory by registering two second-half touchdowns with a ground-control offense.

West Virginia converted a fumble into one touchdown and then drove for a score in the final minutes to tie Maryland 13-13 after Poling had scored twice in the first half. William and Mary then handed the Terps their second defeat 33-14. Maryland had a 14-6 lead in the third quarter, then made a horde of mistakes to allow William and Mary to rally with 20 third-quarter points.

The rest of the season was all Maryland's. The Terps trounced VMI 38-0 as Sam Behr scored twice and VMI managed three yards rushing. They then registered their most significant triumph, a 19-13 defeat of unbeaten Virginia, which had been courting a bowl bid. Poling passed 45 yards to Don Gleasner with 65 seconds left for the victory, which snapped Virginia's 14-game winning streak. Gleasner caught two touchdown passes

Vic Turyn came with Paul Bryant from the service to quarterback Bryant's Maryland team.

and Behr returned a kickoff 90 yards for another score.

Turyn was sick and did not play. Virginia badly outweighed Maryland, which started 10 freshmen. Yet the Terps outgained Virginia 203-133, and were stopped from scoring more by the Cavalier defense, which halted drives on their own 3, 5, 19, and 20. Virginia coach Frank Murray was furious, declaring that Maryland had played "dirty ball" to win.

Maryland finished off the year by whipping South Carolina 19-13 after jumping to a 19-0 lead. Behr scored from 45 yards out and Bonk from the two.

Byrd thought that his football program was now "set for years," but Bryant dropped a surprise in January by accepting a five-year, $12,000 contract from Kentucky. Byrd said it caught him "by complete surprise," but Bryant has a different story.

"I had been away visiting my family in Alabama and came back to the Maryland campus," said Bryant. "The first thing I saw was this player I had suspended walking into his room, which he was supposed to be out of. I asked somebody what was going on and I was told Curley Byrd put him back on the team. Then I found out he was going to fire one of my assistants.

"Now I truly loved Curley but I couldn't put up with meddling with my team. I went inside and started to cry about it. I looked through my mail and there was this telegram from the President of Kentucky asking me to get in touch with him. I did and he offered me a job. I took it and went to Byrd and told him I was leaving."

The football team and student body heard about the resignation and protested. They staged a torchlight parade to Byrd's house that night. Byrd, dressed in pajamas, told them that "I want Coach Bryant to stay but he has a better offer and is leaving." After building a bonfire, the crowd broke up. Few students went to class the next morning. Instead, they staged a rally in front of the administration building.

Bryant finally had to talk to them to get them back to class. "I am leaving of my own free will," he said, "and I'm not under pressure from President Byrd. I'm not taking any players with me. Frankly, I think there is a better opportunity for me at the University of Kentucky.

"Everybody has treated me swell at Maryland. I've been

given everything I wanted. You students have been loyal, the members of the team were among the finest fellows I've ever known and the administration and athletic people have cooperated in every way. Now please go back to your classes. This strike isn't doing anyone any good."

So Maryland and Byrd launched yet another coaching search. "I believe in winning," he told the football team at its annual banquet. "Success comes from success. Since I do know something about what constitutes good coaching, the word I leave with you is that next fall, whoever it may be, we will have some one to give you the kind of coaching to give you another winning football team."

To the astonishment of the football world, that man proved to be Clark Shaughnessy; however, he did not fulfill Byrd's prophecy.

Shaughnessy, the same man who left Maryland in 1943 to coach Pittsburgh, had just been released from his job by the Panthers after seasons of 3-5, 4-5, and 3-7. "He is one of the best two or three coaches in America," said Byrd. "The fact he had trouble at Pittsburgh doesn't alter the fact that he is a great football coach."

During his time at Pittsburgh, Shaughnessy was working as an advisor to the Washington Redskins, an arrangement that the Pittsburgh administration finally grew to dislike. Byrd allowed him to continue the pro relationship at Maryland. "He was a pretty high-priced coach," said Faber, "and if Curley could share his salary with the Redskins, he was better able to afford him."

Shaughnessy missed three weeks of preseason, working instead with the Redskins. He ran a shuttle between Washington and College Park, helping with the Redskins in the morning and coaching Maryland in the afternoon. He had Redskin assistants aiding him with the college players. But these players needed full-time coaches. "We were a real mixture," said Mont, who had returned from the war. "We had veterans, we had 1944 team members, we had Bryant holdovers, and we had new recruits. It was a very difficult situation. The guys were different ages and there was a lot of talent and it needed some tender handling."

Shaughnessy, never the psychologist, worried more about

Curley Byrd had a full head of curly gray hair by the 1940s. His search for a permanent football coach might have contributed to the color change.

his offense. "There were cliques and dissension and he didn't do anything about it," said Turyn. There were also gobs of talent. Bunk, Behr, Poling, Joe Drach, Crosland, Johnston, and Turyn remained from the 1945 team. Mont, James, and Wright returned from 1942. Shaughnessy added such talented recruits as Vern Siebert, Lu Gambino, and Stan Lavine. Ninety-six players were listed on the preseason roster and 46 played on the varsity sometime during the year.

"We should have gone undefeated," said Turyn. Instead, Maryland finished with a 3-6 record. Shaughnessy decided to divide the squad into two teams, the big team, comprised of the returning war players, and the little team, comprised of Bryant's preflight group. He alternated them by quarters. "We grew apart within the team," said Mont, the quarterback of the war players. "It caused resentment. I hadn't realized that until midway through the season, when everything blew up and we had a team meeting and we let it all hang out."

The climax came around the Michigan State game. Maryland took a 3-4 record into the contest. By now, injuries had forced Shaughnessy to integrate the big team into the more successful little team and that had brought everything to a head. Newspaper reporters found out about the difficulties, and then after Michigan State won 26-14 Shaughnessy lashed out.

He criticized some of his players and said that "a lot of people would refer to some of these boys as bums. There are boys on this team who would have been fired a long time ago by another coach for their personal conduct. I've tried to help them and I hope it hasn't been a mistake. You have to remember most of them have been in the Army a long time. They're all mixed up in the upper story about civilian life. They think the world owes them everything."

His outburst started a major controversy. Maryland officials rejected his inferences about GI's, and talk of his resignation began. A story surfaced that Byrd was none too happy with the two-team system or the lack of discipline.

"I asked Shaughnessy once why he didn't get tougher with us," said Turyn. "He said that when you had been a coach as long as he had, you didn't want to get anyone hurt. He was still a great coach. Mont and he and I would sit upstairs at Redskin games and call plays for Sammy Baugh. One day I called three touchdowns against Detroit. His offense worked for the pros but we had 236 plays. It was too complicated for us."

In January, Shaughnessy resigned. He said he was unwilling to give up his Redskin connections and he also wanted no part of Byrd's idea of making the football coach the athletic director. Byrd, for the fifth time in six years, began looking for a new coach. This time, his choice would be most satisfying.

Some Southern Sunshine

Curley Byrd sat in his office, looking out over the expanding Maryland campus, and waited for a call. A couple of newspaper reporters waited with him. Occasionally Byrd would glance at the phone on his desk.

Out in Norman, Oklahoma, Jim Tatum was waiting to see if the Oklahoma Board of Regents would release him from the remaining two years on his contract as the school's football coach so he could come to Maryland and replace Clark Shaughnessy. A telegram came. It was from Tatum, reminding Byrd that Oklahoma was an hour behind College Park in time.

While he waited Byrd talked. "Funny thing," he said, "a year ago we had a professor of educational administration at Maryland and Oklahoma asked us to release him from his contract so he could become a dean out there. We did. Now it's Oklahoma's time to return the favor."

Byrd had been hurt in his negotiations with Tatum because he was forbidden under state law to give long-term contracts. But he had wrangled a commitment that would guarantee Tatum at least five years. Byrd thought it would prevent Tatum from leaving after a year or two, as Bear Bryant had done.

"Do you think they will release him?" he was asked. "It depends on Bud Wilkinson, his line coach," said Byrd. "If Bud wants to become Oklahoma's head coach, I think they'll let Tatum go. I wish we could get Wilkinson too. He's a real fine coach."

Byrd would tell a story on the banquet circuit years later

about how he had breakfast with both Tatum and Wilkinson at a coaches convention. "I told them either one could have the job," he said. "Tatum wasn't sure he wanted to leave Oklahoma so I said I'd take Wilkinson. We decided they should think about it overnight and decide among themselves who wanted it. Tatum called me the next day and said he did."

Byrd then talked of how he had interviewed Tatum for three hours for the job the year before. "Oklahoma was calling him too. I wanted him then, but another coach, a veteran, had promised to come here. All I could offer Tatum was a job as an assistant for a year or two before taking over as field coach. He took the Oklahoma job and then the other coach sent his regrets." After some prodding, Byrd admitted the "other coach" was Harvard's Dick Harlow. He also had sought Harlow this time around but the athletic board said no.

Finally, the phone rang. Tatum was on the line. The board of regents had given him his release. Byrd pulled out a prepared news release:

"James M. Tatum, successful coach of the University of Oklahoma eleven last fall will come to the University of Maryland February 1 as head coach and in general charge of all athletics," it began. "Tatum...will be completely responsible for all factors connected with the development of football at the Old Line institution."

Byrd finally had made the ultimate commitment to the football program. He was relinquishing all direct controls over the sport and making an outsider the athletic director as well as football coach. Tatum would be allowed to hire his own assistants, upgrade the schedule and do whatever else was necessary to build a winning major college program. The series of hirings, firings, and resignations would stop—for nine years.

Tatum was 33 when he came to Maryland. He had first talked to Byrd in 1942 about becoming the Terrapins' head coach. By the time he finally got the job, he had held three head coaching spots and was considered among the best young coaches in the nation. Coincidentally, the man he left behind at Oklahoma, Wilkinson, would match his successes in the years to come.

A native of McColl, South Carolina, Tatum went to the

University of North Carolina where he starred for three years as an All-Southern Conference tackle under Carl Snavely. After graduation he worked for a tire company and played three exhibition football games with the New York Giants. He was asked to help coach the freshmen at his alma mater and accepted, then went with Snavely to Cornell. After three years he returned to Carolina as freshman director of athletics. In 1942 he was made head football coach and compiled a 5-2-2 record, including a 13-6 victory over Duquesne, its first loss in 26 games under Buff Donelli.

Tatum then went into the Navy and wound up as an assistant coach at the Iowa Preflight school under Missouri coach Don Faurot, the father of the split-T. "I was strictly a single-wing disciple," he said, "but Faurot changed me over and I must say, I love the T." He moved with Faurot to Jacksonville Naval Training Station and in 1945 became head coach, running up a 9-2 record.

After his discharge, he signed at Oklahoma and guided the Sooners into the Gator Bowl with a 7-3 record, beating Missouri, Nebraska, and Texas Christian in the regular season and then North Carolina State 41-14 in the bowl.

It was at Oklahoma that Tatum established a reputation as a defensive coach. His defense was the nation's best against the rush, allowing only 58 yards a game, while the Sooners ran up 315 total yards a contest, including 235 on the ground.

"I came to Maryland," Tatum said, "because of the wonderful opportunity for a young coach to grow with an expanding program, and my wife and I like to live in the east. The money and terms of my contract at Maryland are no better than I would have received at Oklahoma but a chance to grow with the job is the big thing." Maryland gave Tatum a contract calling for $12,000 a year.

Tatum was a big, robust, outgoing man, weighing about 240 pounds, standing 6-3. He was known as "Big Jim" or "Sunny Jim." He was the type that could dominate a room just by walking through it. "He was such a massive guy," said one associate. "He made a fantastic impression. He loved to be around people and they naturally took to him. He was a made-to-order recruiter. There was nothing better for him than to go into a kid's home and talk for hours."

Talk was Tatum's strong point. He sometimes was compared to Casey Stengel for his round-about manner of approaching a simple subject. Tatum could talk for hours, non-stop. Sometimes what he said got him into trouble, even when he went on "off the record" sessions. Tatum usually had an opinion on everything and sometimes stated his thoughts in a none-too-complimentary fashion.

"Tatum makes different impressions on different people," wrote one author. "He has been variously described as ruthless and soft-hearted, shrewd and tactless, candid and hypocritical. Actually all these adjectives apply. Underneath this mosaic of contradictions, however, there is one bedrock element that never changes. This is the compelling desire to win."

Another writer said there were many Jim Tatums. The controversial one, the sunny one, the martyr who took every criticism of himself as a slap at the game of football, the dejected, humble, forlorn one losing a big game.

"Jim was no fence rider," said Faurot. "Other coaches seem afraid to venture an opinion on a controversial subject, but not him. But anyone who knows him or worked with him (knows) he gets extreme loyalty from his boys and his staff."

He had never lost his southern drawl and spoke in a slow medium-pitch voice that could go from a whisper to a boom in seconds. With his favorite ten-gallon hat and wire-rim glasses and habit of clearing his voice, Tatum seemed hardly the one to dominate recruiting in Western Pennsylvania, a tough land of coal miners and steel workers. Yet he made the first recruiting inroads to this area for Maryland and through his successes there, turned the school into a national power.

Tatum was a master recruiter. "He was the type of person," said one of his later recruits, "that could talk to a family with a limited background and then go into the home of an upper class family and be equally well received. He made sure he knew everything he could about a recruit before he ever saw him. He had it all down and when he talked to you, you thought you were the most important guy in the whole world."

The standing joke around Maryland for years was that on game days, Tatum should go into the stands and watch. He got so excited on the field that at times he almost stopped coaching. But his teams won because of the preparation and

Jim Tatum, without glasses or cowboy hat, still had a lot to be happy about during his nine years at Maryland.

recruiting that went on before the opening kickoff.

"He was a great organizer," said Tommy Mont, a member of Tatum's staff and later the man who succeeded him as head coach. "He had everything mapped out in great detail, minute by minute. He was ahead of his time. He didn't take a casual approach to coaching. He realized he needed a competent staff and when he got one he let them have responsibility. I always said that Tatum realized back then what the pro coaches know now–one man can't run the whole show."

Bobby Ward, an All-American under Tatum and another player who became a staff member, feels he got as close to him as anyone at Maryland. "I worked with him day in and day out for years," he said. "He was a fantastic person. He was a fantastic worker. We'd go at it 16-18 hours a day and he'd be right there with us. And no one could organize a routine better.

"He loved the good life. He liked to eat and watch the horses and stay up late. But he gave this school something it had not had before, a winner. After a while we never even thought about losing."

Not everyone warmed up to Tatum. He had his pets and was cool to others. But those he liked, he liked very much. "He gave me some of his clothes when I was a junior," said one of his future stars, Bob Pellegrini. "I came from poor people and didn't have any money. But his clothes were much too big for me. I wound up sending them to Italy. He was always there to help out." Another player slept in the basement of Tatum's house so the coach could take care of him.

His forte was defense. "I believe in getting the best people on defense first, especially in the line," said the former tackle. His team always featured strong, large tackles, both on offense and defense. From that position, he felt he could build out and form the rest of his team.

"He kept his teachings simple and sound," said Ward. "I always wished I could have told it as easily as he did. He could teach you how to handle a double team better than anyone I've ever seen."

One of his future quarterbacks, Jack Scarbath, felt that Tatum was "an innovator on defense. He had a way of sensing what to do with a defense to hold an opponent down. He was really proficient at stopping stars. You look at his record: the great people we played usually didn't do much off of us.

"Of course, it all started with his ability to recognize who he should recruit and then go out and get them. He brought in the talent, shifted it around, and then came up with a sound defense to put everyone in."

Tatum came to Maryland talking about creating harder schedules and winning games and going to bowls. In the future was a new stadium and he wanted to fill it. "He always said that Maryland had no reason not to be successful, considering its location," said an associate.

A columnist hailed the appointment. "The task ahead of him on the football field and in the athletic office is sufficiently interesting and difficult to tax his energy and ambition," he wrote. "In passing years Maryland has grown into a large university but has never organized its athletic programs and coordinated it in keeping with the achievement of the school generally."

"I want to schedule teams from the Big Ten, the Big Six, Ivy and Southeastern Conference," Tatum said. "This gives us a good cross section and the possibility of national recognition." He added Vanderbilt to the 1947 schedule soon after arriving in College Park, hailing the addition "as an example of the way we are headed."

Tatum said he took the job without any fancy dreams. "For a good many years Maryland has operated with part-time coaches, so the biggest change here will be in the establishing of full-time men. With such a large student body, the program is too large for anyone but full-time coaches. It's a year 'round job. Our desire is to broaden the whole athletic picture, step it up so we can meet, I hope, other colleges and universities of comparable size."

He would step on toes in years to come with his outspoken ways. But he gave Byrd what he wanted: a winning football team.

"We want the biggest and the best of everything, including our football team," said Byrd. "College is not only for the intellectual. In fact, there are fewer jobs to be filled by the top intellectual types than by boys of fair academic proficiency who can get along with people."

The two men clashed at times, although Byrd had great respect for Tatum's ability. One year, when he was playing Navy, Tatum called Byrd down to the sidelines at the half. "We're leading, 31-0," Tatum said. "Navy beat us back in 1913, 76-0. I think we can make it 77 today. How about it? Should I leave my first team in?"

Byrd looked at the scoreboard, then at the superintendent of the Naval Academy, with whom he was sitting. "Take out the first offensive team," he told his coach, "but leave in the defense."

Going Through A Wall

Lucien Gambino first met Jim Tatum while walking up some stairs. Tatum was walking down. "He looked at me, I looked at him and that was it," Gambino said. "I tell you, I would have gone through the wall for that man."

Gambino was Tatum's No. 1 reclamation project in his first year at Maryland. The 24-year-old running back had clashed with Shaughnessy; his fun-loving, outspoken ways were in direct contrast to Shaughnessy's serious approach to the game. He had spent most of 1946 on the bench, receiving infrequent chances to show off his talents. Tatum, however, was more Gambino's type. The slow-talking extrovert's background was hardly similar to Gambino's Italian ancestry and Chicago boyhood, yet Tatum also was a lover of the abundant, vigorous life. The two understood each other.

"If there was ever an athlete that was made by his coach, Gambino was the guy," said one of his teammates, Stan Lavine. "He always had the talent but Tatum took him and taught him how to run. I think Lu always had the ability but didn't really know what to do with it. But he and Tatum had a great relationship and it showed in how he played."

Under Tatum, wrote one reporter, "Gambino learned to live with himself in harmony. The player who once sulked on the bench became a hero. Strangely, he didn't become a braggart, although his long-delayed triumph might have made that excusable. He even remembered to thank Tatum publicly for giving him a chance."

Lu Gambino, the fun-loving ex-GI from Chicago, found his football godfather in Jim Tatum and responded with a school record 904 yards and let the major colleges in scoring in 1947.

Gambino's emergence was the key to Tatum's initial success. He took a team that was 3-6-0 and discouraged in 1946 and finished 7-2-1, which was good enough to earn a Gator Bowl bid. Tatum had not expected to move so fast. "By 1950, we should have a team of which Maryland can be proud, one which truly can represent the university," he said in the spring.

"But in the meantime, we'll do our best to turn out a good, interesting, scrappy eleven." He had sent a 127-man squad through six weeks of spring practice, and finished with 70 players and concern over the ability of his linemen. It proved unnecessary.

"He brought us to school before classes started," recalled Lavine, "and we'd practice starting at 6:15 a.m. Then we'd go again in the afternoon. We'd live in old temporary barracks near the practice field. I know lots of nights the coaches would meet until midnight, then get up with us at 5:00 a.m." The team had been used to practicing sometimes until 10:00 p.m. under Shaughnessy, running and rerunning his T-formation plays. Tatum normally limited practices to one hour, 45 minutes. Each minute was planned out carefully. "We always knew what to do," said Lavine.

To run his T offense, Tatum settled on Turyn, who had learned his football from Bryant. Turyn had not played football in high school in West Virginia—he had weighed only 130 pounds—but grew to 190 pounds while serving in the Navy. He was stationed in Missouri when Bryant came through looking for players for his North Carolina preflight team. Bryant selected his roommate, Bill Poling, and Turyn "lied a little" and told the coach he was a halfback. "I just wanted to get closer to home," he remembered.

"I didn't even know how to put on my pads," Turyn said. "I had to watch the other guys. But I wound up starting at quarterback for the preflight team. Bryant taught me everything, how to block and tackle. He used to use me to demonstrate how it should be done, because I did it just the way he wanted. I never developed bad habits from anyone else."

Turyn, who had played baseball against Tatum's wishes and started off the spring as the No. 8 quarterback, found a lot of similarities in Bryant and Tatum. "Bryant was a bit more physical and I think Tatum was a better organizer but they both realized who they could yell at and who they couldn't. They had an ability to read and motivate their players. Both had you believing in them. You had confidence that when they taught you, they knew what they were talking about."

With Turyn at quarterback, Maryland started with a 19-13 victory over South Carolina. Gambino scored three touchdowns off a powerful running game that netted 224 yards. Gambino complained about a bad knee against Delaware, but the balding, 200-pound halfback returned a kickoff 88 yards for a touchdown, grabbed a 29-yard pass from Turyn for another, and scored a third in the third period—his only appearance in the second half. Maryland won 43-19 to break Delaware's 32-game winning streak that started in 1940.

Gambino added his seventh and eighth touchdowns in an 18-6 romp over Richmond in which Maryland gained 234 rushing yards. Gambino had 148 yards in 11 carries, including a 71-yard scoring run. Fellow halfback Hubie Werner had a 44-yard punt return.

That set up a clash with Southern Conference power, Duke. Maryland outgained the Blue Devils 251-228, but three interceptions and four lost fumbles prevented the Terrapins from scoring five times after moving inside the 25. Their only touchdown in the 19-7 defeat came on a 12-yard pass from Turyn to George Simler. Virginia Tech appeared ready to hand Maryland another loss, leading 19-7 in the third quarter, before Turyn started passing. He completed 10 passes for 210 yards, including a 39-yard throw to Simler for one touchdown and then tosses of 27 and 15 yards to set up a 32-yard run by Johnny Idzik for the winning score in the 21-19 triumph.

West Virginia was favored by two touchdowns to ruin Maryland's homecoming. Gambino, however, scored three touchdowns before 16,500, the largest crowd in Byrd Stadium history. Turyn tossed two touchdown passes and his replacement, Joe Tucker, also scored as Maryland won, 27-0. Gambino gained 136 yards on 11 carries in a 32-0 victory over Duquesne and had three more touchdowns. Again, however, mistakes hurt the Terrapins against a strong team, this time North Carolina. Maryland lost six fumbles and the game, 19-0. Neither Gambino nor Carolina's Charlie Justice had great afternoons in the rain.

Maryland's most significant win of the year came against Vanderbilt 20-6. The Commodores, who had beaten Alabama, could not contain Gambino, who had two touchdowns and passed to Ray Wingate for another. Idzik, only a freshman, had three interceptions, and another freshman, tackle Ray Krouse, along with junior lineman Gene Kinney, limited Vanderbilt to 183 total yards.

North Carolina, Jim Tatum's alma mater, and Maryland romp in the mud at Griffith Stadium. North Carolina won the game 19-0 in 1947.

Maryland and North Carolina State ended the regular season with a 0-0 tie despite 243 total yards for the Terrapins and 101 rushing yards by Gambino. The tie still did not prevent Maryland from going into the Gator Bowl against highly favored (14 points) Georgia. "For us, it was a tremendous accomplishment to make any bowl," said Turyn. It was only the third Gator Bowl, which was then played on January 1.

The team flew down on a Capital Airlines flight a week ahead of the contest. Tatum worked the team hard. "He let us know that we would have our fun afterwards," said Turyn. It did not quite work out that way.

Gambino played a wonderful game, gaining 165 yards on 19 tries behind blocks by fullback Bonk. He was voted the most

The 1947 Maryland team, the first under Jim Tatum, had just heard it was going to the Gator Bowl. The Terrapins tied Georgia 20-20.

valuable player. He scored Maryland's first touchdown after taking a handoff from Tucker, breaking through the right side of the line, and then running away from the Georgia defense from 35 yards out. Georgia tied it in the third quarter on a sneak by quarterback John Rauch. Maryland took the ensuing kickoff and Turyn completed four straight passes and Gambino plowed over from the one. The conversion was blocked. Gambino scored again minutes later after taking a pass from substitute halfback Johnny Baroni. "When we got up 20-6, Tatum took out the first-string offense," said Turyn. "He told me he didn't want to run up the score."

But Rauch got hot. Georgia scored with three minutes left, then Earl Roth fumbled a snap from center on a punt and the Bulldogs took over on the Maryland 33. Rauch completed three passes before hitting Joe Geri for a 14-yard score to end the game in a 20-20 tie.

Gambino finished fourth overall in the nation in scoring with 96 points on 16 touchdowns. The three players ahead of him were all from small colleges. He gained 904 yards, a modern school record, during the regular season and 1,069 overall on just 114 attempts, for an impressive 9.5 average. He made first-team all-conference and Kinney made second team. Turyn ran for 273 yards and completed 32 of 58 passes, seven for touchdowns. The squad itself averaged 314 yards a game and drew record attendance to Byrd Stadium, making the construction of a new stadium—long a dream of President Byrd—a necessity.

Yet the promise of 1947 disappeared in 1948. A one-point loss to Duke and crushing defeats by North Carolina and Vanderbilt resulted in a so-so 6-4 record despite four shutouts. The season had begun on a sour note. Gambino had been declared ineligible by the Southern Conference, which decided he had used up his allotted playing years. Gambino, some 26 years later, was still furious about the decision.

"I have never understood it," he said. "The rules were that veterans had four years of eligibility when they returned from the war. But they said because I had played at Indiana for two years and at Maryland for two, I couldn't play. I played one year at Indiana, 1942. I never played my freshman year—you couldn't. It was a crooked decision. I got too big too fast, the whole team did. I had turned down a two-year, $25,000 no-cut

Lu Gambino starts off on a 35-yard run that ended in Maryland's first touchdown against Georgia in the 1948 Gator Bowl.

contract with the pros to return for 1948 and then they got me."

Gambino had learned to love the school, he said. He had gone to high school in Chicago. He got a scholarship to play football at Indiana, then went into the service, where he hurt his knee in a plane crackup in South Carolina. When he got out of the service, his father had died and his mother was living in Baltimore. Maryland was the closest major school to her, so he enrolled and went out for football. "The place was a cow school, I couldn't believe it," he said. "Indiana was 50 times better. But our teams, we put Maryland on the map. It's a great school."

He went on to play two years with the Baltimore Colts before the knee injury made him quit. "I wanted Maryland to beat the rest of them so bad it hurt," he said.

He was to have his wish fulfilled.

Climb Toward The Top

Fifty-six years after fielding its first football team, Maryland pushed its way into the big time in 1949. The Terrapins were ranked 15th in the nation by the Associated Press, their first appearance in the top 20, and then thumped a good Missouri team in the Gator Bowl. Their 9-1 record was the school's best—and Tatum had yet to field a team comprised of just his own recruits.

He had forecast at the end of the 1948 season that his next team would be improved. "The main reason is competition on the squad will be keener," he said. "We have three players for each position, whereas before, we were limited in reserves, and regulars sometimes became lackadaisical because of lack of competition." Tatum was beginning to pour talented players into his program. His freshman team in 1949 had such future stars as Jack Scarbath, Dick Modzelewski, Bob Morgan, Stan Jones and Ed Fullerton. Sophomores on the 1949 squad included Ed Modzelewski, Bob Ward and Bob (Boo-Boo) Shemonski.

At least on defense, this was a Tatum team. It was fifth in the nation in total defense (197 yards a game) and third in rushing defense (95 a game), while not allowing more than two touchdowns in any game. Around such standouts as Ward, tackles Krouse and Chet Gierula, end Elmer Wingate, halfbacks Idzik and Jim LaRue, and guard Dave Cianelli, Tatum, the defensive genius, built a marvelous unit that reached its peak in the Gator Bowl.

The only loss came in the third game of the season, to Michigan State, 14-7, in East Lansing, Michigan. Tatum took the defeat hard. Both schools recruited intensely from the same Western Pennsylvania areas and he could think of nothing better to help recruiting than to knock off his rival.

The offense had not jelled at that point. Tatum had hesitated in letting his quarterbacks, Joe Tucker and Stan Lavine, pass a lot, and when Lavine was forced to throw in the last quarter against State, he was unsuccessful. But after the season's eighth game, the Terrapins had scored more points than any other team in Maryland history. Lavine led the team in total offense and scoring (eight touchdowns, 689 yards) and highly regarded halfback Ed (Mighty Mo) Modzelewski plowed his way to six touchdowns and 625 rushing yards.

Maryland started out by picking on Virginia Tech, which had not won a game since 1947. After staying even 7-7 through a half, the Terrapins pulled away from VPI in the second half and won 34-7, with Lavine scoring three times in the last period. One came off a triple lateral. Modzelewski took a hand-off from Lavine and lateraled to Ted Betts as he was being tackled. Three steps later, Betts lateraled to Lavine, who completed the 36-yard run. "It was a planned play in the split T," said Lavine. "The quarterback always would trail the play after he handed off. It really wasn't risky at all."

The Maryland defense, which limited VPI to 41 total yards, allowed Georgetown only two first downs through three periods and the Terrapins romped to a 33-7 triumph. Hank Fox caught two touchdown passes. Michigan State, however, found it could pass over the Terrapin line and gained 121 yards on nine completions. Maryland took a 7-0 lead early in the first quarter after Jake Rowden recovered a fumble on the State 18. Five plays later, Modzelewski went over from the one. The rest of the game was dominated by Michigan State, which tied it in the third period on a two-yard plunge by Frank Waters, and won the contest on a five-yard pass from quarterback Gene Glick to George Smith after a fumble by Lavine. All-American Lynn Chandnois, whose fumble set up the only Maryland touchdown, had key runs in both scoring drives.

"The game came too early in the season," said Lavine. "I think we could have won it later in the year. Tatum wanted me to pass earlier but I didn't want to risk an interception. Then when I did, it wasn't working. We put in more pass plays after that."

Maryland ripped off seven straight victories after the defeat. Tatum got his first triumph over a North Carolina team when Modzelewski went 10 yards for one score, and Cianelli intercepted a pass and returned it 43 yards for another touchdown in a 14-6 victory over North Carolina State. Maryland stopped State after the Wolfpack had a first down on the one in the fourth quarter.

Tucker and Lavine found their passing touch against South Carolina, combining to complete 13 of 18 passes for 307 yards. Going into the game, Maryland had completed only 10 of 44 attempts. Tucker was nine for 12 and threw twice to Pete Augsberger for touchdowns in the 44-7 romp. Lavine added a 92-yard run-pass play to Ed Bolton in the fourth period. It remains a Maryland record for longest scoring pass. The Terra-

Teammates carry Bob Ward off the field after 44-7 homecoming victory over South Carolina in 1949.

pins scored 26 points in the second period against George Washington, en route to a 40-14 rout. Lavine continued the passing streak, hitting 12 of 17 attempts for 207 yards, including two touchdowns to Stan Karnash and one to Augsberger.

Boston University and its standout quarterback, Harry Agganis, represented the last major hurdle in the regular season. Undefeated BU paid the expenses of a representative from the Gator Bowl so he could see the game, but Maryland won 14-13 and later wound up with the bowl bid. Lavine came off the bench—"It was so cold, I really wanted to stay on the sidelines and keep warm," he said years later—to direct the Terrapins to the winning touchdown. Tatum had told him to run end sweeps but BU spread its defenses so he sent fullback Earl Roth inside for the bulk of the 71-yard march. Lavine went the final yard with Roth pushing him from behind. Bob Dean added the extra point for the victory. Earlier Vern Siebert had blocked a Boston conversion.

BU coach Buff Donelli complained afterwards that Maryland had cheated. "They weren't setting up for a full second before the snap," he said. Lavine admitted the charge was probably true. "We ran our plays very quickly," he laughed.

Maryland finished with victories over West Virginia 47-7 with Lavine completing all eight of his first-half passes and Modzelewski scoring two touchdowns, and Miami, Florida 13-0 with Tucker running for one score and Lavine passing to Modzelewski for another.

Next was the Gator Bowl and the matchup with Tatum's former tutor, Don Faurot. Missouri had gained 507 yards in losing to Ohio State 35-34, and had been nipped 28-27 by Southern Methodist and its All-American, Kyle Rote. The Tigers were ranked eighth nationally in total offense and were among the nation's top 10 for the third straight year.

Tatum predicted that Maryland would have to score three touchdowns to win. He also told his team, after reviewing Missouri game films, that the Tigers would be a fumbling team. He proved right on both points. Maryland won 20-7, scoring on drives of 11, 22, and 15 yards as the Terrapins capitalized on Missouri mistakes.

The first came midway through the opening quarter. Idzik

Bob Shemonski scores around right end during Maryland's 20-7 victory over Missouri in the 1950 Gator Bowl. Shemonski scored twice in the contest.

intercepted Dick Braznell's pass and returned it 26 yards to the Missouri 11. On the first play, Shemonski swept right end for the touchdown. The second came shortly after the start of the second period. Braznell fumbled and Gierula recovered on the Missouri 22. Lavine ran 17 yards, Roth got two, and then Modzelewski went over from the three. The third came only minutes later. Krouse recovered a Missouri fumble on the Tiger 15. Five plays later, Shemonski went over from the six.

That was it. Missouri managed to score late in the fourth period after Maryland fumbled on the Tiger four. Otherwise Ward, who was named the game's outstanding player, and the rest of the Maryland defense was unbeatable. Missouri lost five fumbles and tossed three interceptions. The Tigers had run up more total yardage, 267-242, but one writer called it "Jim Tatum's triumph. Against a Missouri team that had scored at least three touchdowns against every opponent except Oklahoma, the large man's squad throttled the Tigers so completely that it wasn't a contest....It is significant that Bob Ward was chosen the most valuable player by a landslide. His stiffest competition came from other linemen."

Ward said the game, for him, "was just like going to heaven. It was the greatest thing that ever happened to me at that time. I remember the facilities were terrible, the water leaked from the showers into the locker room. But it was our first bowl game. You never forget it."

Modzelewski says that he still wears the watch he got from the Gator Bowl "more than any other I have. I've got a lot of awards and watches but that one means something special to me."

The end of the season brought special awards to Krouse, the first of the great tackles developed by Tatum. Krouse was selected first team All-South and second team All-American by Associated Press. Ward, for the second straight year, was selected his team's most valuable player.

Maryland returns from its triumph over Missouri in the 1950 Gator Bowl. It was the first year the Terrapins were ranked in the Top 20.

The Greatest, Pound For Pound

In the 59 years that the University of Maryland had fielded football teams prior to 1950, the Terrapins had never had a first-team All-American. Bill Supplee in 1923, Snitz Snyder in 1928, and Ray Krouse in 1949, had come the closest, making second-team Associated Press. And there was really no reason to believe that a 23-year-old former Army paratrooper who weighed only 178 pounds–despite a program listing of 185–yet played in the line, would end this string of failure. But he did.

"I still believe he was the greatest player, pound for pound, that I have seen in either pro or college ball," said teammate Ed Modzelewski. Jim Tatum called him "the greatest football player I've seen ounce for ounce, and the best I've ever coached." By the time he left Maryland, the school decided to retire his uniform–No. 28–the first player so honored in its history.

"Someone sometime had to make All-American at Maryland, and I was glad it was me," said the man in question, Bob Ward. "It was a thrill that has never left me. To reach the top like that, well, it's anybody's goal. It was mine."

Ward played with an intensity and a particular aggressiveness that has not since been paralleled at Maryland. Not that fast, he had the quickness and reactions to survive in what was even then a big man's game. Yet the big men could not handle him. "I saw days where they would try to triple team him," said Modzelewski. "They could not do it. And while they were trying, it was freeing everyone else to make tackles."

Jim Tatum said that, "ounce for ounce," Bob Ward was the greatest player he had seen.

Ward was a middle guard on defense, a guard on offense, and normally the first man down field on punt and kickoff coverage. "Especially in my senior year, when I was an offensive guard, I felt I had to get down-field first and make those kicking tackles so people would notice me," said Ward. "It gave me some extra incentive."

He made All-American on defense as a junior in 1950, although he averaged more than 50 minutes a game that season. As a senior in 1951, Tatum asked him to concentrate on guard to give leadership to an otherwise inexperienced outfit. So he made the adjustment, despite the fact his first love was tackling, and made All-American on offense that year. He also was chosen as the Southern Conference player of the year, another first for the school.

Ward, however, cherished another honor even more. "I was voted most valuable player on my team for four straight years," he said. "The players did the voting and that has to mean something extra."

After graduating from high school in Elizabeth, New Jersey, Ward was going to enroll at Canisius College on a football and basketball scholarship. But when he saw the school—"It had three buildings and a gym"—and found out he probably still would be drafted into the military, he enlisted in the Army, where he played some football at Fort Benning, Georgia. His coach there was from the University of Alabama and recruited him for the school. Ward got out of the service in January of 1948 and went home to await the start of school in March.

"I was bored to death, I had nothing to do," said Ward. "Then I got a call from Jim Tatum. He had sent one of his assistants, Bill Meek, to Benning and they had recommended me highly. Tatum asked me if I would like to come and look over the campus. I liked the school from the start, I really didn't want to go to Alabama. I was a northern boy."

Tatum had been expecting some sort of superman when he first met Ward—the raves about his service play had been that good—but instead he saw a 180 pounder. "I figured not many of those little guys make good guards," Tatum said. "To myself, I said it would be silly maybe to waste a scholarship on such a little lineman. To Bob, I said, 'Son, why not come to school on the GI Bill?'

"Funny thing is that he did just that. And then I saw him in the first scrimmage. He was wonderful. When it was over, you can bet the first fellow to reach him was ol' Tatum and he said, 'Son, what do you need? Anything I can do for you? If you need anything, let me know.'"

Ward remembers that first meeting "as if it were today. He was so big and he came out and he looked at me and I could tell he was disappointed. The first thing he said was 'I thought you were bigger than that.' I realize now he was shrewd. By asking me to take the GI Bill, he was saving himself a scholarship. But I didn't care. All I wanted to do was play football. I loved the game. It was important to me."

Despite his size, Ward had always been a lineman. And he always had wanted to carry the ball. "Each year in high school, I'd ask my coach to let me but he never did. Then when I went into the service, I thought about going out for fullback. But I knew if I went out for guard, I'd start and I didn't want to sit on the bench as a fullback. I've always said I would have been only average as a back." He did get a chance to carry the ball in one game at Maryland. He gained 46 yards in two carries.

He was not average as a lineman. He had a killer instinct, said Modzelewski. "He was so quick off the ball, he would beat people to spots." Ward's size was deceiving. "He was strong for a little man but I think opponents got lulled by him," said another teammate, Jack Scarbath. "They didn't see how possibly such a little guy would do the things they had heard about. But he did."

One of Ward's favorite maneuvers was to hurdle the opposing center from his middle guard spot. He says it was to combat opponents who were trying to hit him at the legs. "I knew I wasn't going to overpower people," said Ward. "So I developed a technique where I would bring my forearm into the guy's chest to start him up and use my other hand to get away from him. So they started going low to avoid the forearm. I would then go over the top of them to throw them off.

"I never stayed in one spot long enough to get blocked. I think I had a lot of second effort, which helped. I didn't like to get stopped. I figured they would tire out before me."

Scarbath said he never saw a player with a better attitude than Ward's. "He kept coming and coming and coming. He wasn't very outgoing but he was a classic example of leadership by actions, not words. He did things so well that we all got inspired by it. You just can't say enough about how good he was."

Ward credits Tatum with much of his success. "He had me believing that nobody was any better prepared or better fit to play," he said. "When we went out on the field, we had a feeling we were too good to lose. I hated to lose. I really did." Tatum thought so much of Ward that he made him a member of his coaching staff right after graduation.

One of Tatum's former assistants, George Barclay, perhaps summed up Ward's talents best: "He is the perfect example of a perfect guard. He can't be fooled. I coached him a year and that was enough to decide I've never seen anything like him for ability, determination and football savvy."

Ward's abilities were not enough for Maryland to get a second straight bowl trip in 1950. In fact, the Terrapins, for the

first time in their history, found that winning was not enough any more. A 7-2-1 record was considered by even Tatum to be a bit less than expected, especially since he had both an experienced and deep team.

"The schedule had good teams all the way," said Tatum. "But wasn't balanced enough. I would like to start easier and build up."

Tatum had made the mistake of opening against Georgia. "We weren't ready for Georgia. We just weren't in shape and the heat killed us." Indeed, the 92-degree day wilted the Terrapins, who saw a 7-7 half-time tie turn into a 27-7 defeat.

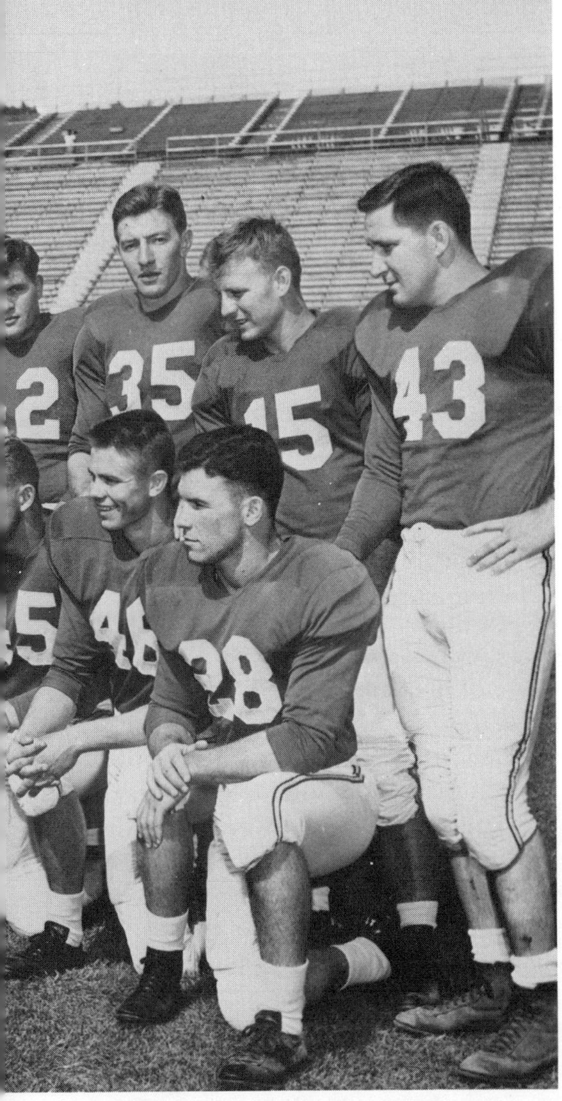

Curley Byrd, Jim Tatum, and members of the 1950 Maryland team. Byrd would criticize Tatum publicly for some of his coaching tactics, but the two got along well enough to let Tatum put together a winning program.

The other loss, to North Carolina State, was a shocker. "Our biggest disappointment," was how Tatum put it. State had won only once entering the contest, but took advantage of two Maryland mistakes to build up a 16-0 lead before the Terrapins scored twice in the fourth period. Three other threats inside the State six were stopped, two on downs and one on an interception by Alex Webster. Modzelewski gained 96 yards, three less than the entire State team.

A tie with North Carolina, his alma mater, did not make Tatum much happier. Carolina scored in the fourth period to knot it at 7-all and then Bob Dean missed a 32-yard field goal with five seconds left. Scarbath, the starting quarterback as a sophomore, missed the game with a shoulder injury.

There also were high spots. The first was perhaps Maryland's most significant win to date. Michigan State, which had handed the Terrapins their only defeat the season before, was ranked second in the nation and would lose only once in 1950, and that was to Maryland 34-7. The victory earned the Terrapins their first ranking ever in the Top 10—a brief stay in the eighth spot—and usually is singled out as the turning point in Tatum's program.

"It was our first major national victory," said Modzelewski. "We found out we could do well against a big power. From then on I think those types of games weren't nearly as hard for us."

Tatum had used a large portion of psychology to psyche up his team. "He told us we were a half-price team," said Modzelewski. "He said they were only charging half-price for tickets for the game. He told us we better show them we were a full-price team." It was a big game for Modzelewski and his brother Dick (Little Mo), who was then a sophomore defensive tackle. "The high school team we had lost to in the Western Pennsylvania championship game had sent seven guys to Michigan State," he said. "Our town rented a train and 850 people would go to the game. We had to win."

Michigan State trailed by only 13-7 going into the final period. Then Scarbath took the Terrapins on a 71-yard drive which he ended by diving over from the one. Three minutes later, Pete Ladygo returned an interception of an Al Darrow pass 35 yards for a score. An interception by Rowden set up a 36-yard run by Shemonski for the final touchdown. Modzelewski had tallied his team's first two scores.

"It was one of the easiest games I can remember," said Scarbath. "They were so predictable on defense. They never varied what they were doing and we just went right around them." Michigan State coach Biggie Munn said that his team was unable "to run a play through, over or around" Ward and called him "terrific." The Spartans had gained 179 yards and 66 of those had come on a run by Sonny Grandelius.

More than 3,000 fans and the school band greeted Maryland at the airport. Seven hundred cars formed a parade to carry

Curley Byrd built Byrd Stadium, which was dedicated in 1950, for $1 million, then regretted that he had not double-decked the facility so it could seat 90,000 people.

the team back to College Park.

The second highlight was a 35-21 victory over Navy in the inaugural game in new Byrd Stadium, a $1 million, 33,000-seat facility that replaced the old 18,000-seat stadium. A record crowd of 43,836, the largest to see a football game in Washington history, turned out, but it troubled Byrd. "I should have double-decked the stadium (to a capacity of 92,000) but I was afraid there would be empty seats and it wouldn't look good." The stadium was the climax of Byrd's new emphasis on football, although the opening had been delayed a year and had forced Maryland to use Griffith Stadium in the District for the 1948 season. The scoreboard did not work that first game and the locker rooms were not finished, but that did not prevent

Scarbath from passing for two touchdowns and running for another against Coach Eddie Erdelatz's first Navy team.

Maryland later recorded its first victory over Duke 26-14, spoiling Coach Wallace Wade's bid for his 200th victory. Shemonski and Joe Petruzzo each scored twice in what Tatum called "one of my sweetest victories."

It had been a particularly sensational year for Shemonski. The 5-10, 165-pound back scored a Maryland record 97 points, including five touchdowns and an extra point in the final game against VPI to win the conference scoring title. He averaged nine yards every time he touched the ball, and also led the team in rushing (560 yards), kickoff returns, punt returns, and interceptions (four). Ward and Wingate made first team All-Conference and Ward was selected the league's best lineman. Krouse, plagued by injuries, was on the second team. Pete Augsburger set a school record with 25 receptions for 422 yards.

Place Among The Elite

Part of Jim Tatum's reputation was built around his outspokenness. He said things that most coaches would never think of uttering, especially about their own team. When he thought Maryland would be good, he said so. In 1951 he knew he was loaded.

"I think," he told his assistants, "this can be our best year. This is the best team I have had, not only at Maryland but any place I have coached. We may not have the best won and lost record, but still this will be our best team."

He wound up being too conservative. Not only was the 1951 team his best, talent-wise, but it also became his best, record-wise. It rolled to nine straight victories, steamrolling over opponents and shattering school records along the way. It established Maryland as an elite football power for the first time. By the end of the regular season, only two schools in the country—Tennessee and Michigan State—were considered better. Never before had Maryland been rated so highly and never before had the Terrapins rated a bid to a major bowl like the Sugar Bowl, where they would meet No. 1 Tennessee and decisively beat the Volunteers to give them claim to the national championship. It would become ironic that in Tatum's highly successful years at College Park, the national title would never unanimously be his. He beat Tennessee after the polls were closed, so the Volunteers are still listed as the nation's best in the record book, although Maryland felt the Sugar Bowl proved otherwise. Then in 1953, when Maryland won the title in the polls, only to lose to Oklahoma in the Orange Bowl, the Terrapins found themselves in a reverse situation of 1951.

Of all the Maryland teams, this one probably was the second best, topped only by the 1953 edition. It was so powerful defensively that Tatum could use Ward on the offensive line exclusively and hardly notice the drop-off. It gave up only 62 points, while scoring 353, a school record and best in the nation for nine games. It averaged 424 yards a game, second nationally, and 324 rushing, third best nationally. In all, it broke 12 team and individual records and was the school's first unbeaten squad since 1896.

Four players stood out. Scarbath, who took over the quarterback chores as a sophomore, matured as a junior and skillfully handled Tatum's tricky split T. Ward made every major All-American team, and won just about every award a lineman can be given. Dick Modzelewski picked up for Ward on the defensive line and made second team on many major All-American squads. His brother Ed finished his career in a blazing fashion, making a few major first-unit All-American squads while fulfilling the promise he had shown as a recruit. Modzelewski scored 11 touchdowns and averaged 7.4 yards a carry, picking up 834 yards. That was 154 more yards than Maryland's nine opponents could gain on the ground. He personally outrushed six of nine foes, making 64 of 114 first downs by running.

On a team that scored at least 35 points in seven games and hit at least 40 five times, Modzelewski did not have the only impressive statistics. Sophomore Ralph Felton averaged 5.8 yards a carry, Ed Fullerton nine and a sophomore speedster from Hackensack, New Jersey, Chet Hanulak, eight. They ran behind the blocking of Joe Moss (205), Ward (185), center Tom Cosgrove (215), Pete Ladygo (210), and Stan Jones (225), a future All-American who had been kept out by Tatum the season before. Felton picked up 485 yards and Shemonski 317.

"We were a pretty confident group," said Scarbath. "When you wind up like we did in 1950 (41-0 over West Virginia, 63-7 over VPI), it starts you off in the right direction. We were strengthened by newcomers. We were so deep that a lot of really good players didn't get in all that much."

Three-fourths of Maryland's 1951 backfield: Ed Modzelewski, Jack Scarbath, Bob Shemonski.

Ward opened the season with a spectacular play. Covering on a Maryland punt against Washington & Lee, he smashed into the W & L receiver so hard he fumbled and Ladygo recovered in the end zone for a touchdown. It was a rout from then on, as the Terrapins breezed to a 54-14 victory. Sophomore Ed Barritt outgained even Modzelewski with 76 yards and Maryland ran up 510 total yards to W & L's 239. Seven different Terrapins scored touchdowns.

George Washington standout Andy Davis was not enough to prevent a 33-6 defeat. Davis set up his team's only touchdown with an interception but by then Maryland had scored its 33 points, including 27 in the first half. The Terrapins had 437 total yards, GW 195, with Davis responsible for 97 of that. Modzelewski rushed for 138 yards to GW's 80.

Maryland revenged its loss to Georgia in 1950 with a crushing 43-7 victory. Tatum had insisted that the game be played at night to avoid some of the Georgia heat, and it also was scheduled later in the season. "He wanted it very badly," said Scarbath of the game. Five different players scored to give Tatum his wish and the defense held Georgia to 125 yards rushing. Fullerton broke off an 86-yard scoring run and Hanulak had two touchdowns. "When we were leaving the locker room, Tatum called us over and told us to look down on the field," said Scarbath. "Wally Butts had Georgia on the field scrimmaging. He told us, 'that's what happens to losers.'"

The closest game of the season came the next week against North Carolina. Maryland scored immediately on a 28-yard run by Felton but Carolina tied it up before the end of the first period. Scarbath, who really had not been called on to do much during the season until now, passed 11 yards in the second period to Lou Weidensaul for the winning touchdown in the 14-7 victory, Maryland's first over Carolina in 26 years. Despite 221 yards from Modzelewski, Shemonski, Felton, and Hanulak, Maryland could not score again. Instead, it was Carolina that threatened. Modzelewski made one saving tackle at the Terrapin 13 on an interception after getting off the ground. Sophomore Joe Petruzzo intercepted two passes and knocked one down in the end zone with 65 seconds left as the Terrapins secondary of Fullerton, Petruzzo, and Bernie Faloney was tested severely. Petruzzo's last-minute deflection became the play of the season. Carolina's Bob Gantt caught the ball in the end zone, only to have Petruzzo's tackle jar it loose.

Ward had played 47 minutes despite a broken finger, and was named national lineman of the week for his efforts.

"Tatum had been riding us pretty hard and after the North Carolina game he eased up a little," said Modzelewski. But not before he had team practice with a wet ball to prepare for the humidity of Louisiana, which was second nature to LSU. Tatum took the players to New Orleans before the game. "He told us to go out on the town and be back by a certain time," said Modzelewski. "We went out and had some drinks and nobody got back on time. He had to get people to go out in cabs and round us up. He got up and told us to forget the incident and to start playing like it was the second half of the season." The tactics worked. Maryland won 27-0, relying mostly on its rushing attack which netted 309 yards, including 84 by Felton on 16 carries and 69 by Scarbath, who scored twice.

Missouri managed only 195 total yards–92 on the ground–while Modzelewski had 102 rushing. Freshman Joe Horning set a school record by returning an interception 105 yards for a touchdown, and Hanulak added two scoring runs and 89 rushing yards in the 35-0 win. Navy dented the Terrapin defenses for 21 points–14 in the last quarter–but could gain only 46 yards rushing and 198 overall. Modzelewski again had a big day with 127 yards on the ground and Scarbath got the passing attack untracked, throwing for 243 yards on 14 of 23 passes and two touchdowns after Navy was able to handle all but Modzelewski among the Terrapin rushers. The Midshipmen took a 7-0 lead on a 100-yard punt return by Frank Brady but Maryland countered with an 18-yard pass to Weidensaul, who caught eight in all, and a four-yard run by Fullerton for a 14-7 half-time lead. The Terrapins then added 20 points in the third quarter to cruise to a 40-21 victory.

Before Maryland could meet North Carolina State, the Terrapins received an official bid to the Sugar Bowl. Curley Byrd's acceptance touched off a tremendous controversy. The presidents of the Southern Conference schools had voted in September–during the middle of great unrest in college sports over recruiting scandals in basketball–to recommend that a ban be placed on bowl games, the reasoning being that the pressure to build bowl teams could lead to recruiting abuses. Byrd decided to defy the action since it was only a recommendation, not a formal vote, and the conference had long allowed its schools to go to postseason games. "It was not a formal meeting legally held," he said. "The recommendation was not formally adopted by the conference, so we feel we can't be legally bound by it. We are not violating any proper conference rules."

Clemson also defied the presidents and accepted a bid to the Gator Bowl. In December the conference met and put the schools on one-year probation and forbid them to play other conference members during that time. The ruling wiped out six of Maryland's 1952 games and eventually led to a breakup of the league into the Atlantic Coast and Southern Conferences.

1951 captains Bob Ward and Dave Cianelli and Testudo, the Maryland mascot. Cianelli was so good on defense that Jim Tatum could afford to move Ward to offense that season.

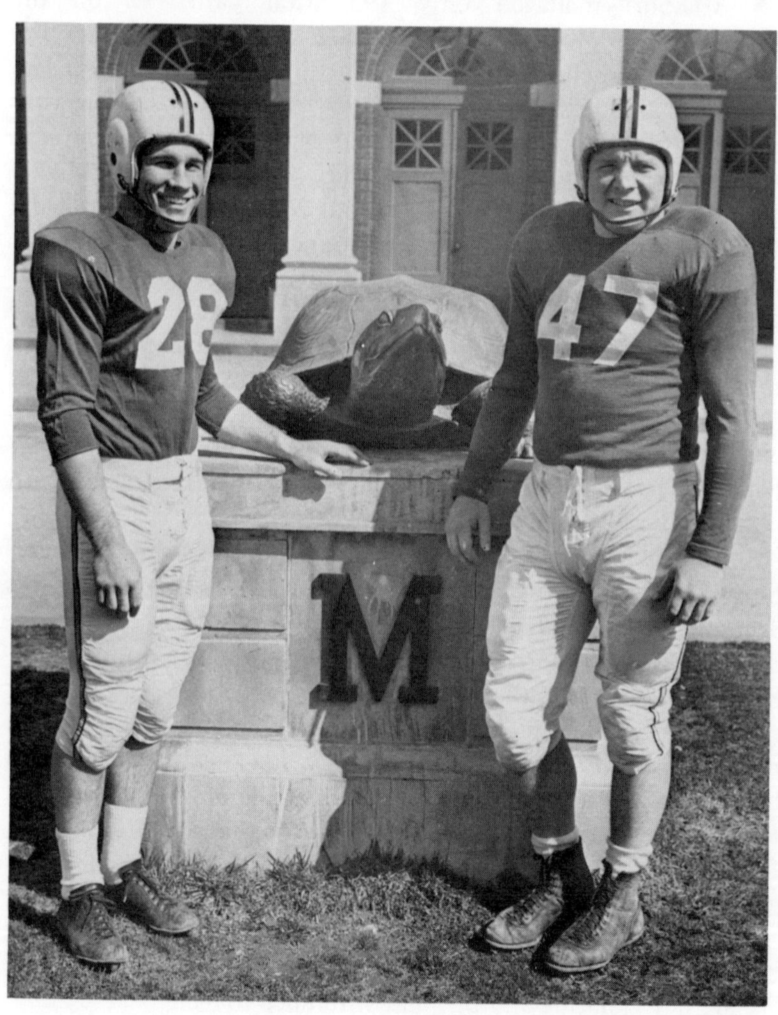

The Maryland football team seemed unaffected by the dispute. It demolished North Carolina State 53-0, gaining 486 yards, including 370 on the ground. State managed only 174 total yards including just 40 rushing, which was 49 less than Modzelewski had in 11 carries. The day, however, was Felton's. The sophomore from Midway, Pennsylvania, nicknamed "The Midway Express," gained 186 yards in 13 carries, including a 21-yard touchdown run. Maryland intercepted five passes, two by linebacker Ed Kensler.

"By now, the starters were playing less and less and the younger kids were getting in a lot more," said Scarbath. "He was always looking to the future. One game he told us right after the half that we were finished for the day. We had a kid come up and give us hot dogs on the bench. That's how finished we knew we were."

Tatum had been so impressed by Modzelewski's play in one game that he told his star fullback to go out and buy himself a $5 shirt. "I was really impressed," said Modzelewski, "until later I realized how little $5 really was. Big deal. I always laugh over it now."

Maryland closed out with a resounding 54-7 triumph over West Virginia. The Terrapins set a school record by gaining 523 rushing yards and 602 total yards while holding West Virginia to minus 21 yards on the ground. The Mountaineers were forced to pass 57 times, completing 19 for 235 yards. Tatum used 14 ballcarriers and Scarbath and Faloney threw only seven passes, three for touchdowns to Weidensaul, Lloyd Colteryahn, and Paul Lindsay. Maryland led 35-0 at the half, with Modzelewski scoring twice. He gained 131 yards on 14 carries.

The Terrapins had finished the season by outscoring their final four opponents, 45-7. "We knew we were an awfully good team by the time of the Sugar Bowl," said Ward. "Tatum didn't have to tell us." Ward, Modzelewski, Cianelli, and Petruzzo made the all-conference team and the first three appeared on All-American squads. But the season's best was yet to come.

New Bully On The Block

Jim Tatum told his players before the game that he did not care if his team was the best in America. "We're like the little boy who said: 'Hell no, I'm not the toughest kid in the neighborhood, but I can lick the kid who is.'"

So Tatum did not gloat much when Maryland embarrassed unbeaten, No. 1 ranked Tennessee in the 1952 Sugar Bowl. The Terrapins' fans, however, did. They had waited a long time to talk about being the country's best and now they went around demanding that Tennessee relinquish its national championship trophy and that the polls reopen to declare Maryland No. 1.

In five short years, Tatum had taken a second-rate football power and built it into the nation's strongest team. He topped it off by registering what remains the greatest victory in Maryland's football history. Few had given the Terrapins a chance against Tennessee and its legendary coach, Gen. Robert Neyland. This was considered one of the general's best teams, and that meant a superior squad, for Neyland rarely lost with his powerful single wing and stingy defenses. But the Terrapins pulled off the upset in a slashing 28-13 conquest that was not even that close. Tatum, who worshipped Neyland and had once scouted voluntarily for him just to be able to witness Volunteer practice sessions, was suddenly thrust among the greats of coaching—and everyone thought the new mantle fit.

Tatum had gambled heavily in his plans for the game. He devised a special defense to stop the single wing and chose to go at the heart of the Volunteer defense. He studied films of four

Jim Tatum, the winner, greets Gen. Robert Neyland of Tennessee, the loser, after the 1952 Sugar Bowl. The game marked the beginning of the end for Neyland's single wing.

Tennessee games, had his scouts look at another, and he personally viewed the Volunteers' regular-season finale. He gambled that Neyland, after 26 years of building an image, would not now change what he had done so successfully so long. Tatum won his bet, and Maryland won the national title.

Until the game, little had gone right for the Terrapins. Bad weather had cost them valuable pre-Christmas practice time. Their plane was five hours late arriving in Biloxi, Mississippi, for a week of practice prior to the contest. Lindsay broke a hand and Felton, the second-leading rusher, wrecked the ligaments in his right knee. Tennessee, training at LSU in Baton Rouge, had much smoother workouts and no injuries, which helped support their position as at least seven-point favorites. George Barclay, a former Tatum assistant and then head coach at Washington & Lee, said the best game would be between Tennessee's first team and its second team.

"The role of an underdog was a tremendous benefit for us," Tatum admitted. "I never had an easier time preparing a team for a game. The boys were higher than a kite right from the start."

The game was considered a classic showdown between the newfangled split T and the steady, reliable single wing. After a surge of switches to the split T, some coaches were thinking about returning to the single wing. Others decided to wait until the outcome of the Sugar Bowl. Many later considered the contest the end of the single wing as an effective offense.

Tennessee had shut out five opponents en route to a 10-0 season. The Volunteers had given up only 88 points while scoring 373. They averaged 424 total yards, including 306 on the ground, third best in the nation. They gave up only an average of 108 yards rushing and 116 passing. But split T teams had given them the most trouble.

Maryland's 39.2 points per game average was the highest in the nation. Its total offense of 382 yards a game was No. 2 nationally and its rushing defense (76 yards a game) was No. 3. Against that defense, Tennessee would send All-American tailback Hank Lauricella, a rich boy from New Orleans who averaged 7.9 yards rushing from his tailback spot and also did the passing and punting. "He's the best I've ever coached," said Neyland.

Tennessee was favored because of its depth and quickness. Maryland outweighed the Volunteers 10 pounds or more a man in the line but that was not unusual for Neyland's teams. He believed in short, sleek linemen and many thought his offensive and defensive lines were among the best in his career.

Although Neyland had called Maryland a team without a weakness and the greatest his team would ever play, Lauricella admitted years later than the Volunteers had underestimated the Terrapins, especially on defense. It was a mistake. Twelve of Maryland's players would be drafted in January by the pros, compared to a handful of Tennessee's.

Maryland was an exceptional defensive team. The front line was built around ends Paul Nestor and John Alderton, a standout all season, and anchored by Dick Modzelewski, Bill Maletzky, and Bob (Blubber) Morgan. Those three each weighed about 235. What they did not tackle was usually stopped by Cianelli or Ed Kensler or Roy Martine. Opponents were forced to pass a lot against this defense, and that strategy was not successful either. Maryland picked off a school-record 34 passes with Fullerton—the best defensive back—getting five, Petruzzo three, and Faloney three. The freshman, Horning, led the club with six. Maryland had allowed only 62 points, including 35 in two games.

"It was difficult to pick against General Neyland," Scarbath said. "He was an institution and we were the newcomers. It was an upset to everyone but the team and the coaches."

A crowd of 85,000 filled the Sugar Bowl to see the power of the single wing against the deception and agility of the split T. The power never got started. By the end of 20 minutes, Maryland was ahead 21-0 and Tennessee's 20-game winning streak was over.

The game started in an odd fashion. Maryland won the toss but elected to kick off. Tennessee punted on third down to begin an exchange of kicks that finally led to Maryland taking over on its own 48 midway through the quarter. The adage was that you did not run against Tennessee, but Tatum ignored the saying. Modzelewski went up the middle for four yards. Shemonski cut off right end for six, Modzelewski used a trap to gain 12 yards, but fumbled, only to have Weidensaul recover on the 25. On fourth and six, Scarbath passed to Fullerton for a first down on the 12. Modzelewski crashed to the five, Fullerton got two, then nothing. On fourth down, Scarbath called a quick count and Fullerton went off right guard for a touchdown.

On the kickoff, Ward and Kensler raced down the field and smacked into Lauricella, who fumbled, with Kensler recovering on the Tennessee 13. On first down, Modzelewski cut over right guard for 11 yards. Scarbath sneaked to the one but Maryland was penalized 15 yards for illegal use of the hands. Scarbath lost two and Modzelewski gained 10 as the quarter ran out. On fourth down from the six, Fullerton started to sweep left end and then passed to Shemonski for the touchdown.

Fullerton, who was starting on offense in place of the injured Felton, was not a good passer. "He could throw a ball into a shower and not get it wet," said Scarbath. But Tennessee

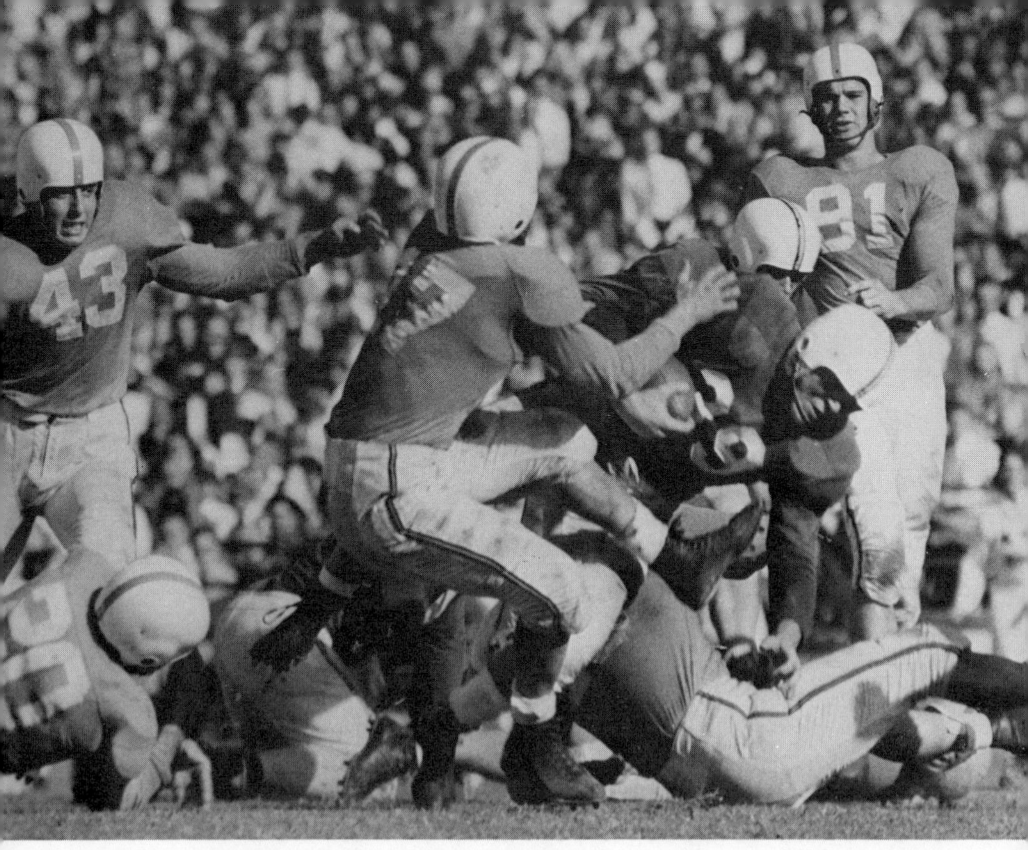

Ed (Big Mo) Modzelewski gains some of his 153 yards against Tennessee in the 1952 Sugar Bowl. Tennessee gained only 156 total yards for the game.

lined up with a four-man secondary and the game plan called for a halfback pass in such a situation. "I changed the play at the line and Fullerton called out, 'I'm not going to do it.' I said, 'yes, you are.' It was a terrible pass but Shemonski caught it and there was no holding him then. For years, Fullerton has claimed he taught me to pass."

Tennessee kept the ball for three plays before backup tailback Hal Payne fumbled and Fullerton, going both ways, recovered on the Tennessee 43. Modzelewski gained five and Horning, replacing Fullerton, got 15 around end. Scarbath then passed to Shemonski for 19. Modzelewski followed a Ward block for eight and then followed Ladygo at the other guard for 11 to the one. Scarbath scored with a hop, skip, and jump keeper play and Maryland led 21-0 five minutes into the second period.

The Volunteers, who hated to pass, went to their aerial

attack to score before the half ended. They covered 70 yards in 11 plays, five of which were passes, including a five-yarder to Bert Rechichar for a touchdown. The extra point missed to make it 21-6.

Neyland elected to kick off to start the second half and Maryland moved to the Tennessee 33 before Modzelewski fumbled. Neither team could move the ball until Fullerton, picking off his second pass of the day, gathered in a Lauricella attempt and returned it 46 yards for a touchdown with one minute remaining in the third quarter. Tennessee took advantage of a Faloney fumble of a punt to score with 11 minutes left in the game but could not muster another threat.

Modzelewski, who Neyland called "the best fullback I've ever seen," was chosen player of the game. He gained 153 yards on 28 carries. But the award could just as easily have gone to Fullerton, who gained 22 yards, scored two touchdowns, passed for another, intercepted two passes, and recovered a fumble.

Tennessee had been manhandled. The single wing had picked up only 156 total yards, including a paltry 81 rushing.

Maryland players seem worried in the 1952 Sugar Bowl despite being ahead 21-0 over Tennessee.

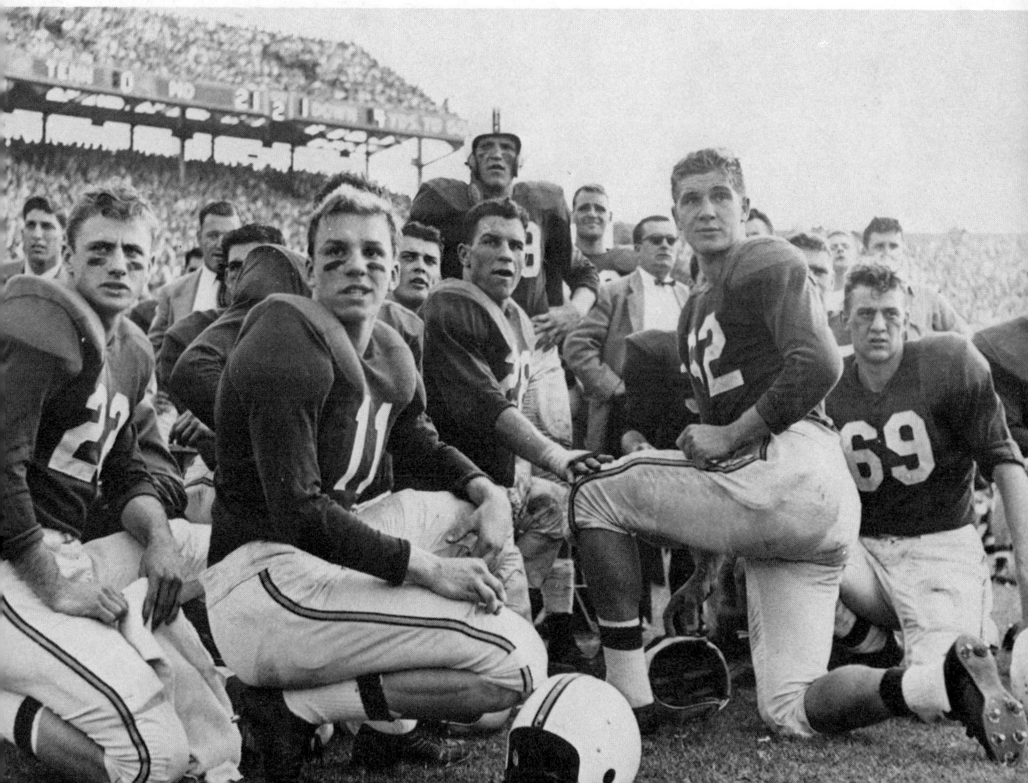

The Volunteers had been forced to pass 19 times, completing nine, and having four intercepted. Lauricella closed out his career with a net gain of one yard on seven attempts. He tried five passes. He completed four–one to a teammate and three to Maryland. It was the most dismal day of his career. He cried afterwards.

Meanwhile the Maryland offense had smashed the Volunteer defense for 352 total yards, including 289 on the ground. Nine different backs gained yards. Scarbath passed only nine times, completing six for 57 yards.

The Tatum tactics had worked. But let the pivotal figures, Ward and Scarbath, explain how.

"They played a loose six-man front defense," Scarbath said. "Neyland never changed unless he absolutely had to. Tatum figured that he should beat them inside, at their

Jim Tatum gets ride off Sugar Bowl field after Maryland beat No. 1 ranked Tennessee 28-13.

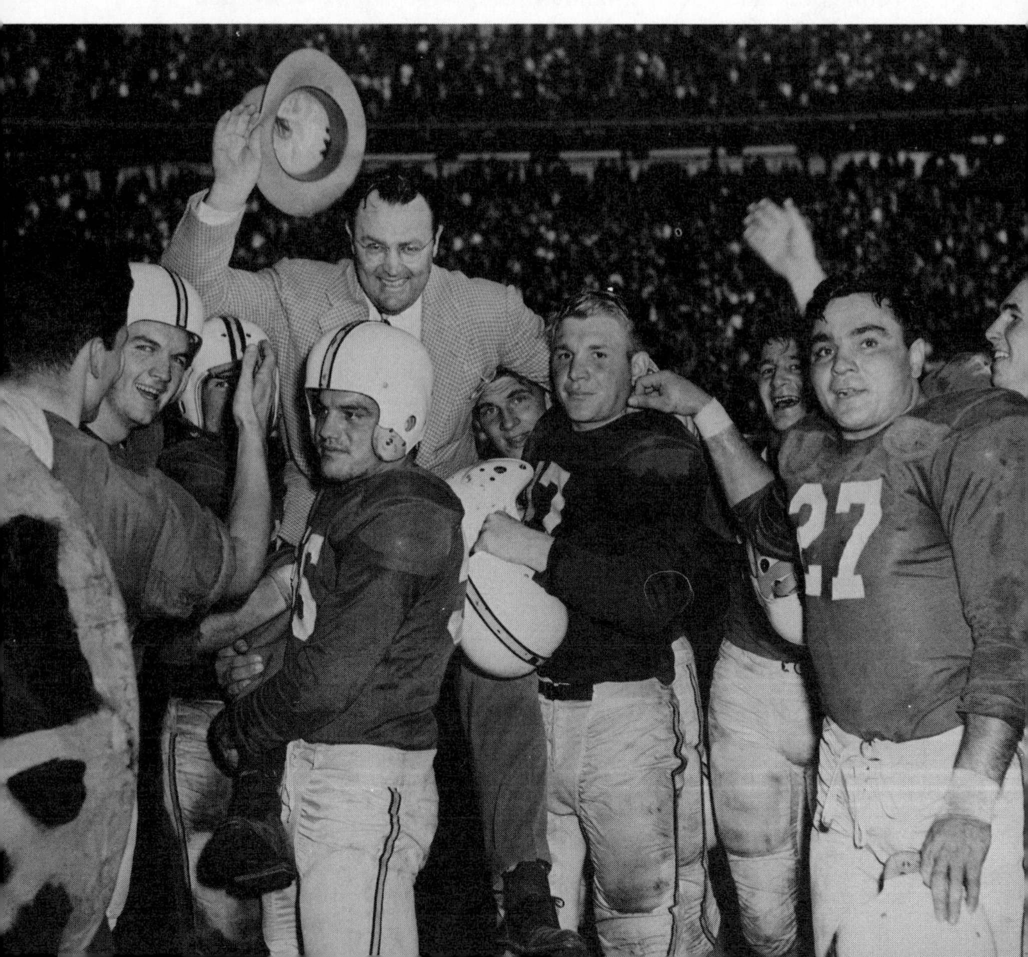

strength, and not outside where it seemed we would go. Neyland spread his ends and tackles just a bit to help against the sweeps and that allowed us to really work inside.

"They had an All-American guard in Ted Dapper and a tackle in Pug Pearman. We decided we didn't want to tangle much with Pearman but that Dapper, in the films, could be handled straight on. So we let Bobby Ward do it. He pushed him all over the field, with some help from Cosgrove. Destroyed him. The holes were huge."

Neyland finally switched to an Oklahoma 5-4 defense. Scarbath saw the change and called audibles on almost every play. "By now we had found out our tackles could handle their tackles too. We'd run Mo on tackle after tackle play. They'd compensate and we'd change. Neyland finally used a box secondary and left the middle wide open. So we exploited that." A pro scout said that he had never seen four more talented tackles on one team before—Moss and Jones on offense, and Modzelewski and Morgan on defense.

Maryland's defense had been altered by Tatum. He decided to force Neyland to throw by putting up an eight-man line and moving some of his linemen slightly off the scrimmage line, so they could pinch in toward the middle where Tennessee loved to run power plays.

"He took Mo and moved him off a step from the center," said Ward. "He became almost impossible to block and the result was that Morgan, Modzelewski, and Maletzky were tying up five guys. It completely destroyed their blocking patterns. They were forced to pass and that is what we wanted." Tatum had moved Fullerton from right to left halfback to take advantage of Lauricella's tendency to go to his right most of the time. Fullerton, who had had a minor knee operation in December, turned in two key defensive plays that led to scores.

Tatum let his players keep their helmets as a souvenir of the triumph. Sen. Estes Kefauver lost his bet with Maryland Sen. Herbert O'Connor and turned over his coonskin hat and live coon. Terrapin fans stormed over New Orleans in celebration.

"You have something like that game happen to you maybe once in a lifetime," Modzelewski said. "It just showed that Tatum was an innovator. He was years ahead of his time."

Big Mo, Little Mo, No Mo

Little brother was slightly taller and some 25 or so pounds heavier than older brother. He was also the outgoing, happy-go-lucky type while older brother was serious and quiet. But older brother was the leader. "He did a lot for Dick, he guided him and took care of him," said a friend about the relationship between Ed and Dick Modzelewski. "Sometimes Dick needed to be kept in line and Ed would do it. That's how it was in old country families. I don't care how big the younger brother was."

Pappa Modzelewski had come from Poland and settled in West Natrona, Pennsylvania, to work in the steel mills. It was 19 steps from the Modzelewski yard to the street and another 19 to the alley that led to the mills. You could stare down at the mill from their front door. The brothers worked on the slag hills in the summer. Ed talked his dad into letting him work one vacation in the mill. "I found out what it was like and knew I didn't want to do it," he said.

At first glance, the divergent backgrounds of a Jim Tatum and the Modzelewskis hardly seem compatible. But Tatum's personality closed the gap between nationalities. "He became very close to us," said Ed. "He'd spend time with us and stay overnight. He'd come to church with us and, even though he wasn't a Catholic, he would sit there with an arm around us and it was very impressive. He'd put in $20 in the collection plate. That was impressive. It was something in our town to put 50 cents in the plate."

On Father's Day at Byrd Stadium, 1951, Pappa Modzelewski receives a tour from sons Little Mo and Big Mo.

"Tatum would eat with them and drink with them," remembered Joe Blair, then Maryland's sports publicist and one of the major reasons why the Terrapins suddenly had so many All-Americans. "I remember one time he told me that he had this soup up there. He asked what it was and they said duck blood soup. I'm sure he had to force it down but he did."

Tatum had a valuable recruiting aide in assistant coach Jack Hennemier. "Hennemier got to know the aunts and the uncles and the local bars, everyone," said Ed Modzelewski. "He went to Polish weddings and ate our food. There would be six coaches at our house and my mom would give him three times as much as the rest because she loved him so much. What he said was golden to her. All the area coaches knew him and trusted him. It was important in a town like ours with 1,500 people. Personal relationships meant something."

Still, Ed, who had played on his high school's first undefeated team, was not going to sign with Maryland. He had visited the campus and did not really like it, although he was impressed with Tatum and assistant George Barkley was from West Natrona. Instead he was more impressed with Michigan State and also liked Penn State so much that the high school manager enrolled there in anticipation. "Maryland's stadium wasn't even any bigger than ours, while Michigan State had a beautiful place," he said.

He got so confused that he still had not decided when preseason practice began. "One Sunday, before I left for church, I decided I would go to Michigan State. Tatum called just before I left and I thanked him and told him my decision. He asked me not to do anything. By the time I got back from church, Barkley was at the airport in Pittsburgh. He called me and asked me to wait. The Michigan State coach came but I said I couldn't do anything because I had promised him. Barkley's sister taught at our high school and she had my future wife in her class. We knew his family. He stayed at her house but he lived at ours. He stayed for six days and Tatum would call every day. Penn State got back into it and I said the heck with it, I'll go there. I was going to meet an assistant coach at the bridge outside of town at 11 p.m. but Barkley came down and baby-sat at my house. Finally I went back to school with him. I stayed in a dorm in old Byrd Stadium and I woke up the first night and saw roaches. I said that was it, but Tatum took me to his house for three days and I finally decided to stay."

Tatum did not have a much easier time with brother Dick, despite Ed's presence. One school offered him a convertible for the summer, and Notre Dame recruited him strongly. Ed stayed at the school during the summer and worked. Dick came down for a visit and liked it, but then he got homesick and decided to go to Notre Dame. Ed was out in rural Virginia working and staying nights in a truck. Tatum panicked.

"He called the state police and they came out and got me," said Ed. "They flashed a light in my face and told me Tatum wanted me at Maryland right away and they drove me over to his office where he had Dick. He told Dick that only priests and lawyers go to Notre Dame, and that he wasn't smart enough to be a lawyer and he sure knew he wasn't going to be a priest. He brought our whole family down for a week so Dick wouldn't be lonely. It was the first time my dad ever saw a television. Dick must have threatened to leave 10 times that first year."

The Modzelewski brothers were then and are now best friends. "We always did things together, Dick would always follow me around," said Ed. "We went to the same college, married girls from our home town, wound up in the pros together. We are really close."

They became one of the most successful brother combinations in college history. Ed climaxed a fine career with his performance in the Sugar Bowl. He left Maryland with a total of 1,913 rushing yards in the regular season, and 2,102 including bowl games. Both records held up for 23 years. Tatum said he was more responsible than any other back his senior year for making the team's offense work. "People got so conscious of Mo going through the middle that they would bunch in the defense and we would walk around their ends," said Scarbath.

"It wasn't much fun tackling him," said Scarbath. "At 210 pounds he wasn't the easiest guy to bring down." Modzelewski also could block. "He gets the other team so aware of his cracking through the middle that a fake handoff allows him to cut down the tacklers—that shakes loose the halfbacks and quarterback for the open field," said one newspaper account. "He was tough, tough as nails," said one teammate. "After coming from the steel mills, football was easy for him. He could get you the tough yardage." Modzelewski had a nose for the goal line. He held the career record for points scored (126) for 23 years, as he did (with Shemonski) for touchdowns (22).

"Football was fun for me," he said. "I remember those college days with relish. We had a good time, we were winning and I was playing for a great man. I always said I had two great coaches, Jim Tatum and Paul Brown."

Besides his All-American honors, Ed led the conference in rushing and finishing second in scoring. Although brother Dick also made first team all-conference and first team on one minor All-American squad, his time really came in 1952, when he was a unanimous All-American and winner of the Outland Trophy, awarded annually to the nation's best interior lineman. It was the most prestigious award ever won by a Maryland player.

Tatum believed in building his teams around his tackles and Dick was his prime example. He was in much the Tatum mold for that position—not too tall (6-0) but strong and hefty

Dick (Little Mo) Modzelewski, Outland Trophy winner as the nation's best lineman in 1952: "He was to tackle what Bob Ward was to guard."

(235). Even during his junior year, one newspaper reported, "some coaches are saying he is to tackle what Bob Ward is to guard." Dick was a defensive specialist, clogging up the interior of the line with superior strength and surprising quickness. "My brother was something out there," said his older brother. "He was a first rate player. They didn't run through that defensive line. It was pretty near impossible." Tatum always said he felt sorry for the lineman who had to play opposite Dick.

They had a Modzelewski Day in West Natrona when it was all over. The townspeople came out to honor one of the few brother combinations to make All-American, and later, to become early round draft picks in the pros. The church bells rang and the steel mill whistles blew together for the first time since the return of Lindbergh. "It was the great thrill for my dad to sit in an open convertible and wave to everyone," said Ed. "He didn't know English, he couldn't read or write, and here he was being honored.

"It was even a bigger thrill for him when we had lunch at the White House with President Eisenhower. For him, a man from Poland who worked in the steel mills all his life, he couldn't put into words what it meant to him. For us, it was simple. We would never have gotten an education without football."

Jack Against The Giant Killers

It finally happened. After 22 straight games without a defeat, including 19 victories in a row, Maryland lost. Jim Tatum cried. "I don't think any loss, even in the bowls, got to him as much as that one," said Joe Blair. "He couldn't believe it had really happened." The defeat devastated the players; but for one, it meant much more. It cost Jack Scarbath the most coveted award in college football, the Heisman Trophy.

Maryland was to lose again the next week and finish the 1952 season with a 7-2 record and no bowl game despite a potentially stronger team than in 1951. Scarbath was to finish as the runnerup in the Heisman Trophy voting to Billy Vessels of Oklahoma. "As you get older, you certainly think about what would have happened if you had won it," said Scarbath. "What if we had won those games? What would I have won? I know that just the things that did come my way have opened up doors in business for years. People want to have you come in and talk about your playing days."

The end came in the eighth game of a schedule that was revised heavily after Southern Conference teams refused to play Maryland. The Terrapins originally were going to meet North Carolina on November 15 but instead found themselves in Oxford, Mississippi, where the Mississippi Rebels had not lost in three years.

Maryland had been off for two weeks prior to the game and was well-rested for the unbeaten but twice tied Rebels. A victory might mean a Sugar Bowl berth, although the Southern

Conference was still refusing to sanction a bid. There was talk of No. 2 ranked Maryland bolting the league.

But the Terrapins, Tatum admitted later, came up flat. "No one gave us his best performance and I stopped thinking during the game," he said.

A record crowd in Hemingway Stadium watched as Ole Miss struck for two fourth-period touchdowns to hand Maryland its first defeat since October of 1950, 21-14. The Rebels went to the Sugar Bowl instead.

Maryland, which was fifth nationally in total offense (423 yards a game), eighth in rushing, and 10th in passing, managed only one sustained drive all afternoon and gained only 128 total yards. Mississippi, meanwhile, penetrated the nation's leading defense (156 yards a game) for a whopping 461 yards. The Rebels were especially effective passing, as quarterback Jimmy Lear tossed for 231 yards while Scarbath, who had completed 47 of 84 passes entering the contest, was only 2 for 13 for 28 yards.

A four-yard run by Hanulak gave Maryland a 7-0 lead on the first play of the second quarter. Mississippi came back to tie it on a pass from Lear to Ray Howell before Dick Nolan took the ensuing kickoff and returned it 90 yards to put the Terrapins ahead at the half, 14-7.

After holding at the one, four, and three, Maryland folded in the fourth period when Mississippi went 41 yards for one score and 47 for another. Maryland had a touchdown pass of 61 yards from Scarbath to Weidensaul nullified just before the final score when an official ruled the Terrapins had an illegal receiver downfield. Tatum later said films indicated there was no such violation.

Tatum, in a letter to boosters, later explained that "we coaches didn't coach. We did a terrible job. What caused us not to do a good job was the fact that during the week off, we got so involved with bowl situations that 90 percent of our energy and time was spent between contacts with bowls and the president of the university. I was late getting on the field three days because I was tied up on the phone.

"You can't walk away and leave people who are offering you $150,000 to come to their party...why were the boys flat? No one on this campus had the power to tell them what we were going to do about a bowl. To our team it was like going to a country picnic and not knowing a soul who was serving the food." Instead of scouting Ole Miss in person, Tatum also had decided to see the Oklahoma-Notre Dame game.

Scarbath, who graced magazine covers during the season and was a preseason choice to win player of the year honors, saw the defeat coming.

"We sort of got away from the split T that we ran the year before," he said. "We started to be a throwing team rather than a running team. We did not have quite the tackles and we didn't control the line of scrimmage. Defenses spread out more and forced us inside. They took a gamble that we couldn't gain yardage up the middle. Instead of me dictating to them what to do, they were dictating to me."

Scarbath was the leading split T quarterback of his day. Byrd once compared him to the legendary Guckeyson. "He runs very much like Guke," said Byrd. "He doesn't look fast, running with that long, sloping stride but he'll outspeed practically anybody on the field on any game day."

It was a matter of the right player being in the right place at the right time. Tatum's split T—or more correctly, sliding T—required a deft ball-handling quarterback who also could withstand the punishment of running. Passing really was secondary. As a junior, Scarbath only threw 67 times; as a sophomore he had tried 80 passes.

"He operates the split T better than any other quarterback I've seen run it," said Missouri's Don Faurot, the offense's inventor. Tatum called Scarbath's work on the keep play "exceptional. His deception is something to watch. He always has the other team off balance." Scarbath was a Mississippi River gambler. He would take chances, risky ones. But he was intelligent and skilled and his daring usually paid off.

Scarbath came to Maryland from Baltimore Poly High after being recruited by, among others, Byrd. "He happened to see me in a game and recommended me," said Scarbath. "I had to come over for a tryout and they passed me." He was given a Charlie Keller scholarship, which usually went to baseball players. He played freshman baseball and then was told to stop by Tatum.

The Tatum split T was quite similar to the much more

Bernie Faloney (left) played defensive back for two years while Jack Scarbath did the quarterbacking in 1951 and 1952. Both eventually made All-American and Scarbath finished second in the Heisman Trophy voting.

modern wishbone, except the Maryland fullback did not line up ahead of the halfbacks. The options were simple, at least as explained by Scarbath.

"First, the fullback. He ran parallel to the line of scrimmage until he got behind the tackle positions and then he ran straight. The quarterback would take the snap and then step forward to where the line of scrimmage used to be before the offensive line moved. He'd slide down the line and fake to his halfback on dive, then give to the fullback who'd break off tackle.

"The quarterback also could continue down the line and option off the last man on the line of scrimmage. If he took the quarterback there would be a pitch to the trailing halfback and he'd go around end. If he took the pitch, the quarterback would keep the ball. That was all there was to it. He had pass plays off the fake to the fullback and we could drop back."

Tatum would spend the whole week prior to a game going over offensive plans with his quarterbacks, who called their own plays. "By the game, we were totally versed as to what to call where according to down, distance, and time," said Scarbath. "We were really an extension of him on the field. He wanted to control the game. He figured three yards on each of four downs was always a first down."

Scarbath, who stood 6-1 and weighed 195 pounds, enjoyed pounding into the secondary for extra yards. He was the fourth-leading rusher on the team in 1952, gaining 237 yards, and he passed for 1,149 more to set single season records in yards, attempts (113), and completions (59). He also left with career marks in all three and they were not broken until the 1960s. He was responsible for 35 career touchdowns, one of the longest lasting marks in the Maryland record book.

Dick Modzelewski and he were Maryland's most honored players in 1952. Both made all-conference, all-south, and unanimous All-American. Modzelewski won the Outland Trophy and Scarbath was the conference's player of the year. Alderton, Fullerton, and Jones also were first-team all-conference picks.

The defense, which allowed only 85 points the entire year and an average of 147 yards rushing and 200 total yards a game, carried Maryland through the first part of the season in which it had been picked to finish either first or second in the nation. The defensive line from 1951 had returned intact: Alderton and Nestor at the ends, and the M-Club in the middle, Modzelewski, Morgan, and Maletzky. Tatum had worried at first about his linebackers since Cianelli and Kensler had graduated and he had lost Roy Martine but he found able replacements in Marty Crytzer, Charley Lattimer, Art Hurd, and Walt Boeri. The secondary, of Faloney, Nolan, Horning, and Fullerton, one of the best in college football, absorbed the loss of Joe Petruzzo to pick off 14 passes and limit opponents to 53 yards a game.

The offensive line was rebuilt with such talent as guards Frank Navarro and Ray Stankus, and returning stars Jones and Cosgrove. Tatum did not lack for ballcarriers. Supporting Scarbath were Felton and Hanulak with Fullerton, who Tatum labelled "the best all-around player in America," moving into Modzelewski's fullback spot.

Tatum predicted that "it would be impossible" for his team to go undefeated considering the upgrading of the schedule—including six games away from home—and the fact "we outmanned five opponents last year but can't do that this season."

The end of the winning streak almost came in the opening game. Missouri, a 27-point underdog, led 10-0 entering the final quarter and did not lose 13-10, until Scarbath hit Colteryahn on the 26 and the senior end ran in for the score with 70 seconds remaining.

Another supposed weak entry, Auburn, led until midway through the fourth period before Scarbath and Colteryahn again teamed up for a 32-yard touchdown pass to pull out a 13-7 triumph. Colteryahn had made up the pass pattern on the sidelines with Tatum. Felton gained 111 yards and Fullerton played 57 minutes.

Scarbath, who had been suffering from two bruised heels, had his best day of the young season in a 28-0 thumping of Clemson. He had 205 total yards, including 128 passing yards on just seven completions. He ran for one score and threw for two, and was named national back of the week.

Maryland had little trouble again until running into Mississippi. The Terrapins crushed Georgia and Zeke Bratkowski 37-0, limiting the Bulldogs to 60 yards rushing while gaining 340 themselves on the ground. Hanulak gained 115 yards, sophomore Dick Bielski showed promise with 67 yards, and seven different players scored.

Unbeaten Navy fell 38-7 before 44,716 in Byrd Stadium, although the Midshipmen broke Maryland's string of 13 consecutive shut-out quarters. Navy gained only 26 rushing yards and 88 total yards and Fullerton ran for 107 yards. LSU was a 34-6 victim with Scarbath passing for 181 yards and three touchdowns, including two to Colteryahn. Scarbath now had 966 total yards, 129 more than in 1951. But the Terrapins lost Fullerton with a dislocated elbow, an injury that would hurt them in the next weeks. Prior to the game, Scarbath, Cosgrove, and Navarro reported an attempt to bribe them to hold the score spread to 21 points. The attempt was made by a Maryland student.

Maryland made it 22 straight without a loss by downing Boston University 34-7, holding Harry Agganis to minus 44 yards rushing and no completions before he left with bruised ribs. The Terrapins failed to gain 400 yards for the first time since the opener but Hanulak had 97 yards rushing, Felton scored twice and BU was limited to 94 total yards.

By now, many were thinking Maryland—not Michigan State or Georgia Tech, the two teams ranked ahead of the Terrapins—was the nation's best squad. One columnist gave the nod to Maryland because of its passing attack "and the way Lou Weidensaul and Lloyd Colteryahn run pro pass patterns."

The dream fell apart the next week against Mississippi and then was shattered completely in the season finale against Alabama, 27-7. The Crimson Tide ran through Maryland's defense for 241 rushing yards while mistakes were costing the Terrapins scoring opportunities. Scarbath completed 10 of 16 passes for 152 yards, including eight to Colteryahn and a touchdown to Weidensaul.

Maryland finished 13th in the final poll while Mississippi was seventh and Alabama, which went to the Orange Bowl—a berth Maryland might have gotten—was ninth. Curley Byrd then dropped a bombshell. He blamed Tatum completely for the losses, saying he stopped thinking and talked too much about things when he should leave well enough alone. "I've been trying to shut him up for three years," said Byrd. Tatum absorbed the slap, did not take a job at North Carolina as had been rumored, and returned the next season. It was to be an historic one for the school.

A Knee And A National Championship

The news rocked the college football world. The two-platoon system had been tossed out by the rules committee. In its place was substituted the one-platoon format which made it mandatory for the return of two-way players and, quite likely, 60-minute athletes. Jim Tatum hailed the news.

"It's the best news I've heard," he said. "This should put coaching back into the game. By that, I mean in substituting wisely and also in teaching boys the game both offensively and defensively. It should help me tremendously. Last season I think we had 26 men as good as any in the country."

One-platoon football was just some of the good news Tatum had before the 1953 season opened. His salary had increased from $12,000 to $16,875 since 1951, making him the third highest paid state employee, behind Byrd ($22,500) and the mental hygiene commissioner ($20,000). Maryland also had left the Southern Conference to form the Atlantic Coast Conference with fellow dissidents South Carolina, North Carolina, Clemson, North Carolina State, Duke, and Wake Forest. Virginia would be added later.

The only bad news was a knee operation undergone by tackle Bob Morgan, who missed all of spring practice, and would sit out most of the first two games of the season and play little in the next two before rounding into shape.

Despite the loss of such players as Scarbath, Dick Modzelewski, Colteryahn, Alderton, Weidensaul, Cosgrove, and Fullerton, Tatum said he had "as good prospects as for any year since I've been here."

Tatum's team was ranked anywhere from first to 10th in the preseason polls. He disagreed. He admitted he would field his most talented backfield, but his line was green and there were a number of players like Hanulak and Jones who had to learn how to play defense. Tatum was especially concerned about his defense, figuring Maryland would surrender a lot of points while also scoring a lot itself.

The quarterback duties fell to Faloney, a two-year defensive starter and backup to Scarbath. Dick Nolan, another defensive specialist, was at one halfback and Hanulak at the other. Felton was the fullback.

Despite Tatum's misgivings, the season became perhaps the most impressive in Maryland's history. The Terrapins went undefeated for the second time in three years, before losing a heartbreaking game to Oklahoma in the Orange Bowl. They emerged the most powerful defensive team in the nation and dominated opponents as no other Maryland team had done. And they won Tatum's first official national championship and the school's only one.

Tatum was hospitalized during much of fall practice with kidney stone attacks. He managed to make the opener at Missouri, which, he predicted, would be very strong. He was right. Hanulak scored on the second play of the game, going 61 yards, but Missouri came back against Maryland's second unit to pull within one, 7-6, at the half.

Faloney then insured the triumph early in the fourth quarter. Felton intercepted a pass and a 26-yard run by junior Ron Waller helped get the ball to the one. Jones was then called for being offside and on fourth down from the four, Faloney faded to pass. "I got desperate," he said. "I finally took off for the end zone. I don't know how the hell I got into the end zone." He was hit on the two, but lunged forward for the score. Maryland added a touchdown at the end for a 20-6 win.

Faloney played all but one minute, 15 seconds of the game. He recovered a fumble and had at least two touchdown passes dropped. Hanulak gained 113 of Maryland's 225 rushing yards.

Washington & Lee was a pushover 52-0 as Waller, Hanulak's backup, scored three times, including a 56-yard punt return. Washington & Lee managed only 145 total yards, and most of that was against the Terrapin reserves.

The Clemson game started off with a surprise—both to the Tigers and Faloney. The opening kickoff came to the Maryland quarterback as he was standing up field, thinking about what he would call on the first series of downs. "I knew I wanted to be in the middle of the field," he said. So he took off in that direction, kept running and returned it 88 yards for the score. It was the first such return in his career. "I've still got the films of it and I love to see it," he laughed.

It became a game of big plays. Ahead only 7-0 at the half, Maryland added a 65-yard scoring pass from Faloney to Nolan. Faloney, who had been hit hard on the play before, called a punt. "Hey, it's only third down," Jones reminded him. So Faloney called "25 pass" at the line of scrimmage—"I think it confused Clemson"—and connected for the touchdown. Nolan returned a punt 90 yards late in the game for the final tally in the 20-0 triumph. Clemson managed 183 total yards to Maryland's 430.

By now Maryland was ranked fourth in the country and already had doubled the total yardage of its opponents. Faloney, who was being touted for All-American, was satisfied with his play but not enthralled with it. That would change against Georgia, which was led by Zeke Bratkowski for the third straight year.

Bratkowski topped the nation in passing his junior year and had thrown for 355 yards entering the game. "We were both being pushed for All-American and it was a big game for both of us," said Faloney. "I was inspired to play well. But I never saw a man who could throw like him."

Maryland jumped to a 14-0 lead on an 18-yard pass from Faloney to sophomore Billy Walker and a one-yard plunge by Faloney. A 92-yard drive ended in a 24-yard scoring pass to Nolan, which was enough to offset two second-quarter Georgia touchdowns. Bratkowski then started his team on a third-period drive, only to have Faloney pick off a pass and return it for a touchdown. That ignited a Maryland rout, 40-13.

Bratkowski completed 16 of 29 passes for 202 yards despite a third-period injury. John Carson caught eight of those completions. But Faloney was better. He completed seven of 10 passes for 148 yards and two touchdowns, scored two himself, gained 23 yards on four carries, and intercepted one pass. And his first touchdown throw was over Bratkowski's head. Maryland wound up outgaining Georgia 452 to 266.

"The Terp backfield has everything, speed, power, deception, and drive," wrote a columnist after the game. "Tatum has added some of the regular T plays to his split-T attack. Add Bernie Faloney's brilliant passing to all this and Maryland showed me one of the finest and most varied offenses I have seen in a long time. This is a more dangerous Maryland eleven than the Terp team of a year ago. Last season, the Terps first downed you, but this year, the backs have more speed and Faloney's passing is super."

The day before it was announced that the Big Seven conference and the ACC had signed a pact with the Orange Bowl, Maryland registered its fifth straight win, a 26-0 romp over previously unbeaten North Carolina. It was Tatum's first win against his alma mater at Chapel Hill and he called it "more satisfying than the Sugar Bowl (1951)." Maryland amassed 367 yards in marching 69, 92, 72, and 85 yards for scores. Faloney was shaken up early in the game and reserve Charley Boxold came through with a fine performance, hitting four of five passes for 97 yards.

Maryland broke to a 27-0 lead in the first 20 minutes and crunched Miami 30-0 in the Orange Bowl, picking up an admirer, actress Gloria DeHaven, in the process. An interception by Felton and two recovered fumbles led to three quick scores, including a pass from Faloney to end Marty Crytzer. "We had called an option pass for Nolan on the play before and it didn't work," said Faloney. "Nolan came back to the huddle and said to call the same play but instead of lateraling to him, to keep it and throw it. It was the first rollout pass we had used and Tatum put it in the next week for good." Miami gained 187 total yards, Maryland 367. Felton had 97 yards from his fullback spot.

Maryland now had registered four shutouts in six games, outscoring opponents 188-19. Tatum credited the one-platoon. "It's made us into the team we are," he said of his second-ranked squad.

Tatum would say afterwards that his squad was not flat for

South Carolina, but Faloney says that is not true. "For some reason, we couldn't get up for them." Maryland still won 24-6 against the ACC's No. 1 defense. Felton scored from the one and then Hanulak went down the right sidelines 66 yards with a punt for another touchdown. A 40-yard field goal by Dick Bielski made it 17-0 before South Carolina scored.

The Gamecocks, the second-best offensive team in the conference, were limited to 37 rushing yards and 122 passing yards. Hanulak gained 67 yards on only seven carries, to keep his yards-per-attempt average at nine for the season.

Maryland was the nation's best defense against scoring (3.6 a game) and the run (96.3) going into the George Washington contest. Still the statistics did not prevent the Terrapins from having their first off-day of the year. Thrice-beaten GW held them to a 7-6 half-time lead. Faloney had set up the score with a pass but had a pass thrown over his head for the Colonial tally. Walker then blocked a punt in the third period to set up a 33-yard touchdown run by Hanulak. Walker caused a fumble on the next series and Faloney scored on a one-yard sneak to insure the 27-6 win. GW gained only 33 yards on the ground.

Next was Mississippi, and a chance for Tatum and his players to gain some much wanted revenge for the Rebels' victory in 1952, which had broken the Terrapins' long winning streak. Tatum was receiving pressure from a lot of places: Byrd kept reminding him that bad coaching had lost the contest; a Washington columnist pointed out that the team had lost its continuity about the time of last year's Mississippi game, giving credence to those who thought Tatum could not win the big ones; and other writers and critics could not understand why Maryland had not run up more big scores on opponents during the season.

Mississippi presented an opportunity for Tatum to put all the criticism—and those who said Maryland had played a simple schedule—to rest. Mississippi was ranked 11th and had won its last five after being shut out by Auburn. The Rebels were ranked just below Maryland in total offense (345 a game) and were the nation's fourth-best passing team while averaging 188 on the ground.

"There was no question we were after them," said Faloney. "Tatum showed us film of the game the year before. I

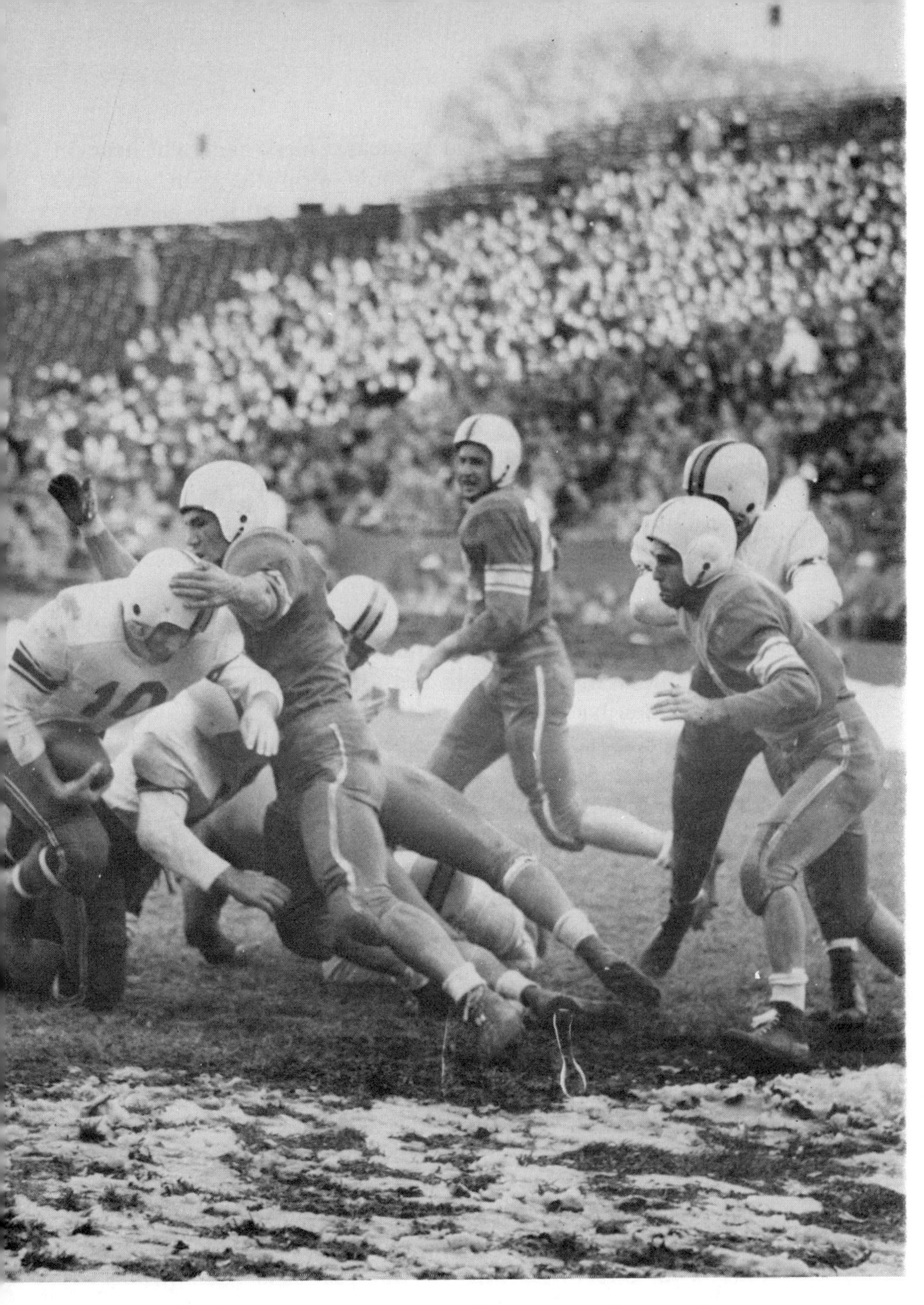

Bernie Faloney sneaks over for a touchdown against George Washington at Griffith Stadium in 1953. Maryland won 27-6.

had a broken nose and had to wear a mask and I got beat on two touchdown passes. He would stop the film and say, 'Faloney, I know you had the broken nose but it shouldn't have happened to you.' He had a way of humiliating the hell out of you nicely."

Tatum's psychology worked. Maryland romped to a 38-0 victory that had pro scouts walking away calling the Terrapins the best in the nation. Mississippi was held to 39 yards rushing and 184 total yards while Maryland ran up 375, including 296 on the ground. Faloney was chosen national back of the week for his performance.

Maryland held the Rebels on the one in the first quarter when Faloney intercepted a pass in the end zone. Then an interception by John Irvine, which he returned 31 yards to the Mississippi two, set up the Terrapins' first touchdown, from the one by Faloney. A 42-yard run by Felton scored the second after Hanulak scooted 40 yards to set it up. Faloney added another score on a nine-yard run. Bielski kicked a 28-yard field goal and later had a 41-yard touchdown scamper.

Faloney scored two touchdowns, intercepted two passes, and recovered a fumble. Maryland intercepted six passes in all, and Mississippi fumbled eight times in losing for only the second time in 20 games.

By now Maryland, which had tied Duke for the first ACC title, was all but assured of going to the Orange Bowl and a meeting with Oklahoma. The final game of the regular season was against Alabama, and another chance for Tatum to revenge a loss. He did, but with costly results.

Alabama came into the game once-beaten and thrice-tied, and just off an upset of Georgia Tech, with Bart Starr at quarterback and Bobby Luna as its star runner. It was no match for Maryland. Alabama lost 21-0. Notre Dame, which had been ranked No. 1, was tied by Iowa the same day, fell out of the top spot, and Maryland was inserted.

Maryland had beaten Alabama despite a first-half injury to Faloney's knee, which limited him to 16 minutes. The Terrapins' 10th straight victory of the year—and their fifth shutout—was sparked by Hanulak, who went 81 yards on Maryland's second play of the game for a touchdown. Faloney then passed 52 yards to Walker, who juggled the ball on his fingertips before carrying it into the end zone.

Faloney was then hit on what he thought was a very late tackle by Sid Youngelman. He tore the ligaments in his knee and was finished for the day. Boxold replaced him and passed 27 yards to Walker for another score before the half ended. Maryland's defense held Alabama on the two for four downs. Alabama previously had been on the seven, six, ten, and four without scoring. Walker was named lineman of the week for his performance.

Tatum was finally convinced that not only his backfield, but his line was his best ever. The Terrapins had run up truly amazing statistics on defense. They had limited opponents to 31 points (while scoring 298) and just 83 yards on the ground, both the best in the nation. Foes gained 2,695 total yards, Maryland 3,595. It was the best defensive showing by a college team since 1947.

"I had heard a lot about Maryland's great backfield," said an Oklahoma scout, "but it's the line that is terrific. Those big boys don't give you half a chance."

Tatum had built his defense around Morgan (6-0, 225) and Jones (6-0, 240) at the tackles, with Tom Breunich subbing. Walker (6-0, 185) had developed quickly at end while at the other flank, Crytzer (6-0, 205) had experience. Irvine (6-2, 210) (with help from second stringer Charlie Lattimer), George Palahunik (6-1, 190) and John Bowersox (6-1, 195) patrolled the middle. The four offensive backs doubled as the secondary men, with Felton a particularly impressive linebacker. Maryland had allowed all of its points in the second quarter, when Tatum usually played his second unit. The Terrapins never trailed or were never tied the whole season.

Although the players felt they deserved the national title, they did not find out for sure until they were eating their traditional spaghetti dinner that marked the end of the regular season. "Tatum came in beaming and said, 'we're No. 1, we're No. 1.' He was overjoyed," said Faloney. "Morgan and I, as team captains, broke out an impromptu sign that said 'Maryland No. 1' and we all posed for a picture."

The team would later be treated to a parade and luncheon in the District, where the school was given the O'Donnell Trophy, symbolic of the national championship. Tatum also

was selected coach of the year by the major news organizations.

"We knew we had to beat Oklahoma to make it official, though," said Faloney.

That job normally would have seemed quite possible. Oklahoma had an 8-1-1 record under Bud Wilkinson, Tatum's former assistant. Maryland had the experience, the defense, and the backfield. Its offensive display had been impressive. Hanulak led the nation in average yards per carry (9.8), gaining 753 on only 77 attempts. Felton averaged 5.6 yards, Nolan 5.2, No. 2 fullback Bielski 6.4, and Waller 4.9. They crunched out 257 yards a game on the ground, requiring Faloney and friends to pass only 11 times a game. In all, 14 runners had at least one carry and 16 players scored at least six points.

But this was an unusual contest. Faloney at best would be barely ready; at worst, he would not play. He had a tear of the internal lateral ligament of the left knee. He was kept inactive

Maryland's 1953 national championship team had a standout backfield of Dick Nolan (22), Ralph Felton (42), Bernie Faloney (10), and Chet Hanulak (33). Other starters included ends Bill Walker (80) and Marty Crytzer (84), tackles Stan Jones (77) and Bob Morgan (76), guards George Palahunik (62) and John Bowersox (64) and center John Irvine (50).

for three weeks while receiving physical therapy, diathermy, and exercises. It became almost a daily guessing game whether the injury would heal sufficiently.

"I hurt the knee on that darn rollout pass that Nolan had suggested in the Miami game," he said. "I had hurt the knee a little earlier in the game but I told Tatum I was okay. I had let go of the pass to Hanulak and wasn't prepared for the hit."

Faloney went with the team to Miami Beach. "It felt better every day," he said. "I was able to do a lot of what I wanted to do." Then on December 29 in a practice, Faloney hurt the knee again. "I was running with the first-team offense and running good. Tatum yelled 'one more play, one more play.' I ran an option, put pressure on the knee and it buckled."

Tatum had been at defensive right end on the play, trying to protect Faloney from getting hit. As his quarterback walked off the field, he said, "there goes my team." It would be a statement that would haunt him. The knee filled up with fluid and Tatum declared Faloney out of the game. "We'll have to scramble," Tatum said. "We'll have to sit down and revise our entire game strategy. Our kids are faced with more problems now than at any time this year."

Faloney, Tatum realized, was the heart of the offense. "You can teach mechanics in a week," he said. "But you can't replace personality. Faloney does things in certain ways. He has the experience, the know-how and the leadership. You just don't get a replacement for that very quickly."

Boxold, who had attempted 26 passes, completing 11, and had run for 154 yards, was now the No. 1 quarterback. He had come to Maryland as a fullback, then became a blocking back as a freshman and a right halfback before being redshirted. He played in one game in 1952 in which he broke his leg, and threw his first pass in an organized contest in the 1953 opener against Missouri—for a touchdown.

Boxold admitted before the Orange Bowl that he was having trouble catching on to the habits of his new backfield mates and of center Irvine. But by game time, he thought he had everything down. "Tatum even put in a few drop back passes for him," said Faloney, who was considered less of a passer than his replacement.

Oklahoma came into the game averaging 353 total yards, 306 on the ground, best in the nation. The Sooners had lost to Notre Dame in the opener, tied Pitt the next week, switched to Gene Calame at quarterback, and gone the rest of the way undefeated to finish ranked fourth in the nation. In J. D. Roberts, they had—along with Maryland's Jones—the best lineman in the country. Wilkinson already had won a national title in 1950, been named coach of the year twice, had never been shut out, had put together a record 31-game winning streak, and still had not lost a conference game since taking over for Tatum in 1947.

Even with Faloney out, Maryland was favored by a touchdown. The coaches had held closed practices and jockeyed all week for the psychological edge. But nothing offset the loss of the Terrapins' No. 1 quarterback.

Oklahoma won 7-0 on a 25-yard, second quarter run by Larry Grigg to end an 80-yard march against the nation's toughest ground defense. But Maryland actually lost the game earlier when it twice was within yards of the Oklahoma goal, only to come up empty-handed.

The first occurred after Maryland took over on the Oklahoma 37. The Terrapins moved to a first down on the four. Hanulak picked up two, Nolan was stopped on a pitchout for no gain by Grigg, Hanulak moved to the one-foot line, and on fourth down Felton was stopped short of the goal line.

Bielski missed a 44-yard field goal minutes later, then Maryland got the ball back on a fumble. The Terrapins moved to the nine with a first down when the quarter ended. Tatum elected to substitute his second unit as usual, a move that would be criticized heavily afterwards.

Maryland could get the ball only to the six and Tatum

Stan Jones, left, and Bob (Blubber) Morgan anchored the 1953 Maryland line from their tackle positions. Jones was a unanimous All-American.

further hurt himself by not having Bielski, who had been removed from the game moments before, around to kick a field goal. So Felton, the only regular in the contest, tried and missed the first kick of his career. Oklahoma then marched to the score, the first time Maryland had been behind all season.

"Charley really played all right," Faloney believes. "Tatum had put in a lot of new offense for the game. We had gotten away from the split T because he felt Oklahoma would be able to handle it. We weren't familiar with the new stuff and it hurt us." Tatum would not admit that Faloney's absence had cost him the game, but Maryland's offense had not run smoothly, gaining only 202 yards to Oklahoma's 236, including 208 on the ground. The Sooners had swarmed over Boxold, gangtackled

Bernie Faloney (10) and Charlie Boxold, who replaced him at quarterback in the 1954 Orange Bowl.

the running backs, covered punts aggressively, and displayed overwhelming speed in the line.

"It was on offense that Maryland was a sad-sack team," wrote a columnist. "The dash was gone from the Maryland attack. There were foul ups on handoffs and Boxold got precious little protection on passes."

Faloney had gotten in for five plays at the end of the third quarter and beginning of the fourth. He moved the team for 16 yards, then was taken out.

"I felt useless, helpless," he said. "I could have just as well sat at the hot dog stand. I thought I could play more but the knee was weak. It was a lousy experience."

Nor was it a good experience for Curley Byrd. He had announced his retirement from the president's office to run for governor, something his friends had been urging him to do for years. The board of regents extended his term so he could sit on the bench at the bowl. Then he left, only to be defeated in the election.

Byrd died in 1970 as president emeritus of the university. He was 81. Byrd had come to Maryland in 1905 when the school had a student body of 260. When he retired, the enrollment had grown from 3,400 when he took over in 1935 to 15,700. The budget had grown from $3,000,000 to $20,000,000. The plant value of the school had grown from $5,000,000 to $65,000,000.

And, just as important to him, he left the school with a winning football team.

Bernie, Superman, And The Jet

One former pro and college star was so bold to write that the four Maryland backs in 1953 were the new version of Notre Dame's famed Four Horsemen. He expounded upon the virtues of each of these new horsemen, and then concluded by giving the nod in talent to the Maryland bunch, mainly because of the multi-abilities of Bernie Faloney.

Faloney was one of those touted three-way men; he could pass, run, and kick, and do them all with a certain efficiency that put him above most other mortals. He came into his senior year in a most difficult position and exceeded expectation. He was asked to replace an All-American, Jack Scarbath, and as an added burden, to go both ways, something Scarbath never did because he had Faloney playing the secondary for him for two years.

There was not much Bernie Faloney could not do on a football field. He was considered Maryland's best defensive back that senior year, a nifty tackler and pass defender. He was also possessor of fine leadership qualities. He had the knack of getting men to respond to him. A B-plus student, he was a cagey signal caller, perhaps not as risky as the daring Scarbath, but so well-drilled by Tatum in opponents' defenses that he admitted "when we lined up on Saturday and I looked at the defense, it was just like we had practiced. All I had to do was just work the game plan."

Faloney differed from Scarbath in other ways. He was not as good a passer, but a better runner, more capable of breaking off long gainers. He also called plays in different sequences. While Scarbath depended heavily on the option, Faloney was more content to rely on quick openers and traps.

When he could not play in the Orange Bowl, and writers were searching for words to describe what he meant to the team, the best they could come up with was simply "personality." He had the intangible leadership ability that could not be broken down into words. Tatum said that without Faloney, "we are a team with a different personality. In the split T, the quarterback gives the team personality."

Tatum said there were six keys to a good split T quarterback: ball handling, ability to analyze defenses, running, passing, defensive ability, and confidence of the team. Faloney rated a top grade in all six from his coach. In his senior year, Faloney showed this versatility through statistics: he ran for 195 yards, he scored 54 points (a team high), he completed 31 of 68 passes for 599 yards and five touchdowns. He had 794 yards total offense (a team high), he punted 19 times for a 39-yard average, he returned two kickoffs 116 yards–including one for a touchdown–and he intercepted six passes (a team high).

"I welcomed the change to go both ways," Faloney said. "In high school, I never came off the field and that's how I always wanted to play football. I had been waiting a long time to show what I could do offensively. When I was a junior, Tatum had to pick between Scarbath and me. Since I could play defense pretty well, it seemed logical to do what he did."

Faloney had come from East Carnegie, Pennsylvania. When he was a senior he was brought to Maryland by his coach to meet Tatum. His coach recommended a scholarship and Tatum agreed. That was, Faloney said, his only offer. "I played four sports in high school, baseball, basketball, soccer, and football, but I liked football the best. Tatum said I was a little small, but my coach told him I was growing. I liked the school, and you don't get fussy with only one offer, so I came to Maryland." He stood six feet and weighed 180 his senior year at Maryland.

The 1953 team became something special but Faloney was not surprised. "Nine of us were on the freshman team together and had stuck together since we got to Maryland," Faloney said. "We had a closeness and I think that made us a good team.

Tatum always remarked that he never saw a team so spirited."

Faloney was drafted in the first round by the San Francisco 49ers, who offered him $9,000 to be a defensive back. He turned it down and went instead to Canada, where he was a quarterback on a Gray Cup winner. He decided to quit after that one season and wound up in the Air Force. When he got out, he went back up north and played 12 more years, appearing in seven Gray Cup games in all, winning four.

"I always felt," he said, "that I was a winning quarterback, and not a defensive back."

He was one of two Terrapins to make All-American in 1953. Faloney appeared on one major team, chosen by the International News Service, and was second-team on the rest of the important squads. Stan Jones did even better. He was a unanimous choice.

Jones was the strongest of the Terrapins. His strength was legend. Tatum liked to tell the story of how Jones burst through the line on a pass play against Georgia, smacked into a blocker, knocking him into Zeke Bratkowski. Both Georgia players were stunned and had to leave the game. Jones just went back to work as if nothing had happened.

"He's so strong that he can move an entire line out of the way on a block," said Tatum. His teammates were properly impressed. They called him Superman. "I can't conceive of any player being stronger and he is the most devastating blocker I ever saw," said Tatum. "It is nothing for him to move a man back from five to 10 yards. He had a keen sense of picking up difficult defenses thrown at Maryland and especially him."

Jones was an easy-going sort who rarely got upset off the field. Indeed, Tatum's major worry about his ability to play defense his senior year was that he was not mean enough. "He took care of that by blasting people," Tatum admitted.

Jones was not highly recruited. His high school coach wanted him to go to a Pennsylvania school. The coach also had a friend who was a line coach at North Carolina. Jones decided that was too far away to go to school. The line coach then set up an appointment for Jones and the coach to meet Tatum. They did and Jones signed with Maryland.

He was selected as lineman of the year by one major magazine. Like Faloney, he also made All-ACC, although Faloney was chosen ACC player of the year.

Another member of that ACC team was Chet Hanulak. He was perhaps the most exciting runner to ever wear a Maryland uniform. For sure, he had the most exciting nicknames. Chet the Jet, Hanulak from Hackensack, the Hanulak Express, Hot-foot Hanulak. He was the victim of ability. The teams he played on had too much talent, won games too easily, and his statistics suffered. His sophomore year, as a second stringer, he gained

Chet (The Jet) Hanulak averaged more than nine yards a carry in 1953. No one recruited him out of high school.

300 yards on only 35 carries. As a junior, he gained a team-leading 491 yards on 78 carries. His senior year, it was 765 on 77 carries. For his three-year career, he had 1,556 yards on 190 carries, a remarkable average per attempt of 8.2. Projected over even 300 carries, normal for most backs his caliber, he would have left with all of the school career rushing records and would have been an All-American.

"I never saw anyone hit a hole and be through it faster than Chet," said Faloney. "He had great quickness, and that amazing ability to break off long gainers. It didn't seem like a good game for him unless he had one long run."

Hanulak weighed only 170 pounds, distributed over a 5-10 frame. He survived because tacklers rarely got a good shot at him. In high school he learned to run weighing 160 pounds or less. He did it well but at his size he did not receive any scholarship offers, and made no plans to attend college.

He got to Maryland by one of the strangest routes Tatum had seen. His high school coach was taking courses at the Columbia University summer school when he ran into a Maryland alumnus. "Any prospects?" the alumnus asked. The coach said yes, this boy Hanulak. He was soon sent to see Tatum, who was not enthusiastic until he saw his high school game films. "I knew he would make us a fine scholar," said Tatum.

Hanulak scored his first college touchdown against Georgia and then forgot to give the ball to the officials. It was discovered sitting in his lap on the bench. He showed similar spunk his senior year during spring practice. He was playing baseball—he was Maryland's best hitter—but still demanded a chance to show he could play defense. "His spring football lasted only through five practice sessions," said Tatum. "The first tackle I saw him make proved he was better than a green hand. I sent him back to the baseball team knowing he could do it."

Hanulak did more than run. He intercepted two passes his senior year, caught a team-best 10 passes for 152 yards, returned a team-high six kickoffs for 131 yards, and brought back 10 punts for 163 yards. "He's a big little man," said his backfield coach, Tommy Mont.

Bud, Tommy, And Too Much Speed

In the nine years he had been at Maryland, Jim Tatum had talked a lot about his "feelings" prior to the start of a season. He usually figured right about a team–how many games it would win, who it would lose to, if it would go to a bowl–and by 1955, his prognostications were being taken seriously by Tatum watchers. So when he admitted during the summer that his next team could be his best yet, it created a stir. Better than 1951? Better than 1953?

"Better than any of them," Tatum said. "We have more talent and speed than any team I've coached. We could be very good." For Tatum, very good meant undefeated once again. At first glance, it seemed that he could not be serious. He had lost seven starters from his 1954 squad, including his entire first-string backfield. But Tatum had learned a lesson from his loss to Oklahoma in the 1954 Orange Bowl. Oklahoma had fielded two almost-equal platoons, while Maryland had experienced a dropoff from first string to second string. Tatum was determined to develop better balance in his 1954 team, and he did–so much so that many of his so-called second stringers were really the stars of the team, especially sophomore quarterback Frank Tamburello and linebacker-guard Bob Pellegrini. Most of those second stringers were back for 1955, experienced and ready to start.

Only one major problem had developed. Fullback Tom Selep, who Tatum said was his best-yet breakaway threat at the position since coming to Maryland, tore a knee cartilage in the first preseason drill and was out for the year. Tatum converted two light backs, Fred Hamilton and Phil Perlo, into fullbacks.

"I never thought that we had better personnel than the 1953 team," said Pellegrini, who was moved to center to fill the one weakness on the offensive line. "But I thought we were more together as a team. We were always pulling for each other. As one of the captains, I served as a go-between from the players to Tatum. I knew the problems. There weren't many."

Tatum had a particular obsession about the season: he wanted to beat UCLA, his second opponent. He was never one to hide his desire for revenge. He had gotten it in 1953 against Mississippi and Alabama, and now he wanted UCLA. The Bruins ultimately had cost Maryland an Orange Bowl bid in 1954, when the Terrapins logged a 7-2-1 record after a 2-2-1 start, including a 12-7 loss to UCLA in game No. 2. A bad snap from center on a punt had set up one UCLA touchdown, and a 14-yard punt in the fourth period allowed the Bruins to score the winning touchdown.

Never had a Tatum team gotten off to such a rocky beginning as did the 1954 squad. The key to getting things settled was Tamburello, a cocky, self-assured sophomore from Baltimore who played himself into an equal stature with Charley Boxold by the sixth game of the season, the point where Maryland began a five-game winning streak that just missed getting it the bowl bid instead of Duke.

Maryland outscored its opponents 200-33 in that stretch, ending with a 74-13 Thanksgiving Day rout of Missouri on national television that left Tatum in tears for the embarrassment it had caused his former coach, Faurot. The Terrapins ran up 601 total yards, including 492 on the ground, and wound up climbing to eighth in the national rankings, after at one point falling from No. 3 to the also-ran class.

Many of the offensive stars of that game had left. Fullback Dick Bielski, a first-round draft choice in the pros, had powered for 406 yards in only 79 carries. Halfback Ron Waller, finally receiving a chance to start after a career of raves about his potential, galloped to 601 yards on 66 attempts, a blistering nine-yards-a-carry pace. He also returned 13 punts an average of 15 yards, including one 68 yarder for a touchdown, and carried back four kickoffs for 121 yards. He had an 80-yard touchdown run against Missouri and a 61 yarder against Clemson. Ten players in all were drafted by the pros.

But Tatum came back in 1955 with a halfback named Ed Vereb, who had carried the ball only 17 times in 1954. By the time he and Tamburello had finished, Maryland's offense had regained most of its scoring touch.

It took a while, however, for the Terrapins to get untracked. They struck for two quick touchdowns against Missouri, a 14-yard dash by Vereb and a 23-yard pass from Tamburello to Bill Walker. But Missouri came back and scored twice in the second half, only to miss both extra points and lose 13-12. Pellegrini, who had hurt his knee the week before in a scrimmage, played 29 minutes, intercepted a pass, and made several sensational tackles. "I was mad as hell," he said. "I thought they'd operate and take away my season."

Tatum now could concentrate completely on UCLA. But he had been doing that since the spring. "We spent 20 days in the spring defending against the single wing," said Vereb. "We really overlooked Missouri. We had UCLA so well-scouted that the coaches had discovered mannerisms of each of their players that helped give plays away. Each of us were assigned a man to watch so we would know what was happening."

The game had long been a Byrd Stadium sellout, a rarity although Maryland had been winning for so long. It got so lively on campus that Tatum decided to move his team into a motel the night before the game, the first time he had done so in his career. "Everyone wanted tickets or was trying to encourage us and it was just making us uptight," said Vereb. "We had to get some sleep."

It rained the day of the game, and the Maryland players thought it was a bad omen. But it turned out that the muddy field slowed down the UCLA single wing and allowed Maryland's strength to dominate the game.

The Bruins, the nation's No. 1 ranked team, unbeaten in 12 games and the top offensive machine from 1954, suffered their first shutout in 40 games and could gain only 79 total yards in the 7-0 defeat. It was to be their only loss of the season. The single wing ground attack was held to minus 21 yards against the play of Pellegrini, 240-pound Mike Sandusky, 215-pound Al Wharton, 215-pound Ed Heuring, 195-pound

Jack Davis, 210-pound Russ Dennis, 240-pound Don Healy, and 230-pound Ed Cooke.

Maryland managed only one touchdown, a 17-yard run by Vereb around right end on a fourth-and-one play following the second-half kickoff. Tamburello checked off the original call at the line of scrimmage. He went with an option, pitching to Vereb, who followed Hamilton's crunching block into a clear path to the end zone.

UCLA threatened once, early in the second quarter. Starting from its own 47, tailback Ronnie Knox completed four passes to move the ball to the Maryland ten.

On first down, Doug Peters almost scored but was stopped a foot short. On second down, UCLA lined up differently, which Pellegrini noticed immediately. Don Shinnick, the right

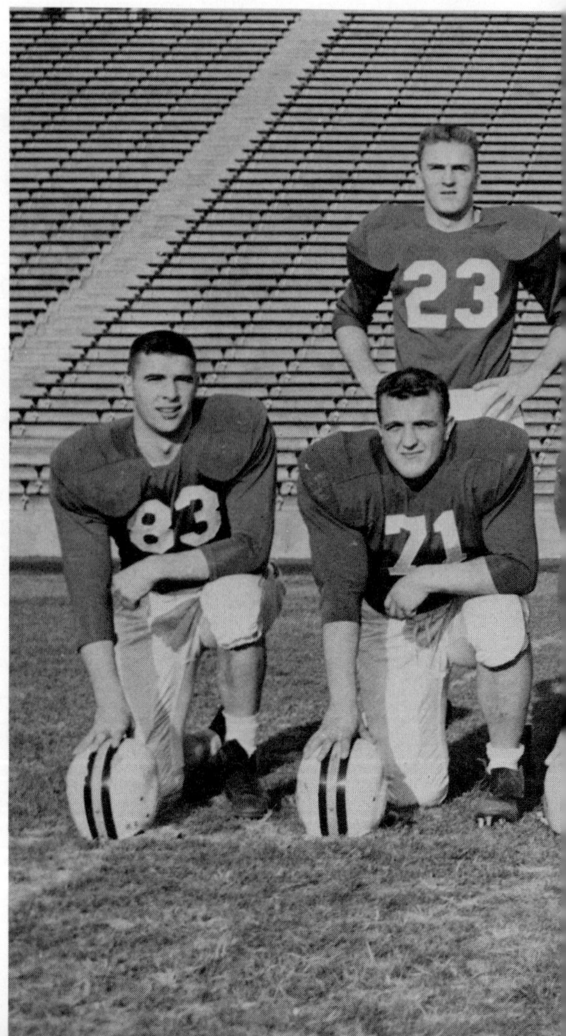

Maryland's starting team on the once-defeated 1955 squad: (line, left to right) Russ Dennis, Mike Sandusky, Jack Davis, Bob Pellegrini, Gene Dyson, Al Wharton, Bill Walker; (backfield) Fred Hamilton, Frank Tamburello, John Merricks, Ed Vereb. Jack Healy played instead of Merricks for most of the season.

guard, had split out from the center. "I wasn't supposed to blitz but when I saw that gap, I took off," said Pellegrini. He went through the hole left by Shinnick's shift, hit Peters and jarred the ball loose. Gene Dyson recovered it. "They said I did," admitted Pellegrini. "They thought it would help me make All-American."

Knox, who played the second half with a slightly separated shoulder, resorted to passes most of the game. But his day was summed up better by one sequence of plays. UCLA had the ball on the Maryland 39 when the Terrapins were penalized five yards for delay. Knox lost 12 yards on a bad snap, then Davis threw him for an 18-yard loss. Davis again charged in and, with help from Wharton, tackled Knox for another 22-yard loss. UCLA wound up with a fourth down-and-57 situation.

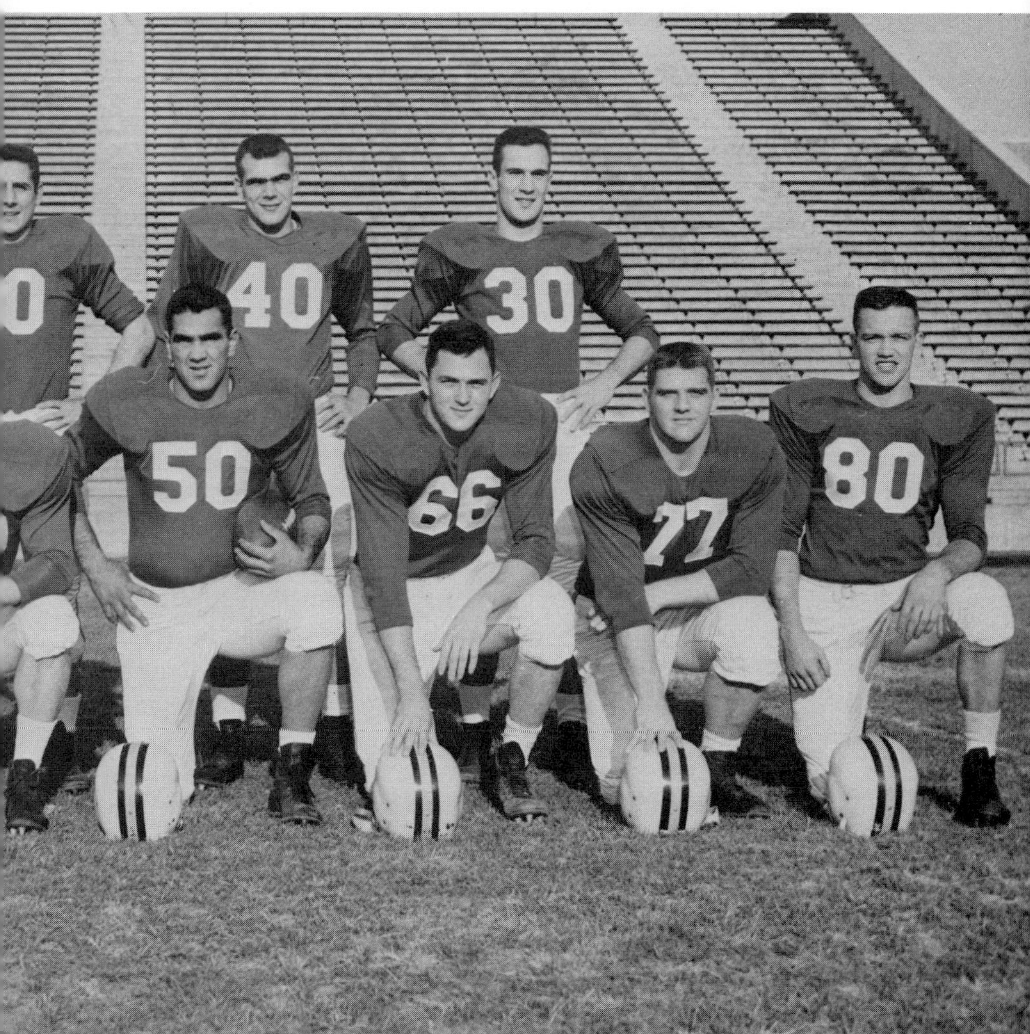

"This is the greatest Maryland team of the era," said UCLA coach Red Sanders, agreeing with Tatum. "I've said right along," said Tatum, "that we've got a powerful line and that Pellegrini is an All-American. It showed out there."

Maryland found itself ranked No. 1 again. It would play hide-and-seek with that spot for the rest of the season.

The rest of the way the Terrapins were aiming for revenge game No. 2—against all-conquering Oklahoma. Maryland wanted another Orange Bowl shot at the Sooners. It would get it.

First, however, was the matter of winning its remaining games and giving Tatum his third unbeaten regular season in five years. Maryland downed Baylor 20-6 as Tamburello turned passer and connected for touchdowns with Dennis and Jack Healy. Halfback Dave Nusz hit Howie Dare for a third score. Baylor was limited to 71 yards rushing and had five passes intercepted. The Terrapins scored three of the first five times they had the ball to coast to a 28-7 victory over Wake Forest. Maryland had four touchdowns from the one yard line and outgained Wake on the ground 237 to 9.

North Carolina fell next 25-7. Maryland went on long marches for its touchdowns, with Vereb scoring three times and passing to Dare for another. North Carolina could gain only 18 rushing yards against the Maryland defense, which was ranked first in the nation, although the team had slipped to No. 2 in the polls behind Michigan. Syracuse was victim No. 6, 34-13. Orangemen fullback Jim Brown picked up 74 of his team's 115 rushing yards. But Vereb gained 132 yards, scored once and passed for another and substitute fullback Perlo tallied twice. It was Maryland's 11th straight win, second only to its 1951-52 streak.

Vereb, the future dentist from Pittsburgh who weighed 185 pounds and ran with both power and speed, broke the ACC scoring record by registering three touchdowns against South Carolina to give him 66 points for the season. He gained 113 yards and set up another score with an interception. Maryland won 27-0 as Carolina gained only 71 yards rushing compared to the Terrapins' 249.

LSU was more of a problem the next week. Maryland was a 19-point favorite but led only 7-0 at the half on a 32-yard pass from Tamburello to Healy. The Terrapins got their other touchdown in the 13-0 win in the third period on a 53-yard drive ended by Vereb's four-yard scoring run. Four interceptions by Maryland, including one in the end zone by Perlo, kept Paul Dietzel's Tigers from scoring, but the close victory knocked Maryland from the No. 1 spot again.

A bid to the Orange Bowl followed a 25-12 triumph over Clemson. It did not come until the Tigers had delighted a home crowd by jumping ahead 12-0. They took the opening kickoff and moved 84 yards to score and then Joel Wells went 50 yards in the second period for another touchdown. Quarterback Lynn Beightol, subbing for a sick Tamburello, brought Maryland back. He drove the Terrapins 35 yards for a Vereb touchdown before the half, then passed 18 yards to Vereb for a go-ahead score in the third quarter. Tamburello added an eight-yard scoring run and Beightol tossed 16 yards to Walker to give Maryland the win. Maryland limited Clemson to 22 total yards in the second half.

Maryland ended the season with a 19-0 victory over George Washington to finish with 15 straight wins and a share of the ACC title (with Duke) going into the Orange Bowl date with Oklahoma, now the nation's No. 1 team. Vereb scored twice, missing Shemonski's school point record of 97 by one. Beightol passed 41 yards to Dennis for another touchdown, the longest of the season for Tatum's usually more explosive split T.

That lack of long-range scoring punch was one reason why Oklahoma was favored by at least a touchdown in the Orange Bowl. The Sooners, already proclaimed national champions, had won 29 straight entering the contest, and their ninth straight Big Seven conference title. Coach Bud Wilkinson, who had yet to lose a league game in 53 tries, had fashioned a record of 83-8-3 since 1947, just a shade better than Tatum's 73-14-4 mark at Maryland.

Oklahoma was considered a superior team, much as Tennessee was rated so highly in 1953. But the Sooners had better speed than the Volunteers and marvelous depth that allowed Wilkinson to play his first stringers for only half of most periods. In Tommy McDonald, he had an All-American halfback with more quickness than any Maryland back. The Sooners averaged 294 yards a game and five yards a play, running off 20 more plays a game than Maryland.

To halt the nation's No. 1 rushing attack, Tatum relied heavily on his No. 1 ranked defense, which allowed only 76 yards rushing a game. Players like Sandusky, Pellegrini, Wharton, Heuring, Davis, and Dennis—he hoped—were too strong for the Sooners. His own offense, which averaged 21 points a game to Oklahoma's 36, was not nearly as quick. But Vereb had gained 642 yards (five yards a carry)—119 less than the rushing total of Maryland's opponents—and led the nation in scoring. Tamburello had passed for 497 yards. He had another five backs—Dare, Hamilton, Perlo, Healy, and Nusz—who had gained at least 178 yards.

Missouri's Faurot saw the game this way: "Maryland is real strong in the line because of its tackles (Sandusky, Heuring, Wharton) but Oklahoma's two first teams plus overall speed and deceptiveness could make a difference. Because of its depth,

Ed Vereb breaks into the open on a 66-yard run against Oklahoma in the 1956 Orange Bowl. Vereb later scored Maryland's only touchdown.

Oklahoma would have an advantage on a hot day." His players, who had played both teams, agreed. Their consensus: Oklahoma had better overall speed and hit harder and more quickly.

For the first time in Maryland's last three bowl appearances, the predictions held up. Oklahoma did have too much speed and quickness, dazzling the Terrapins with both to win 20-6.

Pellegrini, who still hero-worships Tatum, blames his coach for the loss. "We left our game on the practice field," said Pellegrini. "For some reason, he decided to work the heck out of us prior to the game. Oklahoma was on the beach relaxing and we were burning ourselves out." Faurot also proved right about the weather. It had been cool during workouts but the day of the game was hot and humid. Maryland wilted.

It took a while. For a half, the Terrapins held a slight upper hand. Vereb broke loose for a 66-yard run that ended at the 10 when Oklahoma's Jay O'Neal was able to catch him from behind. Tamburello fumbled the ball away before the Terrapins could score. Maryland moved from the Oklahoma 45 just before the half to the 15, from where Vereb started to his right, could not pass, reversed his field, and scored behind blocks from Pellegrini and Walker.

Jerry Tubbs blocked the extra point, but Maryland still took a 6-0 lead into the locker room. Oklahoma had gained only 77 yards rushing to Maryland's 131 in the opening 30 minutes and had had only one scoring threat.

The second half was a different story. Wilkinson discarded his fancy pitchouts and most of his wide plays for quick-hitting, speedy football. Oklahoma began running off a play about every 12 seconds. "I was calling defensive signals from my knees," said Pellegrini. "They weren't even huddling half the time. I've never seen a team move so fast. They'd run the play, get up, call a play, get up, call a play. It was hard to stop."

McDonald, who was limited by Maryland's defense to 11 yards in seven attempts, got his team untracked by returning a punt 32 yards to the Maryland 46 early in the third period. Tatum later said it was the play that turned the game around. From there, Oklahoma went right after Maryland's tackle strength. Quarterback Jimmy Harris sent Bo Burris and Billy Pricer into the line and then McDonald outside to get the ball to the seven. Two plays later, McDonald scored from the four, Oklahoma added the extra point and never trailed again.

The Sooners marched 51 yards on its next possession to score again, then got another touchdown when Carl Dodd returned an intercepted pass 82 yards.

Maryland never penetrated Oklahoma's 30 in the second half and gained only 58 yards on the ground after intermission. The Sooners ran off 17 more plays. Vereb, who gained 108 yards, was the rushing star but everything else belonged to Oklahoma.

"Speed, speed, and more speed...Oklahoma had it and Oklahoma used it from the starting whistle to the final gun," wrote one paper. "That was the story of the 1956 Orange Bowl. Oklahoma didn't save its speed for the actual plays. The Sooners raced back to the huddle and then up to the scrimmage line as though their lives depended upon it. And largely as a result of that hustle, they got off 64 rushing plays to 47 for Maryland." Oklahoma went on to win a record 47 straight games.

Tatum admitted the worst. "We were outplayed in every area," he said sadly. "They were in better physical shape. They handled themselves better. They outhustled us. They had too much speed. I have never seen a team with better equipment."

It was a sad way for him to end his Maryland reign.

Saved From The Coal Mines

The ultimate goal for most college players is to make All-American. It was Bob Pellegrini's. He would have rather played football than do anything else, he remembers, even after that day when Jim Tatum told him he would be a center, not a guard, his senior year at Maryland.

The position change was a shock. Pellegrini realized that he was already proficient at the guard position, and that he had a very good chance at making All-American by playing there. But center? "We did an injustice to him by making him a center," said Bob Ward, by now Tatum's line coach. "He really wasn't that good a center. If he had stayed at guard he would have been maybe the best they had ever seen at the spot."

Even Pellegrini admits his sophomore and junior years were better than his final season. "I hadn't even snapped a ball, and I was on the cover of *Sports Illustrated,*" he said. "It was all kind of unusual." Which is what one writer pointed out. "The silliest preseason poll selection looked like Maryland's Bob Pellegrini. Bob was picked as the nation's No. 1 center and he had never played that position in his life."

Fortunately for Pellegrini, he still could play defense. And that meant he could still be a linebacker, a position made to order for his football instincts. And when he made every All-American team at the end of 1955—and was chosen as the lineman of the year by most news agencies—writers talked about his defensive prowess, gracefully overlooking his deficiences at center.

"Bob bulwarks what may well be the best line in college football," wrote *Sports Illustrated.* "Even before coach Jim Tatum switched him from guard to center this year, he had acquired a national reputation as a linebacker. Packing 225 pounds on a 6-3 inch frame (he) is a clever diagnostician of enemy plays and a superb defensive quarterback. He has taken to the offensive phase of the center position as a duck takes to water."

Ward said that Pellegrini was "bigger, stronger, and faster than I was. He was the best tackler on the team and he did things easier than I did. He was so natural. Wherever the ball went, he made the tackle."

Pellegrini lived in Yatesboro, Pennsylvania. He was a quarterback in a split T offense in high school. "I kept the ball most of the time and ran with it," he said. "I didn't get any media exposure and I was really surprised when Villanova talked to me about going to school. I had never thought about college until then. Our high school really didn't prepare you for school." Maryland and Pittsburgh also recruited Pellegrini, whose father, a native of Italy, worked in the local coal mine. Vereb was among the recruits visiting Maryland on the same weekend.

"Tatum would make you feel like you were the only guy in the whole world he wanted," said Pellegrini. "He told me, 'damn, I want you.' I was ready to sign right there. I was afraid to go away from home. I didn't have the clothes, I had never been away before. But he convinced me.

"I was at quarterback but they put me at fullback after spring practice and then to guard and linebacker. I stayed at guard from then on until they made a center out of me. I never wanted to go back to the backfield. I loved the hitting too much."

Tatum originally moved Pellegrini to the line, he said, because he had so much depth at quarterback and needed Pellegrini more at guard. "It was after he got to guard that we realized how football wise he was on defense," Tatum said. "It didn't matter to him. He's the type who just loves to play the game."

Pellegrini did not begin his junior year as a starter, but UCLA's Sanders called him the best guard the Bruins faced in

Bob Pellegrini watches from the sidelines during the 1955 season with the man who brought him to Maryland and helped to make him into an All-American, Jim Tatum.

1954 "and even better in 1955."

Starting from the fumble-causing tackle against UCLA at the goal line that gained him a year full of publicity, he made the spectacular play during that senior season. He intercepted a pass against Missouri and knocked down three against Wake

Forest just as they were leaving the quarterback's hand. He did the same against North Carolina. He had the knack of being in the right spot to recover fumbles or intercept passes or make key tackles. "You don't teach what Pellegrini did," said Ward. "You just thank goodness he did it."

Pellegrini credits football with getting him away from the coal mines. He is glad. "I was afraid of dark places anyway."

Pellegrini became the first lineman to win player of the year honors in the ACC. Along with teammates Vereb, Tamburello, Sandusky, and Davis, he was on the All-ACC team. "It is pretty well known out in College Park that Pellegrini took it upon himself to see that the Maryland players were in the proper frame of mind, game after game, as the pressure mounted during the unbeaten season," wrote one newspaper. "He called players together for little heart to heart talks, and the squad responded to his urgings in every instance." Both Pellegrini and Vereb were first-round draft choices, the fifth and sixth Terrapins chosen in the first round since 1951.

His first notoriety had come in a regular-season game against Miami in the Orange Bowl his junior year. He had been credited with 12 individual and five assisted tackles, a stadium record. Later there was the most valuable player award in the College All-Star game and a pro career. But Pellegrini looks upon those All-American honors with special relish.

"To make all those teams and to think people thought so much of your ability did something to you," he said. "Those were wonderful days."

"I Don't Want To Leave"

Jim Tatum, fighting back tears, sat inside the car and shook his head. "Joe, I don't want to leave," he told Joe Blair. "I love it here. It's been very kind to me. But I have to." And with that, Tatum drove off to announce his decision to leave the University of Maryland for his alma mater, North Carolina.

Tatum never admitted publicly that anything but the desire to return to his alma mater—"It's like a br'er rabbit returning to the briar patch"—motivated his decision. But others saw it differently. Tatum once said that he was tired of being an athletic director of 14 sports and wanted to concentrate just on football. His friends say that was a part of the reason. The rest was simple: he and the university administration could no longer exist together.

Dr. Wilson Elkins, who had succeeded Byrd in 1954, was determined to bring the football program in line with the rest of the school's academic philosophy. In the last five years, Maryland twice had come under fire for its conduct of athletics. The first, in 1951, was contained in a statement issued by New York Judge Saul Streit before he announced his verdict in a basketball fixing case. He included Maryland among those schools who had overemphasized and commercialized football and made it into a high-powered business. He criticized Maryland's recruiting methods, saying that of the 97 members of the Terrapin team, 60 were from out of the state. He singled out the high-pressure recruiting of quarterback Lynn Beightol as an example of what he was talking about.

Tatum and Byrd reacted bitterly to the accusations. Maryland Gov. Theodore McKeldin ordered the board of regents to investigate and see if the athletic program "is based on deceit, whether it evades the rules of intercollegiate sports and whether it could bring dishonor to the university." The regents reported that although 84 players were on aid, only three of the first 33 were below average standing in class and that they could not find any unethical conduct in the program.

Then in 1954 a report of an evaluation committee of the Middle States Association of Colleges and Secondary Schools became public. Some of its findings were disturbing. It said that Maryland had violated recruiting rules of the NCAA and the ACC. It said that football was overemphasized, that football players received softer part-time jobs and that athletic scholarships were out of proportion with the rest of the school's grants. It criticized the school for its flexible academic entrance requirements and lack of rules limiting the number of times students could repeat courses.

It said that athletes totalled eight percent of the student body but received 78 percent of the total scholarship money. Football players received 54 percent of the grant funds. And while only 33 percent of the student body was from out of state, 73 percent of the football team was from out of state. It recommended 19 corrections, including an end to a combination athletic director and football coach, reduction of athletic scholarship money, an end to bidding for athletes, and setting of criteria for normal progress toward a degree.

Elkins, a former star football player at the University of Texas, also had carefully read the rest of the 163 page report, 19 of which dealt with football. The rest amounted to a criticism of Byrd's one-man rule of the school, which the report thought had created a lack of academic excellence. Elkins was under pressure to correct the entire situation, including football.

"I think a school can have a strong athletic program and a strong academic program," he said. "We are opening up next

Lynn Beightol, besides taking passing lessons from Jim Tatum, was so highly recruited that a judge in New York cited the case as one of the abuses of college football.

year additional scholarships for non-athletes in the amount of $10,000 (10 scholarships). These are state scholarships that formerly went to athletes.

"I hope they (athletic scholarships) can stay the same. Sports will have to depend more on its own funds and on outside help." What Elkins was after was to bring the school's scholarship program into better balance. He already had instituted a rule that out-of-state students of any kind had to have a C average to qualify.

Tatum rebuked almost every part of the report. His solution to the out-of-balance scholarship system? "Add more money for non-athletic scholarships." Soft jobs? "Does anyone in their right mind expect an athlete to hold down a 20-to-30 hour-a-week job after all he puts in on studies and practice?" The report had cited a player who in his fifth year, still was a sophomore in standing. Tatum said in his first eight years, an average of 28 scholarships had been awarded. Of the 224 total, 90 percent of the 100 whose eligibility had expired graduated. Seventy-seven were still in school, 38 had dropped out for various reasons, and nine were no longer playing football.

Although Elkins had not criticized Tatum, it was still clear that he was going to correct the apparent deficiencies despite the effect it might have on the athletic program. Tatum no longer enjoyed a free reign as he had under Byrd. By 1955 he could see that maintaining the type of program he wanted was impossible. When the North Carolina position came open again—he had almost taken it in 1954 and had thought about it earlier—he welcomed it, despite an offer of lifetime tenure from Maryland. His reported salary of $15,000 was $3,200 less than he received in salary and expenses at Maryland.

Tatum recommended that Tommy Mont get his job at College Park. Elkins agreed and Mont was hired at a reported $12,000 a year rate. "He's the most qualified man for the job," said Tatum. "I'll probably pass more, open things up a bit," said Mont, who was inheriting the bulk of the talent from the 1955 squad.

The departure of Tatum marked an end of an era at College Park. One writer said that when Tatum took over "Maryland didn't have a phone in its athletic office and was playing Delaware, Richmond, and Duquesne. The stadium was inadequate, the state had scholastic football in only two counties, and the football team had staggered through three losing seasons in the last four.

"His name was synonymous with Maryland's rise to three perfect seasons, five bowl games, the 1953 national title, a number of All-Americans and pro stars, and a new stadium."

Tatum had compiled a 73-15-4 record in nine years. His teams had gone to five bowl games. Maryland had more players drafted in 1951, 1953, and 1954 than any other school in the nation. He left with Maryland among the football elite. It would be another 18 years before the school breathed such rarified air again.

"Only One Place To Go...Down"

"I knew there would be some changes but I thought I could do the job," said Tommy Mont. "I was a graduate of Maryland and I liked the area. I took the job with the idea if things didn't work out and if Maryland improved its academic standing, things would be worked back up again. I never saw it happen."

Mont lasted three years at Maryland, probably doing as well as anyone who had to follow Tatum. The pressure was intense, the comparisons endless. Mont never seemed to mind, at least in public. He never rapped his team, never made excuses. Throughout what were excruciating months, he stood up well. Others could only shake their heads over the misfortunes that came his way.

In his three years, he compiled records of 2-7-1, 5-5, and 4-6. He was slowed by an incredible amount of injuries his first two years. The third year was a matter of coming very close to a number of wins but always falling short. His three-year contract was not renewed.

Football scholarships were cut, from the 25-to-30 totals under Tatum, to 18 for Mont. With attrition, he barely could keep more than 12 to 15 around each year, and by 1958 the Maryland football roster had shrunk from 93 in Tatum's last year to 51. He was asked to recruit more from Maryland high schools, even though the caliber of football was not good.

"I had talked it over with Tatum very carefully before I said I wanted the job," said Mont. "He wanted me to go to

North Carolina but I thought we had enough material to have a good year in 1956, and then I would be free to move on my own terms."

Mont had come to Maryland from Cumberland, Maryland, as a hotshot back prospect. He was going to attend VPI but Byrd and Al Woods changed his mind. "Mr. Woods said they were trying to get the program revamped and they had signed some good players from Baltimore. I felt I should go to my state university."

He was a tailback his sophomore year, then a quarterback under Shaughnessy in 1942 before going into the service where he played on and coached teams in Europe. When he returned in August of 1946, he was not sure what he wanted to do. He had been drafted by New York and his rights had been traded to the Redskins. "I finally decided to go back and get my degree," he remembered. "It seemed like we would have a good team."

Instead, he was caught up in the problems of Shaughnessy's second term at Maryland. He alternated with Vic Turyn, became the school's all-time passer, and graduated with letters in three sports–football, basketball, and lacrosse. He played behind Sammy Baugh at Washington and saw time as a defensive halfback before joining the Maryland staff in 1951.

He had always been a winner, and that was what made his coaching years at Maryland so hard to take. In 1956 he had 23 lettermen returning from Tatum's last team, including tackle Mike Sandusky, who was being groomed as another Maryland All-American. By the end of the season, he had started 10 different backfield combinations and 13 of his first 22 players had missed at least a game.

Maryland had been picked among the top five in the nation and Mont could not dispute it. Then he lost quarterback Frank Tamburello through the draft to the Armed Forces. He was Mont's only experienced quarterback but to make his loss harder to take, his replacement, Dickie Lewis, sprained an ankle the week before the opener and was ineffective all season. Mont finally wound up using a third stringer, John Fritsch, and a converted halfback, Bob Rusevlyan, at quarterback for most of the season, along with Frank Petrella.

"Injuries, flunkouts, the draft, and illness killed us," said

Mont. It started with Syracuse and Jimmy Brown in the opener at Byrd Stadium. The Orangemen won 26-12 as Brown scored twice and ran up 154 yards on 18 carries. The loss broke Maryland's 15-game regular-season winning streak and was only its second at Byrd Stadium since it opened in 1950. Baylor shut out the Terrapins the next week, the first time that had happened in 70 games dating back to 1948. Tatum got his first victory at North Carolina by beating Maryland 34-6, the loser's worst defeat since 1948. The victories came over North Carolina State and Wake Forest. Mont had hoped to alternate three units in the spring. He felt fortunate to find 11 healthy players by the end of the year. Sandusky made all-conference along with guard Gene Alderton but no one was an All-American this season.

Things looked somewhat brighter in 1957. The Terrapins played well in losing to Bear Bryant's No. 2-ranked Texas A&M team 21-13. A 27-0 triumph over Wake Forest broke a three-game winless streak, and then Tatum brought his North Carolina team to College Park. It was a big game, and it got ever bigger when it was chosen as the contest that Queen Elizabeth II of England would attend on a trip to the United States.

Queen Elizabeth of England (second from left, next to Maryland president Wilson Elkins) stands for National Anthem prior to 1957 North Carolina-Maryland game. Prince Philip is at the far right; Maryland Gov. Theodore McKeldin is in the middle.

Prince Philip of England accepts football from Maryland co-captains Gene Alderton and Jack Healy. Prince Philip and his wife, Queen Elizabeth, watched 1957 game between Maryland and North Carolina.

More than 43,000 packed Byrd Stadium for the game. There were 480 accredited members of the press on hand and more than 300 members of a special security force. And the two teams provided a dandy for the Queen and her husband, Prince Philip, to watch from their seats on the 44 yard line.

It was Tommy Mont's proudest moment as Maryland coach. "Listen," he said afterwards. "I'm going to revel in this the rest of my life." His team had upset the favored Tar Heels 21-7. Carolina had taken a 7-0 lead into the third quarter, then Maryland marched 62 yards to tie it with Rusevlyan scoring from the one. In the fourth period, second-string halfback Ted Kerschner sprinted 81 yards for the go-ahead touchdown, and Maryland drove 67 yards for the insurance score. Sophomore fullback Jim Joyce went the final 13 yards.

The delirious players carried Mont on their shoulders to meet the Queen and she seemed to delight in the break with protocol. "It was the first time in two years I didn't have to think about who I would start," Mont said later. "We were in perfect condition."

On the other side of the field, Tatum walked slowly to the locker room, hands in pockets, shoulders hunched. He was a lonely figure. In less than two years, he would die at age 45 of a massive infection called rickettsia disease, which he probably picked up from a tick bite. He would not win a national championship at Carolina.

Maryland finished strongly, winning five of its last seven and three of its last four. The surge enlivened predictions for

Tommy Mont, in his happiest moment as coach at Maryland, is about to be lifted to his players' shoulders after beating Jim Tatum's North Carolina team in 1957 before the Queen of England.

1958. Standout linebacker and guard Rod Breedlove, who had made All-ACC as a sophomore, along with senior Ed Cooke, was back with seven other starters. Yet the Terrapins struggled to a 4-6 record. They came close to stopping defending national champion Auburn's winning streak before losing 20-7. But Tatum's North Carolina team shut them out 27-0, and going into a meeting with Navy in Baltimore, they were only 2-5.

"I had a feeling that my job depended on how I did against Navy," said Mont. "I got the boys up too much for the game. We played well in the first period, then fell apart." Maryland took a 7-0 first-quarter lead but Navy came back to score 12 points in the second period and went on to a 40-14 victory behind Joe Bellino. Maryland lost one fumble and threw four interceptions. Even season-ending victories over Miami of Florida (26-14) and Virginia (44-6) could not save Mont.

"I always thought the people who were making the big decisions were backing me 100 percent," he said. "I was never once called on the carpet or called down for what I was doing. But it didn't surprise me. There was only one place for Maryland to go and that was down."

He was released after the season ended and Tom Nugent was hired away from Florida State.

The Transition Years

Joe Blair had done wonders publicizing Maryland players before, but this time he outdid himself. He turned over six pages of his 1961 press brochure to promoting Gary Collins for All-American. It had been six years since Blair had anyone of Collins' caliber to crow about—six years since Jim Tatum had left, ending Maryland's string of national rankings and All-American players.

But there was more to 1961 than Gary Collins. It appeared that Tom Nugent, after two years of building—including a 6-4 season in 1960, Maryland's first winning record since 1955—was ready to bring the Terrapins back to national prominence. "I've finally got the horses," Nugent proclaimed. He had a big, strong line; he had Collins; he had a potential fine quarterback in Dick Shiner, and a fine defensive back in Tom Brown. His team had won five of its last six games in 1960, and he had 26 lettermen returning.

Nugent was called the Magician when he came to Maryland. He had taken programs at Virginia Military (1949-52) and at Florida State (1953-58) and made them into winners. He was 34-27-1 at State and 19-17-2 at VMI while gaining a reputation for gimmicks. "Sometimes when you talk to Tom Nugent, you feel as though Mike Todd is still with us," said one writer.

He was given credit for giving football the I formation and the typewriter huddle and the double quarterback and introducing the victory huddle while at Maryland. He always tried to have a different angle for every game. Many at Maryland ultimately got tired of his tricks, which were accepted when he was winning but wore thin when he lost.

Nugent believed in wide-open football. His teams passed a lot but sometimes forgot to play defense at the same time. He had an ability to arouse his players for the bigger contests, only to see them suffer let-downs in the less-important ones. Never was that more evident than in 1961.

Collins was to be a key to the success. He was a big, rangy (6-3, 205 pounds) athlete from Williamstown, Pennsylvania, who did everything well on a football field. He caught the ball in all types of conditions, blocked and tackled effectively, punted and, Nugent said, "he wins games."

"We call Collins our crowded end," Nugent said. "He has the outstanding faculties and instinct to go up for a pass with a

Tom Nugent was called the Magician when he came to Maryland in 1959. His magic wore off by 1965, when he was fired.

crowd around him and come down with the ball. He likes a crowd. He's the best end I've ever coached. He's in a class by himself."

Said one pro scout: "He has the uncanny ability to place himself in the right position when in a group of pass defenders and going up and coming down with the football. He without question is a big play man in a crucial situation, which is often the difference between winning and losing."

Collins had some spectacular games going into his senior year. He blocked three punts in 1960 and partially blocked a field goal and intercepted a pass in the end zone against Wake Forest. He caught two touchdown passes to beat Clemson as a sophomore, then played only a few minutes as a junior, just long enough to set up his winning touchdown reception.

By the time he was a senior, Collins already held career marks for passes caught and touchdown receptions and had been selected to the All-ACC team as a junior. Said Clemson coach Frank Howard: "I don't believe there are any finer ends playing in college today."

The players were glad to get the season underway. Nugent, as always, had been unpredictable. He told them one time he was taking them to a secret workout and loaded them on buses. The final destination wound up being a swimming party. Then he turned around a few days later and ran them through a 90-minute workout on what had been expected to be a light day.

The season started well. Maryland downed Southern Methodist 14-6 while wearing gold jerseys with black numerals, the first time Maryland had worn those colors since the arrival of Clark Shaughnessy. The Terrapins followed with a 24-21 victory over Clemson on a 23-yard field goal by John Hannigan with eight seconds left. They made it three straight by upsetting seventh-ranked Syracuse 22-21, as Collins caught a two-point conversion pass from Dick Novak late in the fourth quarter to win it.

Collins, who was runnerup for national lineman of the

Gary Collins left Maryland with all the school's receiving records. He made All-American in 1961, the first Terrapin so honored since Jim Tatum left in 1955.

week honors against Clemson, caught a touchdown pass prior to the conversion but it was nothing like the two-point play on which he was well covered but refused to drop the ball when hit. Ernie Davis gained 111 yards and scored two touchdowns for Syracuse. A 64-yard run by sophomore Ernie Arizzi set up Maryland's winning score.

Dreams of an unbeaten season ended against North Carolina 14-8. Maryland had climbed into the top 10 for the first time since 1956 but fumbled twice deep in its own territory and Carolina converted both mistakes into touchdowns. Ironically, the Tar Heels got both touchdowns when Gib Carson fumbled going into the end zone, only to have a teammate fall on the ball for the score.

The Terrapins rebounded to beat Air Force 21-0 as Brown intercepted three passes and caught a touchdown pass from Shiner, who had a fine day, completing 11 of 21 passes against what had been the nation's best pass defense. Four-time loser South Carolina, which had not scored in its last two games, then upset Maryland 20-10 with Gator Bowl scouts looking on.

Just when it seemed the season was lost, the Terrapins continued their yo-yo act by upsetting Penn State 21-17 in what remains the only time Maryland has beaten the Nittany Lions. Shiner, who had beaten out Novak, was the star of the day. Getting his first start, Shiner threw three first-half touchdown passes to give the Terrapins a 21-6 lead at intermission. Penn State had hardly been a factor in the first two quarters. Maryland scored the first time it had the ball, then again on a nine-yard pass to Brown, and again on an eight-yarder to Collins. But Shiner hurt his ankle and was in for only one series after the break.

He had to stand on the sidelines as Penn State rallied. First the Nittany Lions drove 65 yards to make it 21-12. Then they kicked a 28-yard field goal to pull to 21-15. Then they moved to the Maryland four with a first down. Four times they tried to score and four times the Terrapins held. With less than a minute left, Maryland gave Penn State a safety and held on to win. Shiner had completed 12 of 20 passes for 158 yards. Collins had caught six for 80 yards despite being sick before the game.

Maryland kept its bowl hopes alive by downing North Carolina State 10-7 on a pass from Shiner to Collins and a field

Dick Shiner liked to pass more than run. He remains Maryland's all-time passer and total yardage leader.

goal by Hannigan. Collins sacked State quarterback Roman Gabriel in the fourth period to blunt a final scoring try. Hannigan won another on a field goal, over Wake Forest 10-7. Brown returned a punt 83 yards on a fancy play that saw him field the kick and hand to Novak, who lateraled back to Brown. Using a block from Walter Rock, Brown scooted into the end zone. Maryland thwarted five different Deacon scoring threats.

That victory brought a bid from the Gator Bowl—on the condition, Nugent said, that Maryland beat Virginia in the regular season finale. Nugent, who welcomed the conditional aspect to fire up his team, said the Terrapins could have gone to some smaller bowl but wanted the Gator. But instead of winning, they lost to Virginia 28-16 and went nowhere. Collins was hurt early in the second half. The Maryland defense—which had played so well during the season behind Rock, Dave Crossan, and Roger Shoals, all future pros—could not handle the Cavaliers. The loss gave Maryland a 7-3 record.

The defeat did not keep Collins from making All-American and all-conference. He shared the latter honors with center Bob Hacker. Collins ended his career with 74 receptions for 1,182 yards, both school records. Brown had eight interceptions, an ACC record, giving him a school-record 11 so far in his career.

Maryland was not supposed to stumble again in 1962. Nugent called his team his best yet, and even went to three different units to take advantage of a horde of returning lettermen and the best from an undefeated freshman squad. With Shiner completing 30 of his first 50 passes to lead the nation in

A standout defensive back, Tom Brown became a top-notch receiver his senior year in 1962.

passing, Maryland got off to a flying 4-0 start before George Mira and the University of Miami stopped the streak with a 28-24 triumph. Brown returned the opening kickoff a school-record 98 yards and Shiner, playing despite a painful back, had his team ahead most of the way. But Mira completed 21 of 31 passes for 288 yards and three touchdowns to pull it out.

Shiner broke season and career records for completions in a 13-11 triumph over South Carolina, in which Brown became the season record holder for pass receptions, and Hannigan won his fourth game in two years with a field goal. But then the Terrapins ran into a snow storm at Penn State which took away Shiner's passing and ended in a 23-7 loss. Then they lost to Duke 10-7 and to Clemson 17-14 on a last-minute field goal, before finishing with a 40-18 defeat of Virginia in which Brown returned an interception 100 yards.

The promising campaign had become a so-so 6-4 one. Shiner had led the nation in passing until the final game and still ended with the career and season passing marks off his year of 121 completions on 203 attempts for 1,324 yards. Brown had 47 receptions to tie the ACC record held by Sonny Randle.

Rock (6-5, 225), who had teamed with Shoals (6-4, 240) and Crossan (6-2, 215) to give Maryland one of its strongest front lines, made all-conference as did Shiner and Brown, who added six interceptions to give him a record 17 for his career. Running back Len Chiaverini won the league rushing crown with 602 yards.

Nugent would last three more years. In 1963, with a young squad dominated by Shiner's third fine year—1,165 yards on 108 completions out of 228 attempts which allowed him to again set season and career marks in passing and total offense—Maryland was 3-7. In 1964, the record was 5-5 but Nugent had high hopes for 1965, since the Terrapins won their last three games the year before and he had 30 lettermen back even with the loss of Bo Hickey, who gained 894 yards, the best ever by a Maryland sophomore. However, Maryland lost three of its last four contests and ended with a 4-6 mark.

The dapper Nugent was fired. In his seven years at the school he had been described by a mixed bag of adjectives. His bubbling manner and optimistic enthusiasm had won over many, yet the gimmicks, his outspoken criticism of players, his running feuds with coaches like Frank Howard, his ill-fated position switching of some athletes, and his constant quips had alienated others.

Nugent attracted controversy, some of which he did not bring on himself. There was the accidental death of a player, Sonny Lohr. There was the use of Maryland's first black football player, Darryl Hill, who broke the ACC record for touchdown receptions in 1963. There was the shifting I formation. There was field goal kicker Bernardo Bramson, who changed his uniform number during games to correspond with his kicking points and wound up leaving Maryland as the kick record holder. There was Jerry Fishman, a 220-pound converted linebacker who led a fierce Maryland defense to a 27-22 triumph over Navy in 1964. Fishman was tagged with two deliberate foul penalties in the game and then made an obscene gesture toward the Midshipmen in the stands when he left the contest. He later apologized but the incident contributed to the breaking off of football relations between the schools.

To replace Nugent, Maryland shocked the football world by hiring Lou Saban away from Buffalo of the then American Football League. Saban had led the Bills to two straight league championships and three consecutive conference titles. Saban said he had come to the conclusion that "there is more to life than drawing circles and squares. In pro ranks, winning is everything. I'm sure that's not completely true on the college level. I enjoy life. This is what I want to do, for my sake and for my family's. We're going to enjoy campus life."

Saban had been a pro coach at Boston and Buffalo for six years and a college coach at Case Tech, Northwestern, and Western Illinois. He had learned the bulk of his football under Paul Brown when he played four years—making all-league at linebacker twice—for the Cleveland Browns. He previously had been an All-Big 10 choice at Indiana.

Maryland gave Saban a four-year contract, beginning at $22,500 a year and increasing to $25,000 at its end. The length of the pact was credited to Elkins, who said he figured "that (four years) is enough time for Lou to prove to us that Maryland is capable of playing winning football again. We wanted a man who was a winner and whom we could trust in making our team a winner."

Maryland hired Lou Saban away from a successful pro football coaching career and gave him a four-year contract. He stayed one year, then left after the 1966 season for another pro job.

Saban lasted a year, in which he produced a 4-6 record. The season produced some quality players, including a talented quarterback in junior Alan Pastrana, who set ACC and Maryland records by passing for 17 touchdowns and 1,499 yards; a solid end in Billy Van Heusen, who had seven scoring receptions; and a fine defensive end in Dick Absher. But he received a 10-year, $500,000 offer from the Denver Broncos and took it, much to the chagrin of the Maryland administration which considered the move a slap in the face.

In leaving, Saban told Maryland it should get out of the ACC and should increase the number of football players dramatically. "I thought they wanted to go big time," he said. "If I had known they were content with the ACC, I wouldn't have taken the job."

Another search for a coach was launched. For a while, it

appeared Jerry Claiborne of Virginia Tech would get the job but the parties could not agree on money and he withdrew his name. Finally the job was given to Bob Ward, who had sought it the year before when Saban was hired.

Ward signed a five-year, $100,000 contract after he demanded security. His hiring was greeted with almost unanimous acclaim. The school's first All-American football player was coming back to the job he always wanted. "My entire career has been directed toward the goal of becoming a head football coach," he said. "It has always been my hope to someday return to Maryland as head coach."

He had been an assistant under Tatum and then under Bud Wilkinson at Oklahoma, and had been hired away from an assistant's job at Army. He was still ruggedly handsome, energetic, demanding, tireless and had never lost that great desire to win that seemed to push him every minute as a player.

Unfortunately, Ward was to guide Maryland through the worst two year period in its football history. He had never experienced a losing season as a player and had lived through only one as an assistant coach. His first year at Maryland was all losing–nine straight defeats in which the Terrapins could score only 46 points and were shut out three times and held to a field goal in two other games. Pastrana had missed the season with a bad knee but that did not affect the defense, which gave up 231 points.

"I feel that when a boy steps on to that Maryland playing field," Ward said before the start of the 1968 season, "he wants to develop himself into the best player possible.... Therefore, I expect him to put forth the necessary effort and determination to become an excellent football player. We expect an all-out effort at all times...."

Maryland had lost 13 in a row entering the 1968 season. The string stretched to 16 after opening losses to Florida State, Syracuse, and a two-point heartbreaker to Duke. It was the longest such streak in the nation but it came to an end the next week against North Carolina.

"Four seconds were left in the game," reported the *Washington Post,* "and Maryland coach Bob Ward was smiling–a wide, toothy thing that seemed to stretch from the 50 yard line to the goal.

"The scoreboard showed the reason for Ward's ecstasy—Maryland 33, Visitors 24. For the Terrapins, nothing like that had happened for 712 days."

Ward said it was "the greatest day of my life." His first success as a head coach would help his players "understand how hard work pays off. Now when I get on them, they won't hang their heads." Ward was carried off on his players' shoulders and showered with Coke in the locker room.

The heroes of the triumph were Billy Lovett, who gained 172 yards and scored two touchdowns en route to amassing 963 yards to break tailback Lu Gambino's single-season rushing record of 904 yards; Pastrana, who passed 16 yards to Rick Carlson for the clinching touchdown; and the defense, which held

Bobby Ward returned to his alma mater in 1967 as head coach, a job he always had wanted. He lasted two seasons, then resigned when his players rebelled.

Carolina at midfield to set up its team's final touchdown.

The streak was over but not the losing. Maryland could salvage only one more triumph out of the season, finishing with a 2-8 record. There was disenchantment with athletics on the campus and, to the public's surprise, with Ward on the football team.

The athletic department was undergoing a shakeup. William Colby, who had succeeded Tatum as athletic director, retired and Jim Kehoe, a crew-cut, hard-nosed winner who had made Maryland a track power without the benefit of much money, was given the job. Kehoe was determined to regain the prestige the school had once enjoyed in the Tatum era. Yet he faced major hurdles. "We were in deep, deep trouble," Kehoe said. "Major teams were performing badly and we were in trouble financially."

He had expected to stick with Ward another year—"the third year will be crucial," he said—but then the players rebelled against Ward, complaining about his coaching conduct and calling for his resignation.

"I wasn't prepared to handle such an incident so quickly," Kehoe admitted. He was still waiting for Colby to leave when the controversy broke out.

The players complained about Ward's discipline methods, his conduct in practice, and his overall handling of the team. They claimed he took away scholarships, hit players during practice, and did not try to understand their problems. He denied the charges, saying he would never step down and that only a few players were causing the problems. The incident was attracting nation-wide attention, just around the time Kehoe was moving to replace basketball coach Frank Fellows with Davidson's Lefty Driesell. The players fought desperately not to be branded as extremists. "We want to do what is right for the school," they said. "We have in no way been influenced by any of the disturbances on this campus."

In a dramatic meeting, the players spoke about their grievances in the presence of Kehoe and Ward. When the football

Despite playing on weak teams, Billy Lovett broke Maryland's single-season rushing record and tied Ed Modzelewski for the career mark.

coach left the room, he looked shaken. He asked for 24 hours to compose a reply, and was granted his request.

He decided not to meet again with the players. Instead, he resigned "in the best interests of the university." One paper commented that Ward resigned "a victim of his own zest for winning." Kehoe thought Ward's ambition was a problem. "I never met a man who wanted to win more desperately and worked at it harder than him," he said. "This could have been the problem."

Kehoe found himself without a football coach, but with a chance to bring Maryland back from the lowest point in its football history. The man he turned to was Roy Lester.

Roy Lester rose from the high school coaching ranks to take over the Maryland program in 1969. After three losing seasons he was fired.

Lester was a high school coach from Richard Montgomery High in nearby Rockville, Maryland. His reputation as a winner was legendary. His teams at Montgomery had compiled an 86-10-1 record over 10 years, and had a 25-game winning streak when he left. "He had the ability, I believed, to get along with youngsters and heal the wounds on the team," said Kehoe. "He had a fascinating record in high school and I heard nothing but good things about him."

It was not a comfortable situation for Lester, a country boy from West Virginia who spoke with a southern accent, chewed tobacco, liked to complain about headaches, was conservative in his politics and his football, and appeared unruffled except when he lost. He had been an assistant for three years under Mont at Maryland and had always harbored a desire to return to the school.

Lester inherited a so-so team and did about as well as possible to finish with a 3-7 record. Pastrana, after a good senior year, and Lovett, who tied Ed Modzelewski's career rushing record of 1,913, were gone and Lester built around inexperienced quarterbacks and only a few top-notch players. One of those, Ralph Sonntag, made the All-ACC team as an offensive tackle, the first Maryland player to be chosen since Absher in 1966.

But the next two years did not get any better. Maryland followed with back-to-back 2-9 seasons and Kehoe began feeling the pressure of dropping attendance in the one sport he relied on to support the rest of his program. In a controversial move, he fired Lester, leaving the ex-coach bitter about his entire tenure at the school.

"I didn't want to do it," said Kehoe. "But I had to make a move. We could not afford to wait financially. I had to get football built so it would bring in some money."

Lester had been successful in one area. He had begun to recruit well, and had brought in an outstanding group his final year. He never doubted his ability to turn the program around "if I had been given the chance. I wasn't."

So Lester went back to high school coaching and Kehoe again was seeking the one man who could somehow push Jim Tatum over a bit on that legend cloud.

Miracle Man

Jerry Claiborne does not look like a miracle man. His rugged face is dominated by a nose flattened after bumping into some immovable object. He has thinning hair and a sort of shy manner that makes him appear uncomfortable in the spotlight.

He is a classic example of the misleading appearance. His body houses a man of fierce desire who is engulfed with a constant craving to succeed. To Claiborne, failure is a sin. He lacks the magnetic personality of a Bear Bryant or Jim Tatum but he has, according to Bryant, "one of the best football minds around." This knowledge has gained him respect among his peers, who consider him one of the nation's premier coaches.

But on the day he was hired by Athletic Director Jim Kehoe to replace Roy Lester, the Maryland football players were not impressed with his prior coaching successes. He was not, in their minds, the sort of coach that would rescue the fading Terrapin football program. "We had our doubts about him," said one of the players, Louis Carter. The athletes were hoping for some famous coach who would be lured to Maryland with a lucrative contract and a free hand to rebuild. Instead they got Claiborne.

Their scrambling for details about their new coach revealed a mixed bag. He had been head coach for 10 years at Virginia Tech, where he had six winning seasons, two Liberty Bowl teams, and an overall 61-37-2 record. But his last two years were not good—4-5-1 and 5-6—and his squads had the reputation of being somewhat dull, disdaining the pass for an Ohio

Jerry Claiborne studies game action with characteristic intensity. He also found a lot to smile about in his first three seasons at Maryland.

State-like ground attack.

He was finally fired after the 1970 season by Tech—"I told them what the recruiting situation was and I lost my job because I was honest," he would say later—and wound up in Colorado where he served as assistant head coach and defensive coordinator under coach Eddie Crowder. Colorado finished as the No. 3 ranked team in the nation. The defense especially made great improvement over the previous year. But Claiborne was restless. He wanted a second chance to prove he was not washed up as a head coach. Then the Maryland job came along.

"I had heard about Coach Claiborne," said Kehoe "and he was recommended highly. But he was successful at Colorado and I understood he was heir-apparent to the head job there.

But he called me. That was extremely important. If he showed that kind of interest I knew he was anxious. If he hadn't called me, we probably would have never considered him.

"We were in trouble, desperate trouble. We weren't drawing any people for football and we needed the money. I couldn't wait any longer. I had to build up the football program. So we talked to Claiborne and hired him. He came to us as a winner."

Claiborne, who was considered for the Maryland job in 1958 and 1966 before withdrawing his name, told a press conference he had three immediate goals: to have a winning season the next year, to be nationally ranked, and to win the Atlantic Coast Conference title. He was strictly business, very confident, very professional. It would be an impression his team would also receive.

For a school that had gone through four head coaches since 1965, Claiborne's promises were very familiar. Others before him had hoped to do the same things, but had failed. Maryland had had nine straight losing years and only three winning ones since Tatum left before the 1956 campaign. From national champions, the Terrapins had fallen to a permanent spot among the nation's worst 10 schools.

Lester had recruited well during his tenure despite three losing years. But the players Claiborne inherited were not as strong or as quick as he wanted. He had found at Colorado the glories of quickness; and from one of his assistants, Jake Hallum, he was converted to the importance of weight lifting to increase strength. He launched an arduous off-season weight and conditioning program and began one-on-one counseling with his players.

Claiborne brought to the Maryland program the type of organization so characteristic of Tatum. He especially was efficient at directing his staff, many of whom had worked or played under him at Virginia Tech. His assistants for the most part were thoroughly schooled in the Claiborne system. "He has everything mapped out minute by minute," said one of his players. "We always knew exactly what to do at every practice. There were never any mixups, any questions. His whole approach was organized. It made things a lot more simple."

To players who had known nothing but losing in college,

Claiborne was a much-needed positive factor. He started off talking about winning to them and never stopped. "It wore off on us," said one of his future stars, Paul Vellano. "Guess you could call it imitation, but after a while we all seemed to reflect his winning attitude, even though we hadn't won."

"These players," Claiborne said, "had been kicked around and criticized long enough. What they needed was a positive approach. We didn't want to look back. I didn't care what had happened before I arrived. I wanted to look forward."

The strategy worked. It took time, a year or more, before the football gospel according to Claiborne really was absorbed by his players. They saw that believing in him and what he preached could produce victories and success, something most of them wanted desperately.

"The whole thing started with Claiborne himself," said Vellano. "The way he carried himself. He is so impressive. He practiced what he preached. He wanted us neat, and he was always neat. He taught us concentration and dedication. He gave us leadership, and that was so important."

Claiborne learned from one of the best, Bear Bryant. He was recruited to Kentucky from Hopkinsville, Kentucky. "I wasn't hard to recruit," said Claiborne. "I always wanted to go to the state university." Bryant liked Claiborne but was unsure as to where to play him. Before his career was over, he had been used at a handful of positions, but was best as a safety. "He might be the best safety I've ever coached," said Bryant. "He'd stick it to people. He was really slow but he was hard-nosed and a competitor." Claiborne thinks his position switching made him a better coach. "I learned a lot about different spots and how to play them," he said. "It broadened my outlook on football."

Under Bryant, Claiborne learned the fundamentals of football. He later was lured from a high school coaching position after two seasons to become an assistant on Bryant's Kentucky staff. He followed Bryant to Texas A&M, left briefly to work with Frank Broyles at Missouri, then went with Bryant to Alabama as assistant head coach.

While at Alabama, Claiborne developed fully a reputation as a defensive wizard. He polished the techniques of the wide-tackle six defense so well that when his peers later switched to more modern alignments, like the pro 4-3 or the 5-2, he stuck to his own defense. "We consider it the best there is," he explained. "Why? Because it works. We think we know how to use it better than anyone and we tell coaches at clinics that it will work for them too."

He finally left Bryant to take the Virginia Tech job in 1961. The school, located in Blacksburg, Virginia, is isolated and most difficult to sell to athletes. That fact finally caught up with him, although Claiborne refuses to be drawn into a long discussion of his difficulties at Tech. "I don't think it's right to talk ill of people," he said.

Jerry Claiborne and four of the players who have helped him turn around the football program at Maryland: All-American Paul Vellano (72), All-ACC tailback Louis Carter (32), three-time All-ACC safety Bob Smith (26), and All-American Randy White (94).

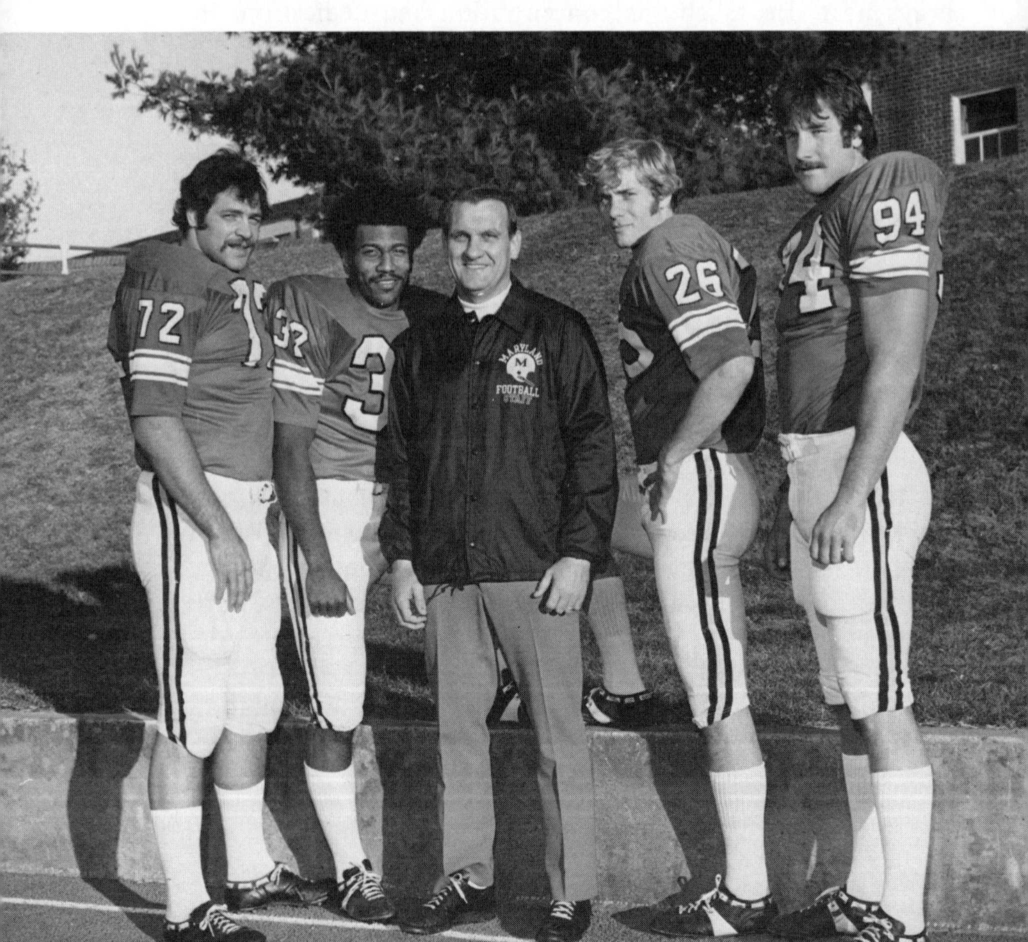

Coming from Claiborne, the message is sincere. He is a religious man who does not swear or drink. He has never quite lost his country-boy background which his still-prominent Southern drawl reveals immediately—and good, old-fashioned religion was one of those habits he learned as a child. Critics of his football are rarely critical of him as a man. He is truly warm and friendly, and demands and receives great loyalty from his staff, in turn repaying them with his own dedication.

Claiborne is also intelligent. At Kentucky, he was an honor student. Bryant likes to tell the story about how he wound up buying Claiborne so many suits for his good grades he thought he would go broke. One time he took tennis during a semester and he thought he had a cinch "A", said Bryant. "He wound up getting a 'C'. It was the only time I've ever heard him swear."

Claiborne is a relentless worker. He puts in long hours, even for college coaches, battling the constant demands on his time. He has a sense of humor, but rarely displays it; instead he presents a facade of all-business, got-to-move-on to the outside world.

"I haven't changed that much as a coach," said Claiborne. "I do think now that I spend more time trying to motivate my players than I once did. Before, we worried more about details and strategy. But today's player has so much more to distract him, with television and more social events and a different type of society. For him to focus his mind just on football is a challenge for both the player and me."

There have been other changes. His own hair, though hardly long by society's standards, has grown out from a crew cut. Likewise, his players' hair is longer and they can have mustaches. Yet he is no advocate of a rule-less team. He still has curfews and other restrictions, nor is he as liberal as many of his players would like. Claiborne is a product of the era of coaches who consider themselves overseers of a dictatorship. "We have to have certain standards," he said. "I believe in order to be a winner, you have to make sacrifices. Following the rules is one way to sacrifice."

And he never has lost his will to compete. One associate loves to recall Claiborne's handball games at Virginia Tech. "He would risk his hair and skin to dive after a point, even though it wouldn't decide who won the game. He never wants to lose."

Smiles, Peaches, And Victories

He was a jolly fellow, the locker room joker, the guy with the ready smile and quick quip who delighted teammates, coaches, and writers alike with his ways. Yet, more than any other player in Jerry Claiborne's first two years at Maryland, Paul Vellano epitomized just what the program had been and just where it had advanced so quickly.

Vellano came to Maryland from Schenectady, New York, as a highly touted recruit, and did little while on the freshman team to discredit the predictions. But as a defensive tackle during his sophomore season in 1971, he had been overweight and weak and did not have nearly the year expected of him. "I realized something had to change when we played Penn State," he said. "I was facing this guy Dave Joyner and before I could read what he was doing, he was past me. Up to then I had kidded myself along that I was in good enough shape."

Claiborne put most of his linemen on diets. Vellano was the chief benefactor. He reported in the fall of 1972 at 235, after being at 275 during the spring. "It killed me, I had to stay away from all my mom's great cooking," Vellano said. "But I'd rather cut out food than have faced Coach Claiborne."

In losing the weight, Vellano regained his high school quickness. But he did not lose his marvelous personality. "Paul was the team leader," said Claiborne. "The fellows looked up to him. He was a very emotional person and his emotion influenced the others."

Emotion had not been enough to transform the Terrapins

Former Maryland football player Dave Clough drew this cartoon of Terrapin All-American Paul Vellano.

into winners Claiborne's first year. He started a freshman (Kevin Benson) most of the way at linebacker and three sophomores (Bob Smith, Ken Schroy, and Pat Ulam) in the secondary. One of his defensive ends was a former linebacker. He had sophomores like Randy White and Dave Visaggio in the defensive line and most of the reserves were just as young. It took four games for the defense to jell and by then the team had tied North Carolina State (24-24), lost to North Carolina (31-26), beat Virginia Military (28-16), and lost to Syracuse (16-12). Two games later, it also lost starting quarterback Al Neville for the season with a broken collarbone.

Yet the foundation for future years had been laid–very carefully. By the end of the season, the defense was No. 1 in the ACC after finishing last the year before. The offense scored 109 points, the most in 18 years, and the team broke 16 records. On offense, such talented sophomores as split end Frank Russell, tailback Louis Carter, and quarterback Bob Avellini had gained experience. The final record–5-5-1–was Maryland's best since 1964 and only a final game loss to Miami (28-8) prevented the first winning year since 1962. The Terrapins had lost two contests in which they failed to score on seven occasions inside the 10.

"We have a long way to go," said Claiborne. "But we've come a long way too. We've made up a lot of ground on some teams but the strong ones are still way ahead of us." But it helped, he admitted, to have 12 starters returning for 1973.

One of those was Vellano. Along with Smith, a safety who also led the ACC in punt returns, he had made All-ACC. He led the team in tackles from his defensive guard position, a rarity in Claiborne's wide-tackle six formation. Especially tough against the run, he had also had some spectacular quarterback sacks, once literally throwing the center into the Virginia quarterback on fourth down and one. In another game, he had 14 unassisted tackles, four assists, three backfield tackles, and caused one fumble. In a third, he was in on 23 tackles, including six for minus yardage.

Only one school had offered him a scholarship out of high school. He accepted and came to Maryland. Under Claiborne's guidance, he excelled as a player, but he hardly was a typical dumb lineman. Once he caught a burglar in his dorm room.

"Hey man, I was going to rob you but I haven't taken anything," the would-be robber told him. Vellano, after briefly considering throwing him out the window, settled for an escorted trip to the nearest exit. "Can you imagine what one of the other guys would have done to him if they had caught him?" he asked.

Vellano's best friend in high school stood 5-2. "He used to pick fights and I had to calm everyone down," he said. "Guys used to say to me, 'Hey, you're the big guy, huh? Wanta fight?' I'd tell 'em 'Come on kid, that's only in the movies.'"

With stories like that, Vellano was his own best publicity man, the one Maryland player that reporters went to for good quotes and lively copy. His teammates soon reflected much of his easy-going manner.

"It was a fun team to coach," said Claiborne of the 1973 squad. "You didn't have to give them pep talks to get them up. With people like Vellano and (Ken) Scott and (Bart) Purvis around, it was easy to arouse them. Those people loved to play."

Vellano was the type who could get a picture of a terrapin tattooed to his upper leg and survive the harassment of his teammates. "Got to really identify with the school," is how he explained the unusually placed picture.

What Vellano and friends produced in 1973 was Maryland's best season in 18 years (8-4) and its first bowl trip in the same span of time. And they came within a field goal of winning the school's first outright ACC title.

Claiborne knew he had a good team entering the season, but was worried about three areas: offensive line where only one starter returned, linebacker, and defensive end. Otherwise, he had veterans manning the rest of the positions, despite the fact only 10 seniors were on the opening-game roster.

Yet things hardly started out on a positive note. In the opener against West Virginia, Danny (Lightning) Buggs, a sprinter on the Mountaineer track team, returned a punt 69 yards for a touchdown with eight seconds left to give his team a 20-13 victory. Claiborne's fears about his offensive line had been realized. The Terrapins could not move the ball although he employed three quarterbacks–Neville, Avellini, and another junior, Ben Kinard.

Defensive guard Paul Vellano grabs an unsuspecting Virginia

Military quarterback and takes him for a spin.

Despite scoring only one touchdown–after White recovered a bad snap from center on a punt at the one–Maryland led until the final 5 minutes, 16 seconds. Then Ade Dillon, a former Navy quarterback, connected with Dwayne Woods for a 75-yard touchdown pass and Buggs returned the game-breaking punt.

The quarterback problem was an old one. Avellini, a widely regarded newcomer, had done well the year before after Neville got hurt. He had thrown for a school-record 312 yards against Duke in his first start and wound up leading the ACC in completions with 98 (for 1,251 yards) and was second in total offense (1,257). It was the fourth-best season by a quarterback in Maryland history. Kinard pushed himself into the picture after a fine spring practice in which he showed better control of his dazzling running abilities. Neville led the ACC in passing as a sophomore in 1971, throwing for 1,275 yards, and had been a starter his first two years on the varsity.

Avellini began the 1973 season as the starter. He hurt his hip in the third quarter of the West Virginia game but neither Neville or Kinard were more effective. Avellini was unable to play the next week against North Carolina (the defending ACC champ and undefeated in 15 straight league games), so Neville was promoted to first string.

The change worked. What Claiborne called "the real Maryland football team" demolished Carolina 23-3 in Chapel Hill, as Neville threw for two touchdown passes and set up a third on another completion. Carolina did not cross the 50 until late in the third period and was held to 196 yards. Neville passed for 121 yards alone.

The triumph was a fine example of the talent the Maryland team possessed. Claiborne had switched junior college transfer Walter White to tight end from split end, and he responded by catching a 13-yard scoring toss from Neville. Russell outplayed a freshman defensive back to catch a 34-yard pass that led to the first touchdown and then caught a 23-yard scoring pass for the second. Tackles Ken Scott and Randy White, who had 18 tackles and was named national lineman of the week, had been instrumental in limiting Carolina to 105 yards rushing. It had been Maryland's first win in Carolina since 1962 and first road victory since 1968.

The team's turnabout had come in a scrimmage the previous Wednesday. Following a poor workout on Tuesday, Claiborne put the team through a 30-minute drill of straight ahead offensive plays until, as one player said, "we got it down just right."

The Terrapins managed to survive an injury to Neville and beat Villanova 31-3 the next week. Neville dislocated his left elbow on a running play and Avellini came in to complete 8 of 13 passes for 119 yards. But Maryland did not break the game open until the last period. After three Steve Mike-Mayer field goals, the Terrapins scored on a 61-yard run by tailback Carter, a 56-yard punt return by Smith, and a 30-yard interception return by reserve Mike Cilensky.

A 38-0 victory over Syracuse, in which the Orangemen did not get inside the Maryland 25 and suffered their worst loss at the hands of the Terrapins in the schools' 53-year series, set up a confrontation with North Carolina State for the ACC title.

The Wolfpack had a potent veer attack which was matched against Maryland's conference-leading defense. Claiborne's pride-and-joy had not allowed a touchdown rushing all year, just one through the air, and none in the past 12 quarters. State had gone over 400 total yards in all but one game.

The offense won, just barely. Avellini hurt his knee on the second play of the game and was replaced by Kinard, who fumbled three times and threw an interception to stake State to a 17-0 lead. Claiborne then turned to Neville, who still was not recovered from the dislocated elbow and had made the trip to hold on kicks if necessary. Despite only partial use of his non-throwing arm, Neville proceeded to rally his team, tossing a 10-yard pass to Walter White for a touchdown in the first half and setting up two scores by Carter, who gained 110 yards in all.

With State leading 24-22 and 3:14 left, Neville moved Maryland to the Wolfpack 23 where Mike-Mayer, who already had one field goal, tried another from 40 yards out with 16 seconds remaining. A high snap from center forced him to kick late and the ball curved just wide. State gained 210 total yards to Maryland's 387, and Neville had completed 19 of 32 passes for 212 yards. State went on to win the ACC title by one game.

Maryland lost only once after that, to nationally ranked Penn State 42-22, after being tied at 22-all at intermission. A crowd of 44,135 saw the contest in Byrd Stadium, and was treated to an exciting first half in which Maryland rallied after falling behind 12-0 in the first 84 seconds of play.

State returned the opening kickoff 98 yards for a touchdown—a rare occurrence against Claiborne's always-tough specialty teams—and then recovered a fumble on the ensuing kickoff, turning that mistake into a second score. The Nittany Lions later added one more touchdown before the half. But Maryland tied it up on a halfback option pass from freshman Ken Roy to Russell, a Mike-Mayer field goal, a pass from Carter to Walter White, and an 83-yard punt return by Smith with five seconds left in the second quarter.

Penn State forced an interception and fumble on the first two series of the second half, turned both into touchdowns, and coasted to the victory. Led by Heisman Trophy winner John Cappelletti, the Lions finished the year undefeated and beat LSU in the Orange Bowl.

All-Americans Randy White (left) and Paul Vellano (right) tackle All-American and Heisman Trophy winner John Cappelletti during the Penn State-Maryland game in 1973. Penn State won in the second half 42-22.

Otherwise, the season proved a breeze. Kinard atoned for his miscues against North Carolina State by throwing for 120 yards and running for 81 more in a 37-0 victory over Wake Forest. Carter gained 91 yards and Wake completed only one of 18 passes, for just one first down. Neville came off the bench to help Maryland beat Duke 30-10 on three fourth-period touchdowns, including a 15-yard interception return by the 235-pound Scott, and the second of two touchdown tosses by Carter from his tailback position. A 33-0 trouncing of Virginia clinched the winning season. This time Kinard, who replaced Neville in the second period, was the hero, racing 52 yards for a touchdown on his first carry. Virginia, which had been averaging 389 yards total offense, managed 246 while Maryland ran up 512, its most since 1954.

That victory set off bowl talk. The Peach Bowl considered Maryland a leading contender but the Terrapins needed some help to get a bid. The Peach Bowl decided to select Georgia and Arkansas with Maryland an alternate choice, replacing Arkansas if the Razorbacks were defeated in their next game. Maryland had to beat Clemson. Everything fell into place. The Terrapins jumped to a 28-7 lead and held off Clemson 28-13, Arkansas was tied by SMU 7-7. The invitation to the bowl was accepted by a Maryland official in the Clemson press box. When the team found out while waiting to fly home, the players staged an impromptu pep rally in a nearby airport.

"This is something we've worked two years for," said Purvis, the team's best offensive lineman. "It would have been unbelievable if Arkansas had gotten a bid with their bad record." Claiborne said the bid "shows how far our program has come. And it's great for our seniors. It was the only opportunity they had."

Carter had his best game to date in the Clemson victory, gaining 127 yards and scoring three touchdowns. Maryland, in turn, played its best game the next week in trouncing Tulane 42-9, which was ranked 16th and 17th and going to the Astro Bluebonnet Bowl. Carter, despite an almost-closed eye caused by a first-quarter scratch, tossed his fourth and fifth touchdown passes of the season, and scored two others. Kinard, now the permanent starting quarterback, completed 9 of 11 passes, one for a touchdown, to equal a school record for accuracy and the team totalled 445 yards. Tulane was held to 58 on the ground. "They beat us physically and mentally all day," said Tulane coach Bernie Ellender.

The Peach Bowl in Atlanta was hardly the glamour bowl of the year, but for Maryland it was something special. It marked the return of the football program to at least some of the satisfaction it had known during the Tatum era. Claiborne already was reaping some benefits. He was selected coach of the year in the ACC, then District III coach of the year by his peers. Vellano, Randy White, Smith, and Carter made the All-ACC team. Vellano, runner-up as the ACC player of the year, also was chosen to the first-team Football Coaches Association All-American squad. White, in somewhat of a surprise, made first-team Associated Press All-American, the school's first wire service All-American since Gary Collins in 1961.

Maryland's defense was ranked nationally in total defense (245 yards a game), scoring defense (11.3 points a game), and rushing defense (112 a game). For the second straight year, the Terrapins led the ACC in all three categories, and were second in passing offense and scoring (29 points a game). They scored the second-most points (319) in the school's history, surpassed only by the 1951 team (381). They set 22 school records. Mike-Mayer alone set seven, including longest field goal (54 yards against Villanova, an ACC record), most field goals in a season (12), most points by kicking in a season (69), and two career marks–most field goals (22) and most points by kicking (124). Carter had one of the more impressive individual performances of the year, rushing for 801 yards and 14 touchdowns, and passing for five touchdowns on just six completions in eight attempts.

The Terrapins now were ranked 17th and 18th in the polls, yet Georgia, despite a 6-4-1 record, was favored in the bowl game. The Bulldogs had two fine offensive players, quarterback Andy Johnson and tailback Jimmy Poulos, second in career rushing to Frank Sinkwich, a Heisman Trophy winner. And they had a typically tough Southeastern Conference defense. They had won three of their last four games and Coach Vince Dooley thanked the Peach Bowl for "waiting until we came around."

Georgia did not disappoint its home state fans. Playing just

Linebacker Harry Walters, Maryland's leading tackler for two years, returns interception in 1973 Peach Bowl. The Terrapins lost to Georgia 17-16.

70 miles down the road from its campus in Athens, the Bulldogs came up with enough big plays to edge Maryland 17-16 despite the fact they were outgained by 177 yards, and, for the most part, outplayed.

Four times Maryland moved inside Georgia's 13 without scoring. On three other occasions, they were inside the 20, but had to settle for Mike-Mayer field goals. Meanwhile, Georgia took advantage of its only second-half break—a recovered fumble on the Maryland eight off a bad pitch from Kinard to reserve tailback Ricky Jennings—to score the winning touchdown.

Carter was selected the game's most valuable player after rushing for 126 yards in 29 carries, completing two of three passes for 83 yards and a touchdown, and catching one pass for 26 yards. Kinard ran for 40 yards and completed four of eight

Tailback Louis Carter, a two-time All-ACC selection, receives the Peach Bowl most valuable player award after the game in 1973. Carter is Maryland's career rushing leader.

passes for 113 before leaving with a sprained ankle in the final period. He later collapsed from exhaustion in the dressing room.

Maryland gained 136 yards to Georgia's seven in the first quarter but neither team scored. That set the pattern for the Terrapins, who fell behind in the second period when Johnson completed a 62-yard screen pass to Poulos. Carter then hit Walter White with a 68-yard touchdown toss, and Mike-Mayer added a 36-yard field goal with 1:31 left before the half. Georgia stormed back for a tying field goal from 26 yards with six seconds remaining.

Georgia managed only 72 yards in the second half but got a touchdown off the Kinard miscue with 4:24 to go in the third quarter. Maryland moved to the five, but Walter White fumbled on a reverse. The Terrapins took over again on the Georgia 15, but had to settle for a 25-yard field goal. They recovered a fumble on the 35, but wound up with only a 28-yard field goal.

In all, Maryland made just two of 15 third and fourth down opportunities, lost three of four fumbles, and tossed one interception. "We made too many mistakes to beat a good ball team," said Claiborne. The first half had been especially bitter. The Terrapins got to the Georgia 11 before a Kinard interception; to the one, where they were stopped on fourth down; and to the 12, where Mike-Mayer missed a 32-yard field goal.

"We had a very satisfying season," said Claiborne, who now had lost six of nine games in two years by a touchdown or less, "but the ones we almost won, they hurt."

With 17 starters returning, including 10 on offense, he admitted he had a good chance to correct even those oversights the next year.

The Bear Returns

Jim Kehoe thought he could have sold 75,000 tickets for the game. "I've never seen anything like it," the Maryland athletic director explained. "People everywhere want tickets." To meet the demand, Kehoe brought in temporary bleachers and placed them around the perimeter of Byrd Stadium, and in the open-end end zone. It was only the second time that bleachers had been in that end zone, but the 1974 season-opening contest already had become the most attractive college game in Washington's history.

Alabama vs. Maryland. Before Jerry Claiborne arrived at College Park, the matchup would have been ludicrous. The Crimson Tide, under the direction of ex-Maryland coach Paul (Bear) Bryant, now a living legend among college coaches, was a national power coming off an 11-1 season in which only a Sugar Bowl loss to Notre Dame prevented it from being national champions. Maryland normally would have been an easy warmup for the major part of its schedule. Now even Bryant, with his tongue somewhat in his cheek, admitted he was concerned.

"I scheduled this game originally so I could take my players sightseeing in Washington," he said. "Now the only sightseeing they will do is on the bus from the airport to the hotel."

This latest Alabama team, he admitted, "had the potential to be my best ever," a sweeping statement indeed for the most successful active football coach at that time. He was worried about his offensive line, but his defense was strong and he had a half-dozen outstanding running backs. Even when he lost quarterback Gary Rutledge with a broken collarbone the week before the game, the odds did not fall, for he had equally talented Richard Todd available.

Maryland had a quarterback problem of a different sort. Claiborne had to choose from among four candidates–veterans Avellini and Kinard; redshirt Leon Harris, who had played well in spring practice; and freshman Mark Manges, Maryland's most highly touted recruit in years. He finally settled on Kinard. Otherwise, he fielded a set team against Alabama that included those 17 starters from the previous year. Preseason polls had ranked Maryland No. 11 and 14, Alabama third and fourth.

"We can be a very good team," said Claiborne of his preseason ACC favorites. "We have a most difficult schedule and it will be a test." Indeed, Maryland opened with games against Alabama, Florida (also ranked), and North Carolina; later they had to face Penn State and North Carolina State. The Terrapins had to integrate a sophomore tackle, Joe Campbell, and two new ends, Leroy Hughes and Rod Sharpless, into its defense; and Claiborne was not happy with the progress of his own offensive line, despite the return of all but Bart Purvis.

A crowd of 54,412, the largest in the stadium's history, turned out on the sunny afternoon to see Maryland's offense sputter enough to lose 21-16. At times the Terrapins outplayed and even dominated Alabama, a 12-point favorite, but they could not cope with their own mistakes–and the running of sophomore fullback Calvin Culliver, who gained 154 yards alone in the first half.

It was Bryant's fourth straight victory over his former player and staff member. "We won," he said, "but they beat us all over the field physically and they deserved to win."

Alabama had started quickly. It marched 72 yards after the opening kickoff for a touchdown, then scored on a 73-yard run by Culliver through the middle of Maryland's defense to take a 14-0 lead. The Terrapins cut into the margin when Mike-Mayer booted a 32-yard field goal after an Alabama fumble on the Tide's 38. He added a second successful kick from 35 yards in the final 31 seconds of the half after another Alabama fumble.

A record crowd of 54,412 filled Byrd Stadium to watch Maryland lose 21-16 to Alabama in the 1974 opener.

Maryland limited Alabama to 105 total yards and Culliver to 15 in the second half–Alabama had 244 before intermission. But the Terrapin offense could not take advantage of the defense's play, beginning when Ricky Jennings returned the second half kickoff 61 yards, only to have Maryland settle for yet a third Mike-Mayer field goal, this one coming from 40 yards out.

A fumble by Kinard set up what proved to be the winning touchdown. Alabama recovered on the Maryland 37. Todd went 19 yards on a second-and-15 situation to set up his own score from the one. Maryland's only sustained march of the game soon followed. The Terrapins went into the end zone on a one-yard dive by Carter to make it 21-16, with 14:21 left in the contest. Minutes later, Bob Smith circled under an Alabama punt on his own 45. He was hit as he caught the ball and fumbled. Alabama recovered to end Maryland's chances.

"I was thinking touchdown," said Smith. "I didn't know where the tacklers were."

The loss did little to damage Maryland's newly gained football reputation. It had done well against a team that went on to finish the regular season undefeated, only to lose a share of the national title with a 13-11 loss to Notre Dame in the Orange Bowl.

The Terrapins had been expected to lose to Alabama. "We probably didn't think we could beat them in our own minds," Carter said later. The team thought, however, it had a chance of sweeping the rest of its schedule. With the experience and talent it had returning from the previous season, Maryland had the potential to be the school's best since 1955.

A poor game the next week in Florida almost ruined the predictions before the year had even gotten warm. The Gators, rebuilding under former Tennessee coach Doug Dickey, scored 10 third-quarter points to overcome a 10-7 Maryland lead. Then they held off Avellini's desperate attempts to rally his team in the final period. Once again, mistakes and offensive inconsistency had hurt Maryland, offsetting fine defensive performances by linebacker Harry Walters and Randy White.

Avellini, the third quarterback used by Claiborne in the game, guided the Terrapins to the 12 before Jennings fumbled; then he went to the 25 in the final minute before running out of downs. Florida won 17-10. Maryland had been victimized by another fine runner, freshman Tony Green, who gained 178 yards and had a 76-yard touchdown run. Maryland managed only 66 yards in the second half until Avellini came in.

"We had to re-evaluate our season after that loss," said Ken Schroy. Claiborne also did some re-evaluating. Kinard was hurt, so he started Avellini against North Carolina. The change got the offense untracked, with help from Carter, who swept right end for 76 yards in the second quarter behind blocks by fullback Alan Bloomingdale and wingback John Schultz.

"That run was definitely what we've been looking for this season," said Claiborne, who had been wondering where last season's scoring power had gone. Carter finished with a career-high 158 yards on 26 carries. He added another touchdown on a

22-yard pass from Avellini in the third quarter to give him 23 career touchdowns, breaking Ed Modzelewski's school record. Avellini completed 8 of 17 passes for 121 yards. North Carolina, which had not allowed a point in eight quarters, suffered its first defeat, 24-12.

The victory started Maryland on a five-game winning streak. Syracuse, trying an eight-man offensive line to control Randy White and to run against the Maryland defense, went 83 yards in 21 plays in the first half without scoring. The Terrapins turned it into a rout in the second half, scoring 24 points and limiting Syracuse to two yards in the third period for a 38-0 victory. Avellini completed 15 of 20 passes for 198 yards. The Terrapins did not wait until the second half to trounce Clemson. They scored 20 points in the first half and went on to a 41-0 triumph, the second most lopsided victory over an ACC opponent in the school's history. The Maryland defense caused nine fumbles, recovering five to set up three touchdowns. Clemson gained only 122 yards on the ground.

A third straight shutout followed 47-0 over Wake Forest, on the same afternoon North Carolina was knocking North Carolina State out of a first-place tie with Maryland for the ACC lead. Maryland used 62 players and ran up 473 yards against winless Wake. Russell caught four passes for 51 yards to break Gary Collins' career yardage record of 1,182.

A one-minute film clip played a prominent part in Maryland's 20-10 victory over North Carolina State that eventually won the title. In the 24-22 loss to State the year before, Wolfpack players had taunted Mike-Mayer after he missed his last-minute field goal attempt. The taunts showed up in the game film. "If you have any kind of pride, you don't want that stuff happening again," said Randy White. "We were more emotional about this game than any this season."

A crowd of 49,674, second only in Byrd Stadium history to the Alabama gathering, watched Maryland outgain State 441-288, but the Terrapins needed a fourth-period interception by Smith to wrap up the triumph. Smith's theft, his second of the day, allowed Maryland to take over on its 46 in the fourth period, from where it marched five plays to score, Carter going in from the six to extend a 13-10 lead. It was the climax of Carter's finest day so far in his career. He rambled 180 yards to

Bob Avellini throws a pass against North Carolina State in a game that paved way to Maryland's first outright ACC title in 1974.

give him 1,952 for his career, breaking the school record of 1,913 held by Modzelewski and Bill Lovett.

"We could see in the films that we could run around end," Carter said. He proved right, but not after his fumble staked State to a 3-0 lead. Then Avellini, not noted for his running ability, scampered 30 yards for a touchdown and a 7-3 lead. Mike-Mayer followed with a 22-yard field goal, his 31st, an ACC record. State tied it by taking the second-half kickoff and scoring the first touchdown off the Maryland defense in 20 quarters. A 44-yard Mike-Mayer field goal got the Terrapins in front again, and then Smith's interception clinched the victory.

Now that it had the ACC title all but won, Maryland set its sights on Top 10 member Penn State, which had fallen to the

Terrapins only once in 20 meetings. The game was in State College, Pennslyvania, where the Nittany Lions hardly ever lost. But this was not a superior Penn State team. It had been defeated by Navy in the rain and was just starting to jell with its new wing T offense. The winner would go to the Cotton Bowl, a prize Maryland wanted dearly. It did not get it.

Mistakes and big plays, which already had cost the Terrapins two other defeats, came back to haunt them again. Before 60,125 fans—the second-largest crowd in the history of Beaver Stadium—Penn State's Jeff Hite, a substitute back starting in place of the injured Jim Bradley, intercepted a flat pass by Avellini and returned it 79 yards for a touchdown. On a second-period kickoff return following another Penn State score, Jennings tried to lateral to Carter but Hite stepped between the two, picked off the ball in the air, and went 21 yards for what proved to be the winning tally. Maryland countered with 34 and 66-yard scoring passes from Avellini to Walter White and a 34-yard field goal by Mike-Mayer that offset a 44-yarder by Chris Bahr.

Avellini, who had a brilliant day passing for 302 yards—second only to his school record of 314—tried to pull it out. He drove Maryland 62 yards with time running out. Carter picked up 31 of his 101 yards before Maryland faced a first down on the 19. Avellini gained six and Carter two, but Schultz was stopped for a yard loss. A fourth-down pass to Bloomingdale in the flat went over his head. He was wide open for a touchdown. Penn State won 24-17.

"He was open, I missed him, what else can I say," said Avellini. Claiborne said that the kickoff lateral was to take place only if Carter handled the ball, not Jennings. Maryland thought Penn State was able to read its plays, as Avellini, who had been sacked once going into the game, was hauled down six times. The Terrapins had outgained Penn State 407-298, but Penn State would go to the Cotton Bowl.

Maryland was not out of the bowl picture entirely. The Liberty, Fiesta, and Gator Bowls all showed an interest. The Liberty decided to make a strong pitch and it paid off. The Terrapins accepted an invitation. It was a step up, they thought, from the less profitable Peach Bowl of the year before.

There were still a few goals left in the season, particularly wrapping up the ACC title. After beating Villanova 41-0 as Jennings, who replaced an injured Carter, gained 150 yards and Maryland ran up 511 total yards, the Terrapins crushed Duke 56-13 to gain that championship. It was the school's first outright football title—Tatum's teams had shared crowns with Duke in 1953 and 1955—and they won it convincingly against the second best defensive club in the conference.

"If I would have told anyone when I came here that we would win an ACC title before I left, they would have told me I was nuts," said offensive guard Frank Romano. "Well I'm not nuts. Just real happy."

Maryland, which had 537 total yards, ran up a 35-7 halftime lead. They had never scored more points against an ACC foe. Avellini completed 10 of 11 passes for 191 yards and ran for 14 more to set two season records: most passing yards (breaking Alan Pastrana's mark of 1,499) and most total yards (breaking Dick Shiner's mark of 1,426). Walter White scored three touchdowns, and Jennings gained 105 yards. "We've come a long way in three years," said Claiborne. "But that is why we came here in the first place."

The Terrapins equalled their 1973 record of 8-3 by downing Virginia 10-0 in the season finale. It was their fifth shutout, the most since 1954, but although fumbles and interceptions kept the game closer than anyone had expected, the afternoon actually belonged to Carter. Back from a rib injury suffered against Villanova, he made a desperate bid to become the first modern-day Maryland runner to go over 1,000 yards. He gained 213, breaking Ray Poppelman's single-game mark of 203 set in 1931, and finished with 991 for the season, a modern-day record.

Carter had come to Maryland from nearby Arundel High in Laurel. He was a quarterback in high school, but that was only to allow him to handle the ball on every play. He was an athlete with 4.5 speed in the 40 and an ability to break off long, exciting runs using his powerful 205-pound frame. At first he clashed with Claiborne over rules. He thought the coach was out of touch with his athletes and their desires. He led the team in rushing all three of his varsity years, but his sophomore season was not impressive. It was not until he decided to adopt Claiborne's love for weight-lifting and minimize his conflicts with

Louis Carter takes advantage of one of the few blocking holes he saw against Tennessee in the 1974 Liberty Bowl to gain some yardage.

the coach that he began to produce. Capitalizing on his throwing ability, Carter proved successful at running the half-back option, especially in his junior year. He wound up holding career records for carries (590), points on touchdowns (162), touchdowns (27), and career rushing (2,392).

Mike-Mayer had done just as well record-wise. He finished with seven career and season kicking marks, including most field goals (15) and kicking points in a season (79) and also career records of points scored (213), field goals (37), and conversions (91).

He had come to Maryland in a round-about fashion. His younger brother was a kicker at Temple University, and he decided to try his hand at kicking too. He wrote letters to the top 10 and bottom 10 schools in the nation. Maryland responded, got a positive endorsement from his brother's coach at Temple, and took a chance. Mike-Mayer, who is a native of Budapest and went to high school in Italy, had never been scouted or tried under pressure, yet he ultimately made some All-American teams his senior year.

The overall assault on the record books by the 1974 team was devastating. Almost every major career and season record was broken. Avellini, despite never playing a full season, finished second to Shiner in career passing (3,222) and total offense (3,285), and gained the passing accuracy record by completing 231 of 394 passes for a 58 percent mark. His favorite target, Russell, held career marks in both receptions (100) and yards (1,346).

Randy White reaped the most benefits from the season. Along with Carter, Mike-Mayer, Smith, tackle Stan Rogers, and linebacker Harry Walters, he was named All-ACC. It was the third time for Smith, a first for Maryland, and it also was the most players ever named from the school to the team. White then was chosen the ACC player of the year, the first Maryland player so honored since Pellegrini in 1955. He also made every All-American team.

His biggest award, however, came just before the Liberty Bowl. He won the Outland Trophy, which goes to the outstanding interior lineman in the nation. Dick Modzelewski had been a recipient in 1952. Later, White received the coveted Lombardi Trophy as the coaches association choice for the outstanding lineman.

Maryland had set a home attendance record, averaging 37,995 per game. The team was the third-highest scoring in the school's history and gained a school record 4,484 yards. The offense was ranked eighth nationally (407 a game) and the defense sixth against scoring (8.8 points a game). The defense again was the ACC's best. The Terrapins ended the regular season ranked 11th after playing against five bowl-bound teams.

The team had hoped to improve its ranking against Tennessee in the Liberty Bowl. The Volunteers came on strong at the end of the season to salvage a bid but Maryland was favored finally to beat a Southeastern Conference team. It did not.

Maryland quarterback Bob Avellini completes a pass to Louis Carter during the 1974 Liberty Bowl. Avellini set school passing and total offense records during the season.

Frank Russell catches a last-minute pass from tailback Louis Carter against Tennessee in the 1974 Liberty Bowl. Officials ruled that Russell landed out of bounds, denying Maryland the winning touchdown.

The offense came up flat. Four times it moved inside the 21, only to fumble twice and toss two interceptions. Maryland's only points came on a 28-yard field goal by Mike-Mayer two plays into the second period. Otherwise, Tennessee stayed close until the fourth period when a bad snap went over Maryland punter Phil Waganheim's head and Tennessee took over on the Terrapin seven. Three plays later the Volunteers scored on a pass with 2:38 left in the game and won 7-3.

Maryland tried to score on one last drive. Avellini moved his team to the 20, where Carter threw a pass to Russell in the end zone. Russell leaped and caught the ball, but the official ruled he had come down out of the end zone. Instant replays on television appeared to indicate he was inbounds.

It was the Terrapins's fourth defeat by a touchdown or less. Twenty-seven more points and they would have finished undefeated. They finished the season ranked 13th in the nation.

Making Of An All-American

Bob Hope once said he was so quick he could beat the instant replay on television. He was described during his senior year as "the best lineman ever," and "the perfect combination of speed and strength." During his career at Maryland, Randy White heard enough praise to also emerge as the biggest ego ever. But he did not. The more good things he absorbed, the more attention he gave to staying humble.

From others, his aw-shucks approach might have been interpreted as a sham. White, however, was different. Nothing about him was a put-on. He would not allow himself to be lulled into complacency. If he thought he was slipping, he would begin working that much harder. During his senior year, he worked as much or more with the weights than any of his teammates, despite the fact he was already the strongest on the squad.

When White won the Outland Trophy, he called his parents in Wilmington, Delaware. "Oh, Randy, we're so happy," said his mother before he could get the news out. "Oh, you know, okay, I'll be seeing you," he said. "There was no way I wanted to talk to her about me. I knew she was happy but that was okay. Let her tell everyone else." White was out buying a suit the night the trophy winner was announced. By the time he returned to his dorm, the place was in an uproar. He got the news when one of his teammates yelled out the window as he was walking toward the entrance. He thought they were putting him on.

White had been the star of his high school team, which had compiled average records, and his play at fullback and linebacker earned him second-team All-State honors. Dim Montero, Maryland's chief recruiter under Roy Lester, had contacted White as a sophomore and continued the relationship throughout his high school career. More than anything else, White decided to attend Maryland because of this early interest.

"I really was heavily recruited just by Maryland and Arizona State," White said. "I considered going to Arizona but it was so far away and I wanted my parents to see me play. They hardly missed a game when I was at Maryland." So White came to College Park as part of Lester's last recruiting group, a bunch of players that would return Maryland to the upper echelon of football teams after an 18-year absence.

He wound up being one of those nearly perfect examples of dedication and loyalty that coaches love to talk about. Claiborne could not have created a better selling point for his program, a fact that has not escaped the coach. "Randy stands as proof that if you work awful hard and put your mind to something, it will pay off," said Claiborne. "Randy never questioned what we asked. He just did it. He was very coachable because he wanted to get better. He was a coach's dream."

White's football life changed soon after Claiborne took control of the Maryland program in the spring of 1972. One morning in his office, Claiborne asked the sophomore-to-be if he wanted to be an All-American.

"Sure, who doesn't," answered White. "But do you know what it takes to become one," said Claiborne. White admitted he really did not. So his coach outlined the one-step procedure: dedication. "I told him that he could make himself into whatever he wanted," said Claiborne. "But he had to go out and want to improve himself. He had the ability if he wanted to develop it."

At that time, White weighed 223 pounds, ran a 4.9 40 and bench-pressed about 300 pounds. By the time he finished his senior year, he weighed 248, ran a 4.6 40 and bench-pressed 450 pounds. Pro scouts admitted that they had rarely seen such a combination of speed and strength in a player.

His development came about through hours in the weight room at Maryland or in a Wilmington YMCA or in the basement of his house using weights he had gotten from a nearby prison. "I really like to weightlift," he said. "I don't mind putting in the time. I know it's helping me and that was enough to keep me at it." White said he sought to be "as good as I could be"—and he blocked anything out of his life that would interfere with his goal. He enjoyed an occasional round of golf with his father and he was not above a beer or two, but football was at once his hobby and profession.

"I like to hit people, I really do," he said. "There is a lot of satisfaction from playing the game. Saturdays for me are something special."

Randy White knocking down a pass against Virginia: "He was a coach's dream."

White exploded a year earlier than expected. Maryland had pushed Vellano for All-American honors in 1973, and Vellano made some All-American teams. But White was selected to the more prestigious Associated Press first team. His play had been spectacular at times, especially when he was able to corner opposing backs from behind, chasing them down with a burst of speed that seemed impossible for a man his size to produce.

His unexpected All-American honors made him a prime preseason candidate his senior year for the Outland Trophy and for unanimous All-American. He played the entire season under great pressure. He was not expected to produce just ordinary performances. To compound his problem, opponents ran away from him most of the time. Many of his tackles came on pursuit, what Claiborne called "just plain determination to make a play." Still, he wound up as Maryland's second-leading tackler with 147–including 12 quarterback sacks, 24 tackles in all for minus yards, 11 for no gain, and five that caused fumbles. He finished off with a spectacular display in the Liberty Bowl.

"Talk about the Outland really didn't bother me," he said. "How can you have any more pressure on you after you've been named an All-American? That puts you in the spotlight immediately. I tried to put all that stuff out of my head. I didn't do that much anyway. The coaches, they are the best around and the defense, it made me look good."

Such explanations are long sentences for White, a Gary Cooper prototype–strong and silent. He is so shy he had to force himself to speak in front of crowds. Once, his teammates pushed him forward as team spokesman at a pep rally. "I think they were trying to have a few laughs," he admitted. "They knew I really didn't want to get up there." He is hardly a mirror of the out-going, All-American type who once roamed campuses. At Maryland, it was easy for him to stay lost in a crowd.

Not so, however, on the football field. "Randy just has great football sense," said Claiborne. "He wants to find the ball and make the tackle. He is so quick and strong that he can do things others can't. He also learns quickly and rarely makes the same mistake twice."

Opponents marveled at his ability. Syracuse put in an unbalanced line in order to block him with two tackles, but still could not subdue him. Wake Forest assigned a man to block

3

him even when the play was being run away from his side. Clemson coaches considered his play against the Tigers so good they would sit later and watch the film and just shake their heads.

"We ran a fourth-down play at him on the goal line," said defensive coordinator Don Murry. "His tendency had been to go outside in such situations. That's exactly what he did. He went outside, our back cut inside. But White came back and made the tackle. You aren't supposed to do that, but he did."

White was able to control option plays off the veer and wishbone offenses with his unusual quickness. "He could stay with the quarterback and still get outside to get the pitch man if the quarterback pitched the ball," said Maryland assistant Gib Romaine, who worked closely with him.

"You dream about someone with that type ability, but you say, no, he can never happen. But Randy is unreal. He does things others don't even consider trying. In our defense, he had to be disciplined. So he did what he was supposed, then went out and made spectacular plays."

White was a superior athlete in high school. He batted over .500 in baseball his senior year and had a few talks with pro scouts. He made third-string all-state in basketball. "The rest of the stuff was fun," he said, "but football was my true love. The season always goes by too fast for me."

As the awards poured in his senior year, making him Maryland's most honored player since Pellegrini in 1955, his future in the pros became a widely discussed matter. "He's a can't miss prospect," said super scout Gil Brandt of the Dallas Cowboys. "You take a guy like him, he stands 6-4, weighs 248, runs a 4.6 40, bench presses 450 pounds and is quick as anything. He's got everything you want in a pro prospect.

"And he's got that attitude you want in every player."

Brandt's Cowboys wound up selecting White. He was the second player chosen in the draft, the highest ever for a Maryland player. The Cowboys talked of making him into a middle linebacker. It did not matter to White. "I just want to play football, I don't care where," he said.

Maryland All-American Randy White blocks a punt against Syracuse.

On the day of the 1974 draft, White posed for pictures, including one where he lifted the football secretary on his shoulders, and answered endless questions—"I like Dallas, they have nice uniforms." At the same time Claiborne was in Pittsburgh, on a recruiting trip, trying to replace the 11 Terrapins taken in the draft, the most since 1951, when a school-record 12 players were picked.

If he was lucky, he might find another Randy White.

Appendix

MARYLAND ALL-AMERICANS

First Team

Bob Ward, guard 1950 (AP), 1951 (AP, UPI)
Ed Modzelewski, back 1951 (INS)
Jack Scarbath, quarterback 1952 (AP, UP, INS)
Dick Modzelewski, tackle 1952 (AP, UP, INS)
Stan Jones, tackle 1953 (AP, UP, INS)
Bernie Faloney, quarterback 1953 (INS)
Bob Pellegrini, center 1955 (AP,UP,INS)
Gary Collins, end 1961 (UPI, Football Writers, Football Coaches)
Paul Vellano, guard 1973 (Football Coaches)
Randy White, tackle 1973 (AP), 1974 (AP, UPI, Football Writers, Football Coaches)

Second Team

Bill Supplee, end 1923 (AP)
Gerald (Snitz) Snyder, back 1928 (AP)
Ray Krouse, tackle 1949 (AP)
Bob Ward, guard 1950 (UP)
Ed Modzelewski, back 1951 (AP, UP)
Dick Modzelewski, tackle 1951 (AP)
Bernie Faloney, quarterback 1953 (AP, UPI)
Chet Hanulak, back 1953 (INS)
Bill Walker, end 1954 (AP), 1955 (UP)
Mike Sandusky, tackle 1955 (UP)
Ed Vereb, back 1955 (INS)
Paul Vellano, guard 1973 (UPI)

Third Team

Dick Modzelewski, tackle 1951 (UP)
Ed Vereb, back 1955 (AP, UP)
Paul Vellano, guard 1973 (AP)

ALL TIME MARYLAND FOOTBALL RECORDS AGAINST ALL OPPONENTS

	W	L	T
Air Force Acad.	2	0	0
Alabama	1	2	0
Alex. High	1	0	0
American Univ.	0	1	0
Auburn Univ.	1	1	0
Bainbridge Training	1	1	0
Baltimore City Col.	2	0	0
Baltimore Med. Col.	0	1	0
Baltimore Poly	3	1	0
Baylor Univ.	1	1	0
Bethel Mil. Acad.	1	0	0
Boston Univ.	2	0	0
Business High	1	0	0
Carnegie Tech	0	1	0
Catholic Univ.	8	1	2
Central High	4	1	0
Charlotte Hall Mil.	1	0	0
Chicago Univ.	0	1	0
Clemson Univ.	12	10	1
Columbia Ath. Club	0	1	0
Connecticut	1	0	0
Curtis Bay Coast Guard	0	1	0
Delaware	3	5	1
Dickinson Col.	1	0	0
Duke Univ.	5	14	0
Duquesne Univ.	1	0	0
Eastern High	3	0	0
Episcopal High	0	2	0
Univ. of Florida	5	9	0
Florida State	0	2	0
Fortress Monroe	0	0	1
Fredericksburg Col.	2	0	0
Gallaudet	9	6	1
Georgetown Univ.	6	9	0
Georgetown Prep	1	1	0
George Washington	10	3	0
Univ. of Georgia	3	2	1
Gibralter Ath. Club	0	1	0
Gonzaga High	1	1	0
Greenville (SC) AAB	1	0	0
Guilford Col.	1	0	0
Gunton Temple Bapt. Ch.	1	0	0
Hampden-Sydney	2	2	0
Haverford Col.	0	2	0
Indiana Univ.	0	2	0
Johns Hopkins	16	11	5
Univ. of Kentucky	1	1	1
Lakehurst Nav. Air St.	1	0	0
Louisiana State Univ.	3	0	0
U. S. Marine Barracks	1	0	0
Merchant Marine Acad.	1	0	0
Miami (Florida)	5	5	0
Miami (Ohio)	0	1	0
Michigan State	1	4	0
Mississippi	1	1	0
Missouri	6	0	0
Mt. St. Joseph's Col.	2	0	0
Mt. St. Mary's Col.	2	2	1
Mt. Washington Club	0	1	0
Navy	5	14	0
New York Univ.	2	0	0
Univ. of N. C.	16	22	1
N. C. State	12	15	4
Ohio Univ.	1	0	0
Oklahoma Univ.	0	4	0
Old Univ. of Md.	3	2	1
Orient Ath. Club	1	0	0
Pennsylvania	1	4	0
Penn State	1	20	0
Penn Military	3	1	0
Princeton	0	2	0
Randolph Macon Col.	0	2	1
Rich. Army Air Base	1	0	0
Richmond Univ.	9	5	2
Rock Hill Col.	3	1	0
Rutgers Univ.	4	3	0
St. Johns Col.	18	11	0
Univ. of S. C.	17	11	0
SMU	2	0	0
Swarthmore Col.	0	1	0
Syracuse Univ.	7	13	1
Tech. High	3	0	0
UCLA	1	1	0
Univ. of Tenn.	1	2	0
Univ. of Texas	0	2	0
Texas A & M	0	2	0
Third Army Corps	1	0	0
Tulane Univ.	1	1	0
Vanderbilt	1	5	0
Villanova	3	2	0
Virginia	22	15	2
Virginia Mil. Inst.	14	9	2
Virginia Tech.	14	10	0
Wake Forest	15	7	1
Walbrook Ath. Club	0	1	0
Washington & Lee	13	5	2
Washington Col.	18	3	1
Western High	0	0	1
Western Md.	18	13	1
West Va.	7	5	2
William & Mary	1	2	0
Yale Univ.	2	8	1

MARYLAND COACHES DOWN THE YEARS

MARYLAND AGGIES

Year	Head Coach	W L T
1892	*W.W. Skinner	0 3 0
1893	*S.H. Harding	6 0 0
1894	*George Harris	3 3 0
1895	No Team	
1896	*Grenville Lewis	5 0 2
1897	*John Lillibridge	2 4 0
1898	*J.F. Kenly	2 5 0
1899	*S.M. Cooke	1 4 0
1900	*F.H. Peters	3 4 1
1901	*E.B. Dunbar	1 7 0
1902	D. John Markey	2 5 2
1903		5 4 1
1904		2 4 2
1905	Fred Nielsen	6 4 0
1906		5 3 0
1907	C.G. Church & C.W. Melick	3 6 0
1908	Bill Lang	2 7 2
1909	Barney Cooper & E.P. Larkin	2 4 0
1910	R. Alston	4 3 1
1911	C.F. Donnelly & H.C. Byrd	3 3 2
1912	H.C. Byrd	5 1 1
1913		6 3 0
1914		5 3 0
1915		6 3 0

MARYLAND STATE

Year	Head Coach	W L T
1916	H.C. Byrd	6 2 0
1917		4 3 1
1918		4 1 1
1919		5 4 0

UNIVERSITY OF MARYLAND

Year	Head Coach	W L T
1920	H.C. Byrd	7 2 0
1921		3 5 1
1922		4 5 1
1923		7 2 1
1924		3 3 3
1925		2 5 1
1926		5 4 1
1927		4 7 0
1928		6 3 1
1929		4 4 2
1930		7 5 0
1931		8 1 1
1932		5 6 0
1933		3 7 0
1934		7 3 0
1935	Jack Faber	7 2 2
1936	Frank Dobson	6 5 0
1937		8 2 0
1938		2 7 0
1939		2 7 0
1940	[Jack Faber, Al Heagy	2 6 1
1941	Al Woods	3 5 1
1942	Clark Shaughnessy	7 2 0
1943	Clarence Spears	4 5 0
1944		1 7 1
1945	Paul "Bear" Bryant	6 2 1
1946	Clark Shaughnessy	3 6 0
1947 - a	Jim Tatum	7 2 2
1948		6 4 0
1949 - b		9 1 0
1950		7 2 1
1951 - c		10 0 0
1952		7 2 0
1953 - d		10 1 0
1954		7 2 1
1955 - e		10 1 0
1956	Tommy Mont	2 7 1
1957		5 5 0
1958		4 6 0
1959	Tom Nugent	5 5 0
1960		6 4 0
1961		7 3 0
1962		6 4 0
1963		3 7 0
1964		5 5 0
1965		4 6 0
1966	Lou Saban	4 6 0
1967	Bob Ward	0 9 0
1968		2 8 0
1969	Roy Lester	3 7 0
1970		2 9 0
1971		2 9 0
1972	Jerry Claiborne	5 5 1

1973 - f	Jerry Claiborne	8 4 0
1974 - g		8 4 0

82 Year Totals 378 339 37

*Teams coached by captains
a Gator Bowl co-champions, tied Georgia, 20-20
b Gator Bowl champions, defeated Missouri, 20-7
c Sugar Bowl champions, defeated Tennessee, 28-13
d National champions, lost to Oklahoma in Orange Bowl
e Orange Bowl, lost to Oklahoma, 20-6
f Peach Bowl, lost to Georgia, 17-16
g Liberty Bowl, lost to Tennessee, 7-3

MARYLAND FOOTBALL AWARDS

The Alvin L. Aubinoe Trophy to the unsung hero of the season.

1956 Al Wharton – Tackle
1957 Wilbur Main – Center
1958 Ted Kershner – Back
1959 Joe Gardi – Tackle
1960 Leroy Dietrich – Center
1961 Dick Barlund – End
1962 Murnis Banner – Halfback
1963 George Stem – Halfback
1964 John Kenny – End
1965 Charles Krahling – Center
1966 Bobby Collins – Back
1967 Pat Baker – Back
1968 Rick Carlson – End
1969 Paul E. Fitzpatrick – Back
1970 Robert J. MacBride – Tackle
1971 Jeff Shugars – Quarterback
1972 Ron Kecman – Center
1973 Ken Scott – Tackle
1974 Frank Russell – End

Anthony C. Nardo Memorial Trophy to the best football lineman of the year.

1950 Bob Ward – Guard
1951 Bob Ward – Guard
1952 William Maletzky – Guard
1953 Stan Jones – Tackle
1954 Bob Pellegrini – Guard
1955 Mike Sandusky – Tackle
1957 Don Healy – Tackle
1958 Fred Cole – Tackle
1959 Tom Gunderman – Guard
1960 Garry Collins – End
1961 Bill Kirchiro – Tackle
1962 Dave Crossan – Tackle
1964 Fred Joyce – Guard
1965 Dick Absher – End
1966 Dick Absher – End
1967 Jim Lavrusky – Linebacker
1968 Ron Pearson – End
1969 Peter Mattia – Tackle

Bob Beall-Tommy Marcos Trophy to the best football lineman of the year.

1970	Guy M. Roberts – End	1973	Randy White – Tackle
1971	Dennis O'Hara – End	1974	Randy White – Tackle
1972	Paul Vellano – Guard		

Jim Tatum Memorial Trophy to the outstanding tackle.

1959	Kurt Schwarz	1967	Tom Myslinski
1960	Tom Sakovich	1968	Tom Plevin
1961	Bill Kirchiro	1969	Peter Mattia
1962	Dave Crossan	1970	Peter Mattia
1963	Olaf Drozdov	1971	Guy Roberts
1964	Larry Bagranoff	1972	Paul Vellano
1965	Larry Bagranoff	1973	Randy White
1966	Tom Cichowski	1974	Randy White

The Teke Trophy to the student who during his four years at the University has rendered the greatest service to football.

1950	John Idzik – Back	1963	Bob Burton – Halfback
1951	Bob Ward – Guard	1964	Olaf Drozdov – Tackle
1952	Ed Fullerton – Back	1965	George Stem – Back
1953	Bernie Faloney – Back	1966	Dick Absher – End
1954	John Irvine – Center	1967	Lou Stickel – Back
1955	Bob Pellegrini – Center	1968	Billy Lovett – Fullback
1956	Mike Sandusky – Tackle	1969	Kenneth B. Dutton – Back
1957	Gene Alderton – Center	1970	Peter Mattia – Tackle
1958	Bob Rusevlyan – Back	1971	Tommy Miller – Back
1959	Kurt Schwarz – Tackle	1972	Don Ratliff – End
1960	Vincent Scott – End	1973	Paul Vellano – Guard
1961	Gary Collins – End	1974	Randy White–Tackle
1962	Tom Brown – Halfback		

SPECIAL TERRAPIN AWARDS

BEST OFFENSIVE BACK

1952	Chester Hanulak – Halfback
1953	Ralph Felton – Fullback
1954	Ron Waller – Halfback
1955	Ed Vereb – Halfback
1956	Fred Hamilton – Halfback
1957	Bob Rusevlyan – Quarterback
1958	Bob Rusevlyan – Quarterback
1959	Jim Joyce – Fullback
1960	Dale Betty – Quarterback
1961	Dick Shiner – Quarterback
1962	Tom Brown – Halfback
1963	Dick Shiner – Quarterback
1964	Tom Hickey – Tailback

BEST DEFENSIVE BACK

1952	Ed Fullerton – Halfback
1953	Dick Nolan – Halfback
1954	Joe Horning – Halfback
1955	Lynn Beightol – Quarterback
1956	Bob Rusevlyan – Quarterback
1957	Bob Layman – Halfback
1958	Jim Joyce – Fullback
1959	Dwayne Fletcher – Quarterback
1960	Jim Davidson – Quarterback
1961	Tom Brown – Halfback
1962	Joe Hrezo – Fullback
1963	Ernie Arizzi – Halfback
1964	Bob Sullivan – Halfback

1965	Walt Marciniak – Fullback
1966	Alan Pastrana – Quarterback
1967	Billy Lovett – Fullback
1968	Billy Lovett – Fullback
1969	Tom Miller – Fullback
1970	Art Seymore – Halfback
1971	Al Neville – Quarterback
1972	Bob Avellini – Quarterback
1973	Louis Carter – Tailback
1974	Louis Carter–Tailback

1965	Fred Cooper – Halfback
1966	Lou Stickel – Halfback
1967	Bob Colbert – Halfback
1968	Kenny Dutton – Halfback
1969	Tony Greene – Safety
1970	Tony Greene – Safety
1971	Larry Marshall – Halfback
1972	Bob Smith – Safety
1973	Harry Walters – Linebacker
1974	Harry Walters–Linebacker

BEST OFFENSIVE LINEMAN

1952	Tom Cosgrove – Center
1953	Marty Crytzer – End
1954	Jack Bowersox – Guard
1955	Russell Dennis – End
1956	Al Wharton – Tackle
1957	Tom Gunderman – Guard
1958	Fred Cole – Tackle
1959	Tom Gunderman – Guard
1960	Bob Hacker – Center
1961	Roger Shoals – Tackle
1962	Roger Shoals – Tackle
1963	Gene Feher – Center
1964	Joe Frattaroli – Guard
1965	Matt Arbutina – Tackle
1966	Tom Cichowski – Tackle
1967	Ron Pearson – Guard
1968	Bill Meister – Guard
1969	Bill Meister – Guard
1970	Pat Burke – Guard
1971	Tim Brannan
1972	Tim Brannan – Guard
1973	Bart Purvis – Guard
1974	Stan Rogers–Tackle

BEST DEFENSIVE LINEMAN

1952	John Alderton – End
1953	Bob Morgan – Tackle
1954	Tom McLuckie – Guard
1955	Mike Sandusky – Tackle
1956	Mike Sandusky – Tackle
1957	Rod Breedlove – Guard
1958	Ben Scotti – End
1959	Rod Breedlove – Guard
1960	Tom Sankovich – Tackle
1961	Dave Crossan – Tackle
1962	Walter Rock – Guard
1963	Joe Ferrante – Guard
1964	Olaf Drozdov – Tackle
1965	Larry Bagranoff – Tackle
1966	Jim Lavrusky – Linebacker
1967	Mike Grace – Guard
1968	Henry Gareis – End
1969	Peter Mattia – Tackle
1970	Guy Roberts – End
1971	Chris Cowdrey – End
1972	Paul Vellano – Guard
1973	Randy White – Tackle
1974	Randy White–Tackle

ACC INDIVIDUAL AWARDS

COACH OF THE YEAR

Jim Tatum 1953, 1955
Jerry Claiborne 1973

JACOBS BLOCKING TROPHY

Bob Pellegrini, center 1955
Ralph Sonntag, tackle 1969

PLAYER OF THE YEAR

Bernie Faloney, q'back 1953
Bob Pellegrini, center 1955
Randy White, tackle 1974

MARYLAND'S ALL-ACC PLAYERS

First Team

1953

Stan Jones, tackle
Jack Bowersox, guard
Bernie Faloney, back
Chet Hanulak, back

1954

Bill Walker, end
Dick Bielski, back
Ron Waller, back

1955

Bob Pellegrini, center
Mike Sandusky, tackle
Jack Davis, guard
Ed Vereb, back

1956

Mike Sandusky, tackle
Jack Davis, guard

1957

Ed Cooke, end
Rod Breedlove, guard

1960

Gary Collins, end

1961

Gary Collins, end
Bob Hacker, center

1962

Walter Rock, guard
Dick Shiner, quarterback
Tom Brown, back

1964

Jerry Fishman, guard

1965

Bob Sullivan, back (defense)

1966

Dick Absher, end (defense)

1969

Ralph Sonntag, tackle (offense)

1970

Guy Roberts, end (defense)

1971

Dan Bungori, end (offense)

1972

Paul Vellano, guard (defense)
Bob Smith, safety (defense)

1973

Randy White, tackle (defense)
Paul Vellano, guard (defense)
Bob Smith, safety (defense)
Louis Carter, tailback (offense)

1974

Randy White, tackle (defense)
Harry Walters, linebacker (defense)
Bob Smith, safety (defense)
Louis Carter, tailback (offense)
Stan Rogers, tackle (offense)
Steve Mike-Mayer, kicker (offense)

TERP LEADERS OVER THE YEARS
(Regular Season Games)

SCORING

97 Bob Shemonski – 1950
96 Lu Gambino – 1947
96 Ed Vereb – 1955
84 Louis Carter – 1973
79 Steve Mike-Mayer–1974
69 Steve Mike-Mayer – 1973
66 Ed Modzelewski – 1951
56 John Schultz–1974
55 Darryl Hill–1963
55 Steve Mike-Mayer – 1972
54 Kambiz Behbahani – 1971
54 Bernie Faloney – 1953
54 Dick Bielski – 1954
53 Ralph Felton – 1953
50 Billy Lovett – 1968

TOUCHDOWNS

16 Lu Gambino–1947
16 Bob Shemonski – 1950
16 Ed Vereb – 1955
14 Louis Carter – 1973
11 Ed Modzelewski – 1951
9 Bernie Faloney – 1954
9 John Schultz–1974
8 Dan Bungori – 1971
8 Jimmy Joyce – 1959
8 Darryl Hill – 1963
8 Billy Lovett – 1968

TOUCHDOWN RECEPTIONS

8 Dan Bungori – 1971
7 Billy Van Heusen – 1966
7 Darryl Hill – 1963
6 Don Ratliff – 1972
5 Walter White – 1973
4 Tom Brown – 1962
4 Gary Collins – 1959--60-61
4 Lloyd Colteryahn – 1952
4 Lou Weidensaul – 1951-52

INTERCEPTIONS

10 Bob Sullivan – 1965
8 Tom Brown – 1961
7 Bob Smith – 1972
6 Larry Marshall – 1971
6 Tom Brown – 1962
6 Bernie Faloney – 1953
6 Joe Horning – 1951

RUSHING PLAYS

224 Louis Carter–1974
221 Art Seymore – 1970
218 Louis Carter – 1973
217 Billy Lovett – 1968
182 Bo Hickey – 1964
169 Tommy Miller – 1969
156 Len Chiaverini – 1962
137 Jimmy Joyce – 1959
137 Billy Lovett – 1967
125 Lu Gambino – 1947
119 Louis Carter – 1972

TOTAL OFFENSE

1689 Bob Avellini–1974
1426 Dick Shiner – 1962
1395 Alan Pastrana – 1966
1386 Jack Scarbath – 1952
1265 Al Neville – 1971
1257 Bob Avellini – 1972
1186 Dick Shiner – 1963
1076 Tommy Mont – 1942
1042 Phil Petry – 1964
1022 Dick Shiner – 1961

YARDS PASSING

1658 Bob Avellini–1974
1499 Alan Pastrana – 1966
1324 Dick Shiner – 1962
1275 Al Neville – 1971
1251 Bob Avellini – 1972
1165 Dick Shiner – 1963
1149 Jack Scarbath – 1952
1076 Tommy Mont – 1942
1053 Alan Pastrana – 1968
921 Dick Shiner – 1961

MOST PASS COMPLETIONS

121 Dick Shiner – 1962
112 Bob Avellini–1974
108 Dick Shiner – 1963
107 Al Neville – 1971
102 Al Pastrana – 1966
98 Bob Avellini – 1972
82 Dale Betty – 1960
81 Al Pastrana – 1968
75 Jeff Shugars – 1970
73 Phil Petry – 1964

MOST YARDS PASS RECEPTIONS

593 Lloyd Colteryahn–1952

557	Tom Brown — 1962
536	Billy Van Heusen — 1966
516	Darryl Hill — 1963
515	Don Ratliff — 1972
499	Roland Merritt — 1969
490	Dan Bungori — 1971
472	Frank Russell — 1972
468	Frank Russell — 1973
462	Bobby Collins — 1965

MOST PASS RECEPTIONS

47	Tom Brown — 1962
43	Darryl Hill — 1963
39	Frank Russell — 1973
36	Don Ratliff — 1972
32	Dan Bungori — 1971
32	Dennis O'Hara — 1971
32	Lloyd Colteryahn — 1952
31	Frank Russell—1974
30	Frank Russell — 1972
30	Gary Collins — 1960-61
27	Walter White — 1973
27	Walter White—1974

MOST TOUCHDOWN PASSES

17	Alan Pastrana — 1966
12	Tommy Mont — 1942
10	Al Neville— 1971
10	Dick Shiner — 1963
10	Jack Scarbath — 1952
10	Vic Turyn — 1948
8	Jack Scarbath — 1951
7	Dick Shiner — 1961
7	Bob Avellini — 1972, '74

YARDS RUSHING

991	Louis Carter—1974
963	Billy Lovett — 1968
945	Art Seymore — 1970
904	Lu Gambino — 1947
894	Bo Hickey — 1964
834	Ed Modzelewski — 1951
801	Louis Carter — 1973
753	Chet Hanulak — 1953
642	Ed Vereb — 1955
629	Tom Miller — 1969
625	Ed Modzelewski — 1949

MARYLAND FOOTBALL RECORDS

SINGLE GAME – INDIVIDUAL

SCORING

Most Points Scored

31 by Bob Shemonski vs. Virginia Tech, 1950 (5 TD's, 1 PAT)

Most Touchdowns Scored

5 by Bob Shemonski vs. Virginia Tech, 1950

Most Points-After-Touchdown Scored

6 by Bob Dean vs. South Carolina, 1949
6 by Don Decker vs. West Virginia, 1951
6 by Vincent Scott vs. Virginia, 1960
6 by Steve Mike-Mayer vs. Duke, 1974

Most Touchdown Passes Caught

2 by Don Gleasner vs. Virginia, 1945
2 by Leroy Mortor vs. Michigan State, 1946
2 by Lu Gambino vs. West Virginia, 1947
2 by Elmer Wingate vs. George Washington, 1948
2 by Stan Karnash vs. George Washington, 1949
2 by Pete Augsburger vs. South Carolina, 1949
2 by Henry Fox vs. Georgetown, 1949
2 by Lloyd Colteryahn vs. LSU, 1952
2 by Bill Walker vs. Alabama, 1953
2 by Gary Collins vs. Clemson, 1959
2 by Billy Van Heusen vs. N. C. State, 1966
2 by Billy Van Heusen vs. Florida State, 1966
2 by Dan Bungori vs. Florida, 1971
2 by Walter White vs. Penn State, 1974

Most Touchdowns Responsibility (Run and Pass)

5 by Bob Shemonski vs. Virginia Tech, 1950

Most Field Goals Scored

3 by Vincent Scott vs. West Virginia, 1959
3 by Steve Mike-Mayer vs. Villanova, 1972
3 by Steve Mike-Mayer vs. Villanova, 1973
3 by Steve Mike-Mayer vs. Alabama, 1974
3 by Steve Mike-Mayer vs. Villanova, 1974

TOTAL OFFENSE

Most Net Yards Gained Rushing and Passing

312 by Bob Avellini vs Duke, 1972

Most Total Plays

46 by Al Neville vs. Penn State, 1971 (35 passes, 11 rushes)

Best Offensive Average (Minimum Four Plays, Rushing and Passing)

24.0 by Ernie Arizzi vs. Syracuse, 1961 (4 plays, 96 yards)

RUSHING

Most Yards Gained Rushing (Net)

213 by Louis Carter vs. Virginia, 1974 (29 carries)

Most Rushes

39 by Billy Lovett vs. North Carolina, 1968
39 by Billy Lovett vs. South Carolina, 1968

Best Rushing Average

24.0 by Ernie Arizzi vs. Syracuse, 1961 (4 carries)

Longest Scoring Run From Scrimmage
90 yards by Dick Burgee vs. Missouri, 1954

Longest Non-Scoring Run From Scrimmage
76 yards by Harry Bonk vs. North Carolina, 1948

PASSING

Most Yards Gained Passing
314 by Bob Avellini vs.Duke, 1972 (21 for 31)

Most Passes Attempted
35 by Jim Corcoran vs. Penn State, 1965 (completed 18)
35 by Jeff Shugars vs. Miami (Ohio), 1969 (completed 19)
35 by Al Neville vs. Penn State 1971 (completed 23)

Most Passes Completed
23 by Al Neville vs. Penn State, 1971 (attempted 35)

Best Completion Percentage (Minimum, 10 attempts)
.909 by Bob Avellini vs. Duke, 1974 (10 for 11)

Most Touchdown Passes Thrown
3 by Tommy Mont vs. Connecticut, 1942
3 by Vic Turyn vs. George Washington, 1948
3 by Stan Lavine vs. George Washington, 1949
3 by Jack Scarbath vs. West Virginia, 1951
3 by Jack Scarbath vs. LSU, 1952
3 by Dale Betty vs. North Carolina State, 1959
3 by Dale Betty vs. Clemson, 1959
3 by Dick Novak vs. West Virginia, 1959
3 by Dick Shiner vs. Penn State, 1961
3 by Alan Pastrana vs. North Carolina State, 1966

Most Passes Caught
10 by Darryl Hill vs. Clemson, 1963

Most Yards Gained By Pass Receptions
144 by Walter White vs. Penn State, 1974 (5 catches)

Longest Scoring Pass and Run
92 yards by Stan Lavine to Ed Bolton vs. S. Carolina, 1949 (pass 15 yds., run 77 yds.)

Longest Scoring Run After Pass
77 yards by Ed Bolton on pass from Stan Lavine vs. S. Carolina, 1949 (pass 15 yards)

Longest Non-Scoring Pass and Run
73 yards by Tommy Mont to Hubie Werner vs. Lakehurst, 1942 (pass 32 yds., run 41 yds.)

Longest Non-Scoring Run After Pass
41 yards by Hubie Werner vs. Lakehurst, 1942, on 32-yards pass from Tommy Mont

Longest Scoring Pass
40 yards by Dick Novak to Jim Davidson vs. West Virginia, 1959

Longest Non-Scoring Pass
50 yards by Alan Pastrana to Ralph Donofrio vs. Wake Forest, 1966

Most Passes Had Intercepted
4 by Dick Shiner vs. Navy, 1963
4 by Alan Pastrana vs. Clemson, 1966

Most Passes Intercepted
3 by Bob Shemonski vs. Georgia, 1951

3 by Tom Brown vs. Air Force, 1961
3 by Bob Sullivan vs. Navy, 1965
3 by Bob Smith vs. V.M.I., 1972

Most Yards Gained On Interception Runbacks

111 yards by Dick Lewis vs. North Carolina State, 1956

Longest Scoring Run Of Intercepted Pass

100 yards by Joe Horning vs. Missouri, 1951 (105 actual)
100 yards by Dickie Lewis vs. N. C. State, 1956 (103 actual)
100 yards by Tom Brown vs. Virginia, 1962

Longest Non-Scoring Run Of Intercepted Pass

89 yards by Kevin Benson vs. Virginia 1973

Longest Scoring Run Of Intercepted Pass By Opponent

93 yards by Walter Matson of Pennsylvania, 1941

OTHERS

Most Punts

11 by Greg Fries vs. Clemson, 1968, Syracuse, 1969

Most Total Yards Punting

510 by Bill Guckeyson vs. Syracuse, 1936

Best Punting Average

53 yards by Lynn Beightol vs. Oklahoma, 1956 Orange Bowl (3 punts)

Longest Punt With Roll

88 yards by John Fritsch vs. Miami, 1956

Longest Punt With Roll By Opponent

84 yards by Charlie Justice of North Carolina, 1948

Most Punts Returned

8 by Larry Marshall vs. Villanova, 1971 (141 yards)

Most Yards Gained Returning Punts

146 by Bob Shemonski vs. North Carolina State, 1950 (5 returns)

Longest Punt Return For Touchdown

100 yards by Frank Brady of Navy, 1951

Longest Punt Return For Touchdown by Opponent

100 yards by Frank Brady of Navy, 1951

Longest Non-Scoring Punt Return

67 yards by John McVicker vs. Syracuse, 1956

Most Punts Blocked

1 by several players

Most Kickoffs Returned

6 by Larry Marshall vs. Miami (Ohio), 1969 (129 yards)

Most Yards Returning Kickoffs

153 by Tom Brown vs. Miami, 1962 (5 returns)

Longest Kickoff Return For Touchdown

100 yards by Dick Novak and Dennis Condie vs. Virginia, 1960 (102 actual). Novak ret. to nine yard line, then lateraled to Condie who returned 91 yards.

100 yards by Kenny Ambrusko vs. Navy, 1964 (101 actual)

Longest Kickoff Return For Touchdown By Opponent

93 yards by Jim McPherson of North Carolina, 1926

Longest Non-Scoring Kickoff Return

76 yards by Howie Dare vs. Miami, 1957

Longest Scoring Run With Recovered Fumble

23 yards by Howie Dare vs. North Carolina State, 1954

Longest Non-Scoring Run With Recovered Fumble By Opponent

75 yards by Dave Russell of Washington and Lee, 1942

Most Opponents Fumbles Recovered

3 by Tom Gunderman vs. Miami, 1957

Longest Field Goal

54 yards by Steve Mike-Mayer vs. Villanova 1973

SINGLE GAME RECORDS – TEAM

SCORING

Highest Score

Maryland 80 – Washington College 0, 1927

Most Total Points Scored By Both Teams

90 in 1971; Maryland 27 Penn State 63

Largest Victory Margin

80-0 vs. Washington College, 1927

Largest Defeat Margin

0-76 vs. Navy, 1913

Most Touchdowns Scored

12 vs. Washington College, 1927

Most Points-After-Touchdown Scored

8 vs. Washington College, 1927
8 vs. Missouri, 1954
8 vs. Duke, 1974

Most Field Goals Scored

3 vs Villanova, 1972

Most Touchdowns Scored Passing

4 vs. George Washington, 1948 (3 by Vic Turyn, 1 by John Idzik)
4 vs. Navy, 1952 (2 by Jack Scarbath, 1 by Lloyd Colteryahn, 1 by Bernie Faloney)
4 vs. George Washington, 1954 (2 by Frank Tamburello, 1 by Charles Boxold, 1 by Lynn Beightol)
4 vs. Tulane 1973 (2 by Louis Carter, 1 by Ben Kinard, 1 by Al Neville)

Most Touchdowns Scored Passing By Opponents

4 by Wake Forest, 1958 (3 by Norm Snead, 1 by Charlie Parker)
4 by Virginia 1965 (by Bob Davis)
4 by Florida 1971 (by John Reaves)

Most Safeties Scored

2 vs. Delaware, 1947
2 vs. Georgetown, 1950
2 vs. Villanova, 1974

TOTAL OFFENSE

Most Total Yards Gained

602 vs. West Virginia, 1951 (523 rushing, 79 passing)

Fewest Total Yards Gained

29 vs. Syracuse, 1959

Most Total Plays

93 vs. North Carolina State 1973

RUSHING

Most Net Yards Gained Rushing
577 vs. Virginia Tech, 1950

Fewest Net Yards Gained Rushing
Minus 58 vs. Navy, 1965

Most Rushes
76 vs. Miami, 1958

Fewest Rushes
24 vs. North Carolina State, 1965

Best Average Per Rush
10.5 yards vs. Virginia Tech, 1950 (577 yards, 55 rushes)

Fewest Net Yards Gained Rushing By Opponents
Minus 21 by West Virginia, 1951
Minus 21 by UCLA, 1955

Most First Downs Rushing
24 vs. Washington and Lee, 1951

Fewest First Downs Rushing by Opponent
0 by Wake Forest 1973

Fewest First Downs Rushing
1 vs. Michigan State, 1944
1 vs. Syracuse, 1959

PASSING

Most Yards Gained Passing
336 vs. Penn State 1971 (27 for 40)

Fewest Yards Gained Passing
0 vs. Michigan State, 1944
0 vs. Vanderbilt, 1948
0 vs. Missouri, 1951

Most Passes Attempted
48 vs. South Carolina 1971 (23 completions for 210 yards)

Most Passes Completed
27 vs. Penn State 1971 (40 attempts for 336 yards)

Fewest Passes Completed
0 vs. Michigan State, 1944 (1 attempt)
0 vs. Vanderbilt, 1948 (12 attempts)
0 vs. Missouri, 1951 (3 attempts)

Fewest Passes Attempted
1 vs. Michigan State, 1944
1 vs. Wake Forest, 1969

Best Completion Percentage (Minimum 10 attempts)
.824 vs. Tulane 1973 (14 completions, 17 attempts)

Most Passes Intercepted
7 vs. Georgia, 1951

Most Passes Had Intercepted
6 by Pennsylvania, 1941

Most First Downs Passing
18 vs. Penn State 1971

Fewest First Downs Passing
0 – 13 times, last vs. Wake Forest, 1969

Most Passes Attempted By Opponents
57 by West Virginia, 1951 (19 completions)

Fewest Passes Completed by Opponents
0 by Syracuse, 1939 (5 attempts)
0 by Michigan State, 1944 (0 attempts)
0 by Delaware, 1948 (3 attempts)
0 by Boston University, 1952 (6 attempts)
0 by Kentucky, 1956 (3 attempts)

Fewest Yards Gained Passing By Opponents
Minus 1 by Clemson, 1956

OTHERS

Most Punts
14 vs. Virginia, 1937
14 vs. Western Maryland, 1940

Fewest Punts
1 vs. Washington and Lee, 1953
1 vs. Georgia, 1953
1 vs. Syracuse, 1955
1 vs. North Carolina State, 1954
1 vs. South Carolina, 1962

Most Total Yards Punting
510 vs. Syracuse, 1936 (10 punts)

Best Punting Average
51.7 yards vs. Washington and Lee, 1951 (155 yds., 3 punts)

Most Total First Downs
29 vs. Wake Forest, 1963

Fewest Total First Downs
1 vs. Michigan State, 1944

Fewest Total First Downs by Opponent
1 by Wake Forest 1973 (passing)

Most Fumbles
8 vs. Georgia, 1952 (lost 2)

Fewest Fumbles
0 vs. VMI, 1945
0 vs. Kentucky, 1954
0 vs. South Carolina, 1958
0 vs. South Carolina, 1959
0 vs. West Virginia, 1960
0 vs. Virginia, 1960
0 vs. Syracuse, 1972
0 vs. Duke, 1973

Most Fumbles Lost
6 vs. North Carolina, 1947

Most Fumbles By Opponents
8 by South Carolina, 1948
8 by Mississippi, 1953

Most Opponents Fumbles Recovered
5 vs. Missouri in Gator Bowl, Jan. 1, 1950
5 vs. West Virginia, 1950
5 vs. North Carolina, 1960

Most Penalties
18 vs. Virginia Tech, 1950

Most Yards Penalized
130 vs. Virginia Tech, 1948
130 vs. Virginia Tech, 1950

Fewest Penalties
0 vs. Duke, 1941

Most Penalties By Opponents
15 by Miami, 1957

Most Yards Opponents Penalized
135 by North Carolina, 1953

Fewest Penalties By Opponents
0 by Western Maryland, 1937
0 by Western Maryland, 1939
0 by Florida, 1939
0 by Washington and Lee, 1941
0 by William and Mary, 1945
0 by South Carolina, 1953

SEASON RECORDS – INDIVIDUAL

SCORING

Most Points Scored, Regular Season
97 by Bob Shemonski, 1950 (10 games)
96 by Lu Gambino, 1947 (10 games)
96 by Ed Vereb, 1955 (10 games)

Most Points Scored, One Season, Including Bowl Games
114 by Lu Gambino (96 in 1947 season plus 3 TD's in 1948 Gator Bowl)
102 by Ed Vereb (96 in 1955 season plus one TD in 1956 Orange Bowl)

Most Touchdowns Scored, Regular Season
16 by Lu Gambino, 1947 (10 games)
16 by Bob Shemonski, 1950 (10 games)
16 by Ed Vereb, 1955 (10 games)

Most Touchdowns Scored One Season, Including Bowl Games
19 by Lu Gambino (16 in 1947 season plus 3 in 1948 Gator Bowl)
17 by Ed Vereb (16 in 1955 season plus one in 1956 Orange Bowl)

Most Points-After-Touchdown Scored, All Games
41 by Don Decker (37 in 1951 season, 4 in 28-13 1952 Sugar Bowl victory over Tennessee, 55 attempts)

Most Touchdown Passes Caught
8 by Dan Bungori, 1971 in 11 games

Most Touchdowns Responsibility (Run and Pass)
21 by Alan Pastrana, 1966 (17 TD passes, 4TD's)

Most Field Goals
15 by Steve Mike-Mayer, 1974

Most Points by Kicking
79 by Steve Mike-Mayer, 1974

TOTAL OFFENSE

Most Yards Total Offense (Rushing and Passing)
1,689 by Bob Avellini, 1974, 11 games

Most Total Plays

314 by Dick Shiner, 1963, 10 games

RUSHING

Most Net Yards Rushing, Regular Season

991 by Louis Carter, 1974, 10 games
963 by Billy Lovett, 1968, 10 games
945 by Art Seymore, 1970, 10 games
904 by Lu Gambino, 1947, 10 games
894 by Bo Hickey, 1964, 10 games

Most Net Yards Rushing, Including Bowl Games

1,069 by Lu Gambino (includes 904 yards of 1947 season plus 165 yards on 22 carries in 1948 Gator Bowl)

1,056 by Louis Carter (includes 991 yards of 1974 season plus 65 yards on 22 carries in 1974 Liberty Bowl)

Most Rushes

224 by Louis Carter, 1974

Best Rushing Average

9.8 yards by Chet Hanulak, 1953

PASSING

Most Yards Gained Passing

1,648 by Bob Avellini, 1974 (112 completions in 189 attempts)

Most Passes Attempted

222 by Dick Shiner in 10 games, 1963 (completed 108)

Most Passes Completed

121 by Dick Shiner in 10 games, 1962 (203 attempts)

Best Completion Percentage

.621 by Dale Betty in 10 games, 1960 (completed 82 of 132)

Most Touchdown Passes Thrown

17 by Alan Pastrana, 1966, 10 games

Most Passes Caught

47 by Tom Brown in 10 games, 1962 (557 yards)

Most Yards Gained on Pass Receptions

593 by Lloyd Colteryahn, 1952 (32 receptions, 9 games)

Most Passes Had Intercepted

16 by Dick Shiner in 10 games, 1962

Most Passes Intercepted

10 by Bob Sullivan in 10 games, 1965 (Led nation)

Most Yards Returning Intercepted Passes

147 by Joe Horning, 1951 (6 interceptions in 9 games)

OTHERS

Most Punts

72 by Greg Fries, 1968 and 1969 (each 10 games)

Best Punting Average

43.7 by Bill Walker in 10 games, 1955 (15 punts). Walker added four punts in 1956 Orange Bowl for an 11-game average of 41.2, 19 punts.

Most Punts Returned

40 by Bob Smith in 11 games 1973 (420 yards)

Most Yards Gained on Punt Returns

420 by Bob Smith in 11 games 1973 (40 returns)

Best Punt Return Average (More Than Three Returns)

24.5 by Tom Brown on 8 returns, 1961

Most Kickoffs Returned

24 by Kenny Dutton, 1967 (454 yards)

Most Yards Gained on Kickoff Returns

587 by Larry Marshall on 22 returns, 1971

Best Kickoff Return Average (More Than Three)

44 yards by Howie Dare, 1957 (6 returns for 264 yards)

Best Point-After-Touchdown Average

1.000 by John Hannigan, 1961 (17 for 17)
1.000 by Bernardo Bramson, 1965 (15 for 15)

SEASON RECORDS – TEAM

SCORING

Most Points Scored

353 in 9 regular season games, 1951
381 in 10 games, including 1951 season plus '52 Sugar Bowl

Fewest Points Scored (Full Season)

39 in 9 games, 1940

Most Points Scored By Opponents

299 in 10 games, 1968

Fewest Points Scored By Opponents

31 in 10 regular season games, 1953
38 in 11 games, 1953 season plus 1954 Orange Bowl

Most Touchdowns Scored

52 in 9 regular-season games, 1951
56 in 10 games, 1951 season plus 1952 Sugar Bowl

Most Field Goals Scored

15 in 11 games, 1974

Most Points-After-Touchdown Scored

38 in 9 regular-season games, 1951
42 in 10 games, 1951 season plus 1952 Sugar Bowl

TOTAL OFFENSE

Most Yards Gained Rushing and Passing

4,484 in 11 games, 1974 (2,507 rushing, 1,977 passing)

Most Yards Gained Rushing and Passing By Opponents

4,192 in 10 games, 1968 (2,272 rushing, 1,920 passing)

Fewest Yards Gained Rushing and Passing By Opponents

1,691 in 10 games, 1955 (761 yards rushing, 930 passing)
Oklahoma gained 202 yards rushing, 53 passing, in 1956 Orange Bowl for 11-game total of 1,946 yards

RUSHING

Most Yards Gained Rushing

2,921 in 9 regular-season games, 1951

3,210 in 10 games, 1951 season plus 28-13 victory over Tennessee in 1952 Sugar Bowl

Most Rushing Plays

601 in 1973

Most Yards Gained Rushing By Opponents

2,371 in 9 games, 1967

PASSING

Most Yards Gained Passing

1,982 in 11 games. 1972

Most Passes Attempted

287 in 11 games, 1972 (159 completions)

Most Passes Completed

159 in 11 games, 1972 (287 attempts)

Best Passing Percentage

.593 in 11 games 1973 (118 of 199)

Most Yards Gained Passing By Opponents

1,920 in 10 games, 1968

Fewest Yards Gained Passing By Opponents

731 in 10 games, 1957 (Note: early records incomplete)

Best Passing Percentage By Opponents

.527 in 9 games, 1967 (77 completions, 146 attempts)

Most Pass Interceptions

34 in 9 games, 1951

38 in 10 games, including the 28-13 victory over Tennessee in the Sugar Bowl, Jan. 1, 1952

Most Pass Interceptions By Opponents

23 in 10 games, 1948

OTHERS

Most Punts

79 in 11 games, 1970

Most Yards All Punts

2,832 in 10 games, 1969 (73 punts); 3180 in 11 games, 1970

Best Punting Average

42.6 in 11 games, 1974

Most Punts By Opponents

87 in 11 games, 1973

Most First Downs

210 in 11 games, 1972

210 in 11 games, 1974

Most First Downs By Opponents

222 in 10 games, 1968

Most Fumbles

44 in 10 games, 1950 (Lost 22)

Most Opponents Fumbles

40 in 10 games, 1960 (Maryland recovered 19)

40 in 11 games, 1971 (Maryland recovered 22)

Fewest Fumbles

17 in 10 games, 1960 (Lost 7)

Most Penalties

78 in 11 games, 1953 (492.5 yards)

Most Yardage Lost By Penalties

757 in 11 games, 1972

Best Seasons

1951–Won 9 Lost 0 during regular season, defeated Tennessee 28-13 in 1952 Sugar Bowl for 10-0 record

1953–Won 10 Lost 0 during 1954 regular season, lost to Oklahoma 7-0 in 1954 Orange Bowl for 10-1 record

1955–Won 10 Lost 0 during regular season, lost to Oklahoma 20-6 in 1956 Orange Bowl for 10-1 record

Worst Season

1967–Won 0 Lost 9

CAREER RECORDS – INDIVIDUAL

SCORING

Most Points Scored Regular Season

203 by Steve Mike-Mayer in 33 games, 1972-74 (37 FG & 92 PAT)

Most Points Scored All Games

216 by Steve Mike-Mayer in 35 games, 1972-74 (41 FG & 93 PAT) includes two bowl games

Most Touchdowns Scored, All Games

27 by Louis Carter in 35 games, 1972-74

Most Points-After-Touchdown Scored

91 by Steve Mike-Mayer in 33 games, 1972-74 (103 attempted)

Most Touchdown Passes Caught

12 by Gary Collins, 1959-60-61 (30 games)

Most Touchdowns Responsibility, Run And Pass

35 by Jack Scarbath, 1950-51-52

Most Field Goals

37 by Steve Mike-Mayer in 33 games, 1972-74

Most Points By Placekicker

203 by Steve Mike-Mayer in 33 games, 1972-74 (37 FG & 92 PAT)

Most Consecutive Points-After Touchdown Scored

29 by Steve Mike-Mayer, 1974

TOTAL OFFENSE

Most Net Yards Gained Rushing and Passing

3,634 by Dick Shiner, 1961-63, 30 games

Most Total Plays, Rushing and Passing

790 by Dick Shiner, 1961-63, 30 games (avg. gain 3.0 yards)

RUSHING

Most Net Yards Gained Rushing, Regular Season

2,266 by Louis Carter in 30 games, 1972-74

Most Net Yards Gained Rushing, All Games

2,461 by Louis Carter in 32 games, 1972-74 (includes two bowl games)

Most Rushes

590 by Louis Carter in 30 games, 1972-74

Best Rushing Average, Regular Season Games

8.1 yards by Chet Hanulak, 28 games, 1951-53 (1,544 yards, 190 carries)

Best Rushing Average, All Games

7.9 yards by Chet Hanulak, 30 games including 35 yards on 4 carries in 1952 Sugar Bowl and 39 yards on 12 carries in 1954 Orange Bowl

PASSING

Most Yards Gained Passing

3,410 by Dick Shiner, 30 games, 1961-63

Most Passes Attempted

536 by Dick Shiner, 30 games, 1961-63

Most Passes Completed

287 by Dick Shiner, 30 games, 1961-63

Best Completion Percentage

.586 by Bob Avellini, 1972-74 (231 of 394)

Most Touchdown Passes Thrown, Regular Season

23 by Alan Pastrana, 20 games, 1966 and 1968

Most Passes Caught, Regular Season

100 by Frank Russell in 33 games, 1972-74

Most Yards Gained By Pass Receptions

1,346 by Frank Russell in 33 games, 1972-74

Most Passes Intercepted

17 by Tom Brown, 30 games, 1960–62

YEAR BY YEAR RECORDS

MARYLAND AGGIES

1892 (0-3-0)

0	St. Johns	50
0	Johns Hop.	62
0	Episcopal Hi.	16

1893 (6-0-0)

36	Eastern Hi.	0
10	Central Hi.	0
18	Balt. City Col.	0
6	St. Johns Col.	0
18	W. Md. Col.	10
16	Orient Ath. Col.	6

1894 (3-3-0)

52	W. Md. Col.	0
12	Wash. Col.	0
6	St. Johns	22
6	Georgetown	4
0	Col. Ath. Cl.	26
0	Mt. St. Marys	24

1895 – No Team
No Games

1896 (5-0-2)

0	Gallaudet	0
32	Business Hi.	0
10	Central Hi.	6
18	Alexandria Hi.	0
20	Bethel Mil. Ac.	10
16	West. Md.	6
0	U. of Md.	0

1897 (2-4-0)

24	Central Hi.	6
4	Eastern Hi.	0
0	J. Hopkins	30
4	St. Johns	6
6	Gallaudet	16
0	Balt. Med. Col.	10

1898 (2-5-0)

5	Columbian U.	17
0	West. Md.	32
36	Eastern Hi.	0
0	Gallaudet	33
0	Johns Hopkins	16
0	Episcopal Hi.	37
27	Rock Hill Col.	0

1899 (1-4-0)

0	West. Md.	21
26	Eastern Hi.	0
0	Johns Hopkins	40
0	Delaware Col.	34
0	St. Johns	62

1900 (3-4-1)

0	Western Hi.	0
0	Gib. Ath. Cl.	17
0	Georgetown Prep	5
6	Episcopal Hi.	34
5	Gonzaga Hi.	11
15	Georgetown Prep	0
21	Gonzaga	0
21	Char. Hall. Ac.	0

1901 (1-7-0)

6	Del. Col.	24
10	Gallaudet Re.	11
0	Johns Hopkins	6
6	Rock Hill Col.	11
0	Central Hi.	11
27	U.S. Marines	0
0	Wal'k Ath. Cl.	36
0	West. Md.	30

1902 (2-5-2)

0	Georgetown	27
5	Mt. St. Jos.	0
11	Columbian U.	10
0	Wash. Col.	0
0	Mt. St. Marys	5
6	West. Md.	26
0	U. of Md.	5
0	Johns Hopkins	17
0	Del. Col.	0

1903 (5-4-1)

0	Georgetown	28
0	St. Johns	18
28	Wash. Col.	0
27	Tech. Hi.	0
0	Mt. St. Marys	2
6	West. Md.	0
11	U. of Md.	0
0	Dela. Col.	16
6	Columbian U.	0

1904 (2-4-2)

0	Georgetown	22
0	Ran. Macon	0
0	Ftress Monroe	0
11	Mt. St. Marys	6
0	West. Md.	5
22	Gallaudet	5
0	U. of Md.	6
0	Dela. Col.	18

1905 (6-4-0)

20	Balt. Poly In.	0
16	Gallaudet	0
0	West. Md.	10
0	Navy	17
17	Wm. & Mary	0
28	Mt. St. Josephs	0
27	St. Johns	5
0	Wash. Col.	17
23	U. of Md.	5
0	Dela. Col.	12

1906 (5-3-0)

5	Tech. Hi.	0
22	Balt. City Col.	0
0	Navy	12
0	Georgetown	28
0	Mt. Wash. Cl.	29
20	St. Johns	4
16	Rock Hill Col.	0
35	Wash. Col.	0

1907 (3-6-0)

13	Tech. High	0
0	Georgetown	10
5	Richmond Col.	11
0	Navy	12
6	Mt. St. Marys	12
10	Geo. Washington	0
10	Wash. Col.	5
0	St. Johns	16
0	Gallaudet	5

1908 (2-7-2)

0	Richmond Col.	22
0	Johns Hopkins	10
0	Navy	57
5	Gallaudet	0
0	Fred'bg Col.	10
12	Balto. Poly	6
0	St. Johns	31
0	Wash. Col.	11
0	Geo. Washington	57

1909 (2-4-0)

0	Richmond Col.	12
0	Johns Hopkins	9
5	Rock Hill	0
0	George Washington	26
0	N. C. State	31
14	Gallaudet	12

1910 (4-3-1)

12	Central High	0
20	Richmond Col.	0
11	Johns Hopkins	11
21	Catholic U.	0
11	George Washington	0
0	V.M.I.	8
0	St. Johns	6
3	West. Md.	17

1911 (3-3-2)

0	Richmond	0
5	Fred'bg Col.	0
3	Johns Hopkins	6
6	Catholic U.	6
0	St. Johns	27
5	Wash. Col.	17
6	West. Md.	0
6	Gallaudet	2

1912 (5-1-1)

46	Richmond Col.	0
58	U. of Md.	0
13	Johns Hopkins	0
0	St. Johns	27
13	Gallaudet	6
17	West. Md.	7
13	Penn. Mil. Col.	13

1913 (6-3-0)

27	Balto City	10
45	Richmond Col.	0
26	Johns Hopkins	0
46	West. Md.	0
0	Navy	76
13	St. Johns	0
26	Wash. Col.	0
0	Gallaudet	13
7	Penn. Mil.	27

1914 (5-3-0)

0	Balto. Poly	6
6	Catholic U.	0
13	West. Md.	20
14	Johns Hopkins	0
10	St. Johns	0

3	Wash. Col.	0
0	Gallaudet	23
26	Penn. Mil.	0

1915 (6-3-0)

31	Balto Poly	0
0	Haverford	7
0	Catholic U.	16
10	Gallaudet	3
14	Penn Mil.	13
27	St. Johns	14
28	Wash. Col.	13
51	West. Md.	0
0	Johns Hopkins	3

MARYLAND STATE

1916 (6-2-0)

6	Dickinson	0
7	Navy	14
15	V.M.I.	9
6	Haverford	7
31	St. Johns	6
10	N.Y.U.	7
13	Catholic U.	9
54	Johns Hopkins	0

1917 (4-3-1)

20	Dela. Col.	0
0	Navy	62
14	V.M.I.	14
29	Wake Forest	13
6	N. C. State	10
13	St. Johns	3
0	Penn. State	57
7	Johns Hopkins	0

1918 (4-1-1)

6	American U.	13
7	V.M.I.	6
19	West. Md.	0
6	New York U.	2
19	St. Johns	14
0	Johns Hopkins	0

1919 (5-4-0)

6	Swarthmore	10
13	Virginia	0
0	West Va.	27
0	Va. Poly	6
0	Yale	31
27	St. Johns	0
13	Catholic U.	0
20	West. Md.	0
14	Johns Hopkins	0

UNIVERSITY OF MARYLAND

1920 (7-2-0)

54	Randolph Macon	0
0	Rutgers	6
0	Princeton	35
14	Catholic U.	0
27	Wash. Col.	0
7	Va. Poly	0
13	North Carolina	0
10	Syracuse	7
24	Johns Hopkins	7

1921 (3-5-1)

3	Rutgers	0
0	Syracuse	42
3	St. Johns	7
10	Va. Poly	7
7	North Carolina	16
0	Yale	28
16	Catholic U.	0
0	Carnegie Tech.	21
6	N. C. State	6

1922 (4-5-1)

7	Third Army	0
0	Richmond	0
0	Pennsylvania	12
0	Princeton	26
3	North Carolina	27
0	Va. Poly	21
3	Yale	45
3	Johns Hopkins	0
54	Catholic U.	0
7	N. C. State	6

1923 (7-2-1)

53	Randolph Macon	0
3	Pennsylvania	0
23	Richmond	0
7	Va. Poly	16
14	North Carolina	0
26	St. Johns	0
14	Yale	16
26	N. C. State	12
40	Catholic U.	6
6	Johns Hopkins	6

1924 (3-3-3)

23	Wash. Col.	0
7	Wash. & Lee	19
38	Richmond	0
0	Va. Poly	12
6	North Carolina	0
0	Catholic U.	0
0	Yale	47
0	N. C. State	0
0	Johns Hopkins	0

1925 (2-5-1)

13	Wash. Col.	0
16	Rutgers	0
0	Va. Poly	3
0	Virginia	6
0	North Carolina	16
14	Yale	43
3	Washington & Lee	7
7	Johns Hopkins	7

1926 (5-4-1)

63	Wash. Col.	0
0	South Carolina	12
0	Chicago	21
8	Va. Poly	24
14	North Carolina	6
38	Gallaudet	7
15	Yale	0
6	Virginia	6
0	W. & L.	3
17	Johns Hopkins	14

1927 (4-7-0)

80	Wash. Col.	0
26	South Carolina	0
6	North Carolina	7
13	Va. Poly	7
10	V.M.I.	6
6	W. & L.	13
6	Yale	30
0	Virginia	21
20	Vanderbilt	39
13	Johns Hopkins	14
6	Florida	7

1928 (6-3-1)

31	Wash. Col.	0
19	North Carolina	26
7	South Carolina	21
13	West. Md.	6
0	V.M.I.	0
6	Va. Poly	9
6	Yale	0
18	Virginia	2
6	W. & L.	0
26	Johns Hopkins	6

1929 (4-4-2)

34	Wash. Col.	7
0	North Carolina	43
6	South Carolina	26
13	Gallaudet	6
6	V.M.I.	7
13	Virginia	13
13	Yale	13
24	Va. Poly	0
39	Johns Hopkins	6
0	West. Md.	12

1930 (7-5-0)

60	Wash. Col.	6
13	Yale	40
21	North Carolina	28
21	St. Johns	13
20	V.M.I.	0
14	Virginia	6
41	W. & L.	7
13	V. Poly	7
0	Navy	6
21	Johns Hopkins	0
7	Vanderbilt	22
0	West. Md.	7

1931 (8-1-1)

13	Wash. Col.	0
7	Virginia	6
6	Navy	0
6	Kentucky	6
41	V.M.I.	20
20	Va. Poly	0
12	Vanderbilt	39
13	W. & L.	7
35	Johns Hopkins	14
41	West. Md.	6

1932 (5-6-0)

63	Wash. Col.	0
6	Virginia	7
0	Va. Poly	23
0	Duke	34
24	St. Johns	7
12	V.M.I.	7
0	Vanderbilt	13
7	Navy	28
6	W. & L.	0
23	Johns Hopkins	0
7	West. Md.	39

1933 (3-7-0)

20	St. Johns	0
0	Va. Poly	14
0	Tulane	20
13	V.M.I.	19
7	West Md.	13
0	Virginia	6
7	Duke	38
27	Johns Hopkins	7
33	W. & L.	13
0	Florida	19

1934 (7-3-0)

13	St. Johns	0
0	W. & L.	7
13	Navy	16
14	Va. Poly	9
21	Florida	0

20	Virginia	0
23	V.M.I.	0
14	Indiana	17
6	Georgetown	0
19	Johns Hopkins	0

1935 (7-2-2)

39	St. Johns	6
7	Va. Poly	0
0	North Carolina	33
6	V.M.I.	0
20	Florida	6
14	Virginia	7
7	Indiana	13
0	W. & L.	0
12	Georgetown	6
0	Syracuse	0
22	West. Md.	7

1936 (6-5-0)

20	St. Johns	0
6	Va. Poly	0
0	North Carolina	14
21	Virginia	0
12	Richmond	0
20	Syracuse	0
6	Florida	7
7	V.M.I.	13
6	Georgetown	7
19	W. & L.	6
0	West. Md.	12

1937 (8-2-0)

28	St. Johns	0
21	Pennsylvania	28
6	West. Md.	0
3	Virginia	0
13	Syracuse	0
13	Florida	7
9	V.M.I.	7
14	Penn State	21
12	Georgetown	2
8	W. & L.	0

1938 (2-7-0)

6	Richmond	19
0	Penn State	33
0	Syracuse	53
14	West. Md.	8
19	Virginia	27
14	V.M.I.	47
7	Florida	21
7	Georgetown	14
19	W. & L.	13

1939 (2-7-0)

26	Hamp.-Syd.	0
12	West. Md.	0
7	Virginia	12
12	Rutgers	25
0	Florida	14
0	Georgetown	20
0	Penn State	12
0	V.M.I.	13
7	Syracuse	10

1940 (2-6-1)

6	Hamp.-Syd.	7
0	Pennsylvania	51
6	Virginia	19
0	Florida	19
6	West. Md.	0
0	Georgetown	41
0	V.M.I.	20
14	Rutgers	7
7	W. & L.	7

1941 (3-5-1)

18	Hamp.-Syd.	0
6	West. Md.	6
0	Duke	50
13	Florida	12
6	Pennsylvania	55
0	Georgetown	26
0	Rutgers	20
0	V.M.I.	27
6	W. & L.	0

1942 (7-2-0)

34	Connecticut	0
14	Lake NAS	0
27	Rutgers	13
0	V.M.I.	29
51	West. Md.	0
13	Florida	0
0	Duke	42
27	Virginia	12
32	W. & L.	28

1943 (4-5-0)

7	Curtis B. CG	13
13	Wake Forest	7
19	Rich. AAB	6
2	West. Va.	6
0	Penn State	45
43	Greenv. AAB	18
0	Virginia	39
0	Bainbridge	46
21	V.M.I.	14

1944 (1-7-1)

0 Hamp.-Syd. 12
0 Wake Forest 39
6 West. Va. 6
0 Mich. State 8
6 Florida 14
7 Virginia 18
0 Mich. State 33
19 Penn State 34
8 V.M.I. 6

1945 (6-2-1)

60 Guilford Col. 6
21 Richmond 0
22 Merch. M.A. 6
13 Va. Poly 21
13 West Va. 13
14 W. & M. 33
38 V.M.I. 0
19 Virginia 13
19 South Carolina 13

1946 (3-6-0)

54 Bainbridge 0
7 Richmond 37
0 North Carolina 33
6 Va. Poly 0
7 W. & M. 41
17 South Carolina 21
24 W. & L. 7
14 Mich. State 26
7 N. C. State 28

1947 (7-2-2)

19 South Carolina 13
43 Delaware 19
18 Richmond 6
7 Duke 19
21 Va. Poly 19
27 West Va. 0
32 Duquesne 0
0 North Carolina 19
20 Vanderbilt 6
0 N. C. State 0
(Gator Bowl, Jan. 1, 1948)
20 Georgia 20

1948 (6-4-0)

19 Richmond 0
21 Delaware 0
28 Va. Poly 0
12 Duke 13
47 George Washington 0
27 Miami 13
19 South Carolina 7
20 North Carolina 49
0 Vanderbilt 34
14 West Va. 16

1949 (9-1-0)

34 Va. Poly 7
33 Georgetown 7
7 Mich. State 14
14 N. C. State 6
44 South Carolina 7
40 George Washington 14
14 Boston U. 13
47 West Va. 7
13 Miami 0
(Gator Bowl, Jan. 1, 1950)
20 Missouri 7

1950 (7-2-1)

7 Georgia 27
35 Navy 21
34 Mich. State 7
25 Georgetown 14
13 N. C. State 16
26 Duke 14
23 George Washington 7
7 North Carolina 7
41 West Va. 0
63 V.P.I. 7

1951 (10-0-0)

54 W. & L. 14
33 George Washington 6
43 Georgia 7
14 North Carolina 7
27 L.S.U. 0
35 Missouri 0
40 Navy 21
53 N. C. State 0
54 West Va. 7
(Sugar Bowl, Jan. 1, 1952)
28 Tennessee 13

1952 (7-2-0)

13 Missouri 10
13 Auburn 7
28 Clemson 0
37 Georgia 0
38 Navy 7
34 L.S.U. 6
34 Boston U. 7
14 Mississippi 21
7 Alabama 27

1953 (10-1-0)
National Champions
Co-Champions, ACC

20 Missouri 6
52 W. & L. 0
20 Clemson 0
40 Georgia 13
26 North Carolina 0
30 Miami (Fla.) 0

24	South Carolina	6
27	George Washington	6
38	Mississippi	0
21	Alabama	0
*0	Oklahoma	7
	*(Orange Bowl)	

1954 (7-2-1)

20	Kentucky	0
7	U.C.L.A.	12
13	Wake Forest	13
33	North Carolina	0
7	Miami (Fla.)	9
20	South Carolina	0
42	N. C. State	14
16	Clemson	0
48	George Washington	6
74	Missouri	13

1955 (10-1-0)
Co-Champions ACC

13	Missouri	12
7	U.C.L.A.	0
20	Baylor	6
28	Wake Forest	7
25	North Carolina	7
34	Syracuse	13
27	South Carolina	0
13	L.S.U.	0
25	Clemson	12
19	George Washington	0
*6	Oklahoma	20
	*(Orange Bowl)	

1956 (2-7-1)

12	Syracuse	26
6	Wake Forest	0
0	Baylor	14
6	Miami (Fla)	13
6	North Carolina	34
7	Tennessee	34
0	Kentucky	14
6	Clemson	6
0	South Carolina	13
25	N. C. State	14

1957 (5-5-0)

13	Texas A&M	21
13	N. C. State	48
0	Duke	14
27	Wake Forest	0
21	North Carolina	7
0	Tennessee	16
10	South Carolina	6
7	Clemson	26
16	Miami (Fla.)	6
12	Virginia	0

1958 (4-6-0)

0	Wake Forest	34
21	N. C. State	6
0	Clemson	8
10	Texas A&M	14
0	North Carolina	27
7	Auburn	20
10	South Carolina	6
14	Navy	40
26	Miami (Fla.)	14
44	Virginia	6

1959 (5-5-0)

27	West Va.	7
0	Texas	26
0	Syracuse	29
7	Wake Forest	10
14	North Carolina	7
6	South Carolina	22
14	Navy	22
28	Clemson	25
55	Virginia	12
33	N. C. State	28

1960 (6-4-0)

31	West Va.	8
0	Texas	34
7	Duke	20
10	N. C. State	13
19	Clemson	17
14	Wake Forest	13
15	South Carolina	0
9	Penn State	28
22	North Carolina	19
44	Virginia	12

1961 (7-3-0)

14	SMU	6
24	Clemson	21
22	Syracuse	21
8	North Carolina	14
21	Air Force	0
10	South Carolina	20
21	Penn State	17
10	N. C. State	7
10	Wake Forest	7
16	Virginia	28

1962 (6-4-0)

7	SMU	0
13	Wake Forest	2
14	N. C. State	6
31	North Carolina	13
24	Miami	28
13	South Carolina	11
7	Penn State	23
7	Duke	10
14	Clemson	17
40	Virginia	18

1963 (3-7-0)

14	N. C. State	36
13	South Carolina	21
12	Duke	30
7	North Carolina	14
21	Air Force	14
32	Wake Forest	0
15	Penn State	17
7	Navy	42
6	Clemson	21
21	Virginia	6

1964 (5-5)

3	Oklahoma	13
24	South Carolina	6
13	N. C. State	14
17	Duke	24
10	North Carolina	9
17	Wake Forest	21
9	Penn State	17
27	Navy	22
34	Clemson	0
10	Virginia	0

1965 (4-6)

24	Ohio U.	7
7	Syracuse	24
10	Wake Forest	7
10	North Carolina	12
7	N. C. State	29
27	South Carolina	14
7	Navy	19
6	Clemson	0
27	Virginia	33
7	Penn State	19

1966 (4-6)

7	Penn State	15
34	Wake Forest	7
7	Syracuse	34
21	Duke	19
28	West Va.	9
14	South Carolina	2
21	N. C. State	24
10	Clemson	14
17	Virginia	41
21	Florida State	45

1967 (0-9)

0	Oklahoma	35
3	Syracuse	7
9	N. C. State	31
0	North Carolina	14
0	South Carolina	31
3	Penn State	38
7	Clemson	28
17	Wake Forest	35
7	Virginia	12

1968 (2-8)

14	Florida St.	24
14	Syracuse	32
28	Duke	30
33	North Carolina	24
21	South Carolina	19
11	N. C. State	31
14	Wake Forest	38
0	Clemson	16
13	Penn State	57
23	Virginia	28

1969 (3-7)

7	West Virginia	31
7	N. C. State	24
19	Wake Forest	14
9	Syracuse	20
20	Duke	7
0	South Carolina	17
0	Clemson	40
21	Miami (Ohio)	34
0	Penn State	48
17	Virginia	14

1970 (2-9)

3	Villanova	21
12	Duke	13
20	North Carolina	53
11	Miami	18
7	Syracuse	23
21	South Carolina	15
0	N. C. State	6
11	Clemson	24
0	Penn State	34
17	Virginia	14
10	West Virginia	20

1971 (2-9)

13	Villanova	28
35	N.C. State	7
14	North Carolina	35
14	Wake Forest	18
13	Syracuse	21
6	South Carolina	35
23	Florida	27
38	V.M.I.	0
27	Penn State	63
14	Clemson	20
27	Virginia	29

1972 (5-5-1)

24	N.C. State	24
26	North Carolina	31
28	V.M.I.	16
12	Syracuse	16
23	Wake Forest	0

37	Villanova	7
14	Duke	20
24	Virginia	23
16	Penn State	46
31	Clemson	6
8	Miami (Fla.)	28

1973 (8-4)

13	West Virginia	20
23	North Carolina	3
31	Villanova	3
38	Syracuse	0
22	N.C. State	24
37	Wake Forest	0
30	Duke	10
22	Penn State	42
33	Virginia	0
28	Clemson	13
42	Tulane	9
*16	Georgia	17

*Peach Bowl

1974 (7-3)

ACC Champions

16	Alabama	21
10	Florida	17
24	North Carolina	12
31	Syracuse	0
41	Clemson	0
47	Wake Forest	0
20	North Carolina State	10
17	Penn State	24
41	Villanova	0
56	Duke	13
10	Virginia	0
*3	Tennessee	7

*Liberty Bowl

FOOTBALL LETTERMEN, 1892-1974

(The author has made every effort to make the following list of lettermen—the first ever published for Maryland—as accurate and complete as possible. However, records of some years are questionable, and could be in error. Any corrections, additions, or deletions should be reported to the Maryland sports information office.)

"A"

Abbott, Robert 1971
Absher, Dick 1964, '65, '66
Adams, Chester 1908
Adams, Donald 1925, '26, '27
Adams, Ron 1963, '64
Aitcheson, Leither 1917
Aitcheson, Whitney 1913, '14
Albarano, Ralph 1937, '38, '39
Albrecht, George 1952, '53, '54
Albrittain, Lemeul 1902, '03
Alderton, Gene 1955, '56, '57
Alderton, John 1950, '51, '52
Alexander, Richard 1941
Alkire, John 1973, '74
Ambrusko, Ken 1962, '64, '65
Andorka, Bill 1934
Andrews, Olin 1908, '09, '10
Andrus, Robert 1946
Arbutina, Matt 1963, '64, '65
Arizzi, Ernie 1961, '62, '63
Armsworthy, Frank 1950
Athey, Ronald 1955, '56
Augsburger, Pete 1948, '49, '50
Avellini, Bob 1972, '73, '74
Axt, R.W. (Dutch) 1915, '16, '17

"B"

Bach, Billy 1966
Bafford, Harold 1925, '26, '27
Bagranoff, Larry 1963, '64, '65
Baierl, Ralph 1953, '54
Bailey, Caleb (Zeke) 1918, '19, '20, '21, '22
Baker, Charles 1906
Baker, Pat 1965, '66, '67
Banner, Murnis 1960, '61, '62
Bannon, J.G. 1892, '93, '94
Barkalow, Gerald 1945
Barlund, Dick 1959, '60, '61
Barnes, George 1941, '42, '45
Barnes, Hank 1969, '70, '71
Baroni, John 1947, '48
Barritt, Ed 1952
Bartlett, W.D. 1923
Bates, Duane 1944
Battaglia, Sam 1967
Bauer, J.W. 1908
Beamer, Francis 1938, '39
Beardsley, Al 1956, '58
Beatty, Bill 1924, '25
Becker, Ed 1958
Bednar, Ray 1970, '71, '72
Behbahani, Kambiz 1971
Behr, Sam 1945, '47
Behrmann, Joe 1957, '58
Beightol, Lynn 1951, '53, '54, '55
Benson, Kevin 1972, '73, '74
Bielski, Dick 1952, '53, '54
Bell, Fred 1896, '97
Bell, Karl 1965
Benner, Willis 1932, '33
Bennett, Gordon 1960
Berger, Louis (Bosey) 1930, '31
Bernardo, Ralph 1943
Berry, Harold 1940, '41
Besley, Kirk 1922, '24, '25
Betty, Dale 1958, '59, '60
Betz, Theodore 1948, '49, '50
Bilancioni, Bert 1965
Binder, Paul 1910
Birkland, John 1934, '35, '36
Bishop, Randolph 1944, '46
Bissell, John 1945
Bittner, Dick 1955
Blackburn, Ray 1953, '54
Blackistone, Wade 1894
Blandford, James 1897, '98
Bloomingdale, Alan 1973, '74
Bobenko, Alex 1943
Boeri, Walter 1951, '52
Boinis, John 1962
Boinis, Pete 1958, '59, '60
Bolton, Ed 1949, '50
Bonk, Harry 1945, '46, '47, '48
Bonnet, Arthur 1924, '25
Boothe, Dan 1942
Bosley, John 1905
Bosley, Lester (Sally) 1918, '19, '20, '21
Bovic, Charles 1902
Bouscaren, William 1897
Bowersox, Jack 1953, '54
Bowland, Bill 1904, '05, '06
Bowland, Jay 1911, '12, '13, '14
Bowman, Charles 1967
Boxold, Charles 1953, '54
Boyda, John 1937, '38, '39
Bozeman, Richard 1943
Bracken, Lou 1967, '68
Bradford, Robert 1949
Bradley, J.A. 1898, '99
Bradley, Walter 1933
Bramson, Bernardo 1964, '65, '66
Brancato, Joe 1973, '74
Brand, Robert 1937, '38
Brandt, Marshall 1942

Brannan, Tim 1970, '71, '72
Branner, Cecil (Tubby) 1919, '20, '21, '22, '23
Brant, Mike 1967, '68, '69
Brant, Tim 1970, '71, '72
Branthover, Lee 1970, '71
Brasher, James 1947, '48, '49
Brechbiel, Jim 1973, '74
Breedlove, Rod 1957, '58, '59
Brenner, John 1941, '42
Bresnahan, Tom 1964
Breunich, Tom 1952, '53
Brewer, Edward B. (Untz) 1916, '20, '21
Brewer, Mac 1922, '23
Broglio, Paul 1947, '48
Bromley, Walter 1922, '23, '24, '25
Brougher, Don 1952, '53, '54
Broumel, Tom 1960
Brown, David 1900, '01, '02, '03
Brown, Robert 1937, '38, '39
Brown, Tom 1960, '61, '62
Bryan, Thomas 1901
Bryant, William 1937
Brzostowski, Art 1965, '66, '67
Budkoff, Nick 1936, '37
Bungori, Dan 1971, '72, '73
Burgee, Dick 1953, '54, '55
Burger, Joe 1921, '22, '23, '24
Burgly, Bill 1956, '57
Burke, Pat 1968, '69, '70
Burlin, Ralph 1939, '40, '41
Burns, Jimmy 1910
Burton, Bob 1961, '62, '63
Bury, Lou 1962, '63
Buscher, Bernie 1933, '34, '35
Buscher, F.A. 1932, '33
Butsko, Harry 1961, '62
Byrd, Bill 1942
Byrd, Harry C. (Curley) 1905, '06, '07

"C"

Calandra, William 1971
Callahan, Charles 1933, '34, '35
Campbell, Joe 1973, '74
Carliss, Ernest 1929, '30, '31
Carlson, Rick 1966, '67, '68
Carroll, Charles 1957
Carroll, Douglas 1899
Carter, A.R. 1914
Carter, Crawford 1918
Carter, Louis 1972, '73, '74
Cashell, Dorsey 1897, '98
Chacos, Louis 1942
Chadick, Mike 1968
Chalmers, George (Shorty) 1929, '30, '31
Chiaverini, Len 1962, '63
Chisari, Thomas 1943, '44, '45
Chovanes, Eddie 1941, '42, '46
Christianson, Dave 1951
Church, C. Grant 1897, '99
Church, L.M. 1905
Ciambor, Steve 1967, '68, '69
Cianelli, Dave 1949, '50, '51
Cichowski, Tom 1963, '65, '66
Cielensky, Mike 1973, '74
Clark, Morrison 1920
Cloud, Everett 1958, '59, '60
Coggins, Bert 1916
Coggins, Irving 1914, '15, '16
Colbert, Bob 1967, '68, '69
Cole, Bob 1958
Cole, Fred 1956, '57, '58
Cole, George 1932
Collins, Bobby 1964, '65, '66
Collins, Gary 1959, '60, '61
Colteryahn, Lloyd 1951, '52
Compton, Barnes 1892, '93
Condie, Dennis 1960, '61
Condon, John 1949
Conrad, David 1974
Conrad, Luther 1940, '41, '42
Continetti, Reno 1943, '44
Cooke, Ed 1955, '57
Cooke, Sam 1897, '98, '99
Cooper, Barney 1905, '06, '07
Cooper, Fred 1964, '65, '66
Cooper, Larry 1943, '44
Corcoran, Jim 1962, '64, '65
Cordyack, John 1940, '41
Cory, Ernest 1907, '08
Cosgrove, Tom 1950, '51, '52
Coster, H.O. 1916, '17, '18
Couch, George 1942
Cowdrey, Chris 1970, '71, '72
Crapster, Jack 1908
Crecca, Joseph 1932, '33
Crosland, Robert 1945, '46
Crossan, Dave 1960, '61, '62
Crothers, Omar (Gus) 1926, '27, '28
Crytzer, Marty 1951, '52, '53

"D"

Daly, Ed 1934, '35, '36
Daly, Leslie 1943, '44, '45
Darby, Samuel 1899
Dare, Howie 1954, '55, '57
Davidson, Jim 1959, '60, '61
Davis, Fred 1946, '47, '48, '49
Davis, Jack 1954, '55, '56
Davis, Lynn 1949, '50, '51
Dean, Robert 1948, '49, '50
DeArmey, Frank 1935, '36, '37
DeArmey, John 1938
DeCarlo, Dan 1974
DeCicco, Nick 1955, '56, '57
Decker, Don 1951, '52
Deckman, Joe 1930
Deitz, Guy 1972, '73, '74
Demczuk, Bernard (Sonny) 1968, '69
Dennis, Russell 1953, '54, '55
Derrick, H.B. 1914, '15, '16
DeStephano, Robert 1950, '51, '52
Detko, Chester 1960, '61, '62
Devon, Joe 1898
DiCaprio, Richard 1973, '74
Dickey, Edmund 1900
Dietrich, Leroy 1958, '59, '60

Dill, Chris 1965
Dill, John 1967, '68, '69
DiOrio, Joe 1967, '68
Dittmar, Jack 1941, '42
Divito, Paul 1973, '74
Doak, Harry 1906, '07
Dodson, Charlie 1927, '28, '29
Dominic, Brian 1971
Donofrio, Ralph 1966, '67
Doory, Frank 1943, '44
Drach, Joseph 1945, '46, '47
Drass, Pat 1959, '60, '61
Drimal, Chuck 1967
Drozdov, Olaf 1962, '63, '64
DuBois, Oscar 1942
Duley, Tom 1931
Dunbar, Emmons 1900, '01, '02
Dutton, Ken 1967, '68, '69
DuVall, Mearle 1939, '40, '41
Dwyer, Frank 1939
Dyer, John 1968, '69, '70
Dyson, Gene 1955

"E"

Earley, Harold 1949
Edel, Sam T. 1919
Ellinger, Charlie 1934, '35, '36
Emrich, William 1971
Ennis, Lou 1933, '34, '35
Eppley, Geary (Swede) 1919, '20
Erhard, Jerry 1970, '72
Evans, Bill 1974
Evans, Clay 1907
Evans, Francis 1945, '46, '47, '48
Evans, William 1928, '29, '30
Everson, William 1947, '48

"F"

Faber, Parker 1930, '31
Faloney, Bernie 1951, '52, '53
Farrell, Albert 1932
Fastuca, Sal 1944
Feher, Gene 1961, '62, '63
Fehr, Walter 1945, '46
Felton, Ralph 1951, '52, '53
Ferrante, Joe 1961, '62, '63
Fesmeyer, Charles 1901, '02
Fiedor, John 1973
Fincke, Edward 1950
Firor, Guy 1905, '06
Fischer, Stanley 1952
Fisher, Ralph 1973, '74
Fisher, William 1930
Fishman, Jerry 1963, '64
Fitzpatrick, Paul 1967, '68, '69
Fletcher, Andy 1916, '17
Fletcher, Dwayne 1958, '59, '60
Fletcher, Edward 1935, '36
Flick, Paul 1942
Flor, Tom 1957, '58, '59
Flynn, Tim 1953, '54, '55
Forbes, John 1957, '58
Forrester, James 1937, '38
Fox, Hank 1949, '50, '51
Franklin, Jamie 1972
Frattaroli, Joe 1962, '64
Friedgen, Ralph 1968
Fries, Greg 1968, '69, '70
Fritsch, John 1955, '56, '57
Fritz, Emile 1945, '46
Fromang, Steve 1970, '71, '72
Fry, Clarence (Chick) 1949, '50, '51
Fuller, Clifton 1892, '93, '94
Fullerton, Ed 1950, '51, '52
Fulton, Ed 1973, '74
Funk, Mike 1962
Furst, Walter 1911

"G"

Gaetz, Norman 1944
Gaines, Mike 1970, '71, '72
Gallagher, Bob 1958
Galt, Pete 1905
Gambino, Lu 1946, '47
Gardi, Joe 1957, '58, '59
Gareis, Hank 1967, '68, '69
Garner, Enoch 1902
Garrott, William 1933, '35
Gawlick, Fred 1965, '66, '67
Gayzur, Rudolph 1949
Gebhardt, John 1967, '68
Getz, Harry 1935
Gibbons, Charles 1896, '97
Gibson, Ray 1962
Gienger, Craig 1970
Gienger, George 1939, '40
Gieula, Chester 1947, '48, '49, '50
Gilbert, Herbert 1918, '19, '20, '21
Gill, Vernon 1903, '04
Gillespie,Bill 1967, '69
Gilmore, Ed 1962, '63
Gilmore, Jack 1940, '42
Gleasner, Donald 1945
Goldman, Luther 1933
Goodman, Jim 1946, '47, '48
Gormley, John 1934, '35, '36
Grace, Mike 1966, '67, '68
Graff, Gustavius 1892, '93
Graham, Duey 1970
Grant, Bill 1967, '68
Grason, Andy 1898, '99
Greene, Tony 1968, '69, '70
Greer, William 1944, '45
Gretz, Harry 1933
Groves, John (Boots) 1919, '20, '21, '22, '23
Guckeyson, Bill 1934, '35, '36
Gunderman, Ed 1965, '66
Gunderman, Tom 1957, '58, '59
Gundry, Jesse 1921

"H"

Hacker, Bob 1959, '60, '61
Hafer, Robert 1943
Hagerman, Tom 1942
Haley, Bob 1967, '68

Hall, Irving (Bottle) 1923, '24
Hamilton, Fred 1955, '56, '57
Hamley, James 1969
Hannigan, John 1961, '62
Hanulak, Chet 1951, '52, '53
Harding, Samuel (Pop) 1892, '93, '94
Hardisty, John 1899, 1900
Harris, Derick 1974
Harris, George 1893, '94
Harrison, Roland 1892, '93, '94
Hart, R.G. 1915
Hatfield, Norm 1962, '63
Hatter, Jim 1956, '57, '58
Hatton, Hannibal 1905, '06
Hawkins, Ralph 1956, '57
Hayden, Courtney 1930, '31
Hayman, Edgar 1904
Headley, Coleman 1934, '35, '36
Heagy, Al 1927, '28, '29
Healy, Don 1955, '56, '57
Healy, Jack 1955, '56
Heffner, Fred 1952, '53
Heine, George 1923, '24
Heintz, William 1928, '29
Helbock, Bill 1942
Herzog, Fred 1924, '25
Hetrick, John 1966
Heuring, Ed 1954, '55, '56
Heward, Harry 1894, '96
Hewitt, Frederic 1937, '38
Heyer, Frank 1940, '41
Hickman, William 1943
Hicks, Chaplain 1907, '08
Hill, Darryl 1963
Hillis, Robert 1943
Hinebaugh, Wade 1896, '97
Hindman, E.R. 1913, '14, '15
Hines, Frank 1898, '99
Hines, Frank Jr. 1932
Hinkle, Monte 1971, '72, '73
Hoch, Mike 1966
Hoen, Ralph 1907, '08
Hoen, Stanley 1908
Hoffecker, Frank 1911, '12, '13
Hoffman, Charles 1968, '69
Hoffman, Edward 1943
Hoffman, Herb 1952, '53, '54
Hoge, Hamilton 1906
Hons, Craig, 1970
Hoopengardner, Joe 1940, '42
Hoover, Kim 1973, '74
Horning, Joe 1951, '52, '53, '54
Hough, John 1922, '23, '24
Hrezo, Joe 1960, '61, '62
Hufman, Jack 1942
Hughes, Leroy 1972, '73, '74
Humphries, Howard 1963, '64, '65
Hunt, Max 1940
Huntemann, Charles 1912, '13
Hurd, Art 1951, '52
Hurson, Edward 1943

"I"

Idzik, John 1947, '48, '49, '50
Iglehart, John 1905
Imphong, Mike 1967
Irvine, John 1952, '53, '54

"J"

Jackson, Fred 1946
James, Robert 1941, '42, '46
Jameson, George 1906
Jankowski, Gary 1960, '61, '62
Jarmoska, George 1940, '41, '42
Jennings, Ricky 1973, '74
Jernigan, Cy 1971, '73
Johnson, Dave 1911, '12, '13
Johnson, Ed 1965
Johnston, Richard 1945, '46
Jones, David 1971
Jones, Stan 1951, '52, '53
Joyce, Fred 1962, '63, '64
Joyce, Jim 1957, '58, '59

"K"

Kane, Ed 1966, '67, '68
Karangalen, Peter 1943
Karnash, Stanley 1948, '49, '50
Kaufman, Norman 1959, '60
Kecman, Dan 1967, '68, '69
Kecman, Ron 1970, '71, '72
Keith, Jeff 1949, '51
Keenan, Charles 1930, '31, '32
Keenan, John 1926, '27, '28
Kefauver, Harry 1898, '99
Kelly, Harold 1970
Kemp, William 1909, '10, '11
Kenley, Frank 1896, '97, '98
Kenny, John 1964, '65
Kensler, Ed 1948, '49, '50, '51
Kern, Fred 1957, '58
Kershner, Ted 1956, '57, '58
Kessler, Gordon 1926, '27, '28
Kichman, Charles 1956
Kiernan, Paul 1931, '32
Kilgallen, Jim 1953
Kinard, Ben 1973, '74
King, John 1968, '69
Kinney, Eugene 1945, '46, '47, '48
Kirchiro, Bill 1959, '60, '61
Kishpaugh, W. M. 1913, '14, '15, '16
Klingerman, Doug 1964, '65
Kloppmeyer, Charles 1906
Knode, Bobby 1916, '17, '18, '19
Knode, Ken 1911, '12, '13, '14, '15
Koehler, Hugh (Pop) 1909, '10, '11, '12
Koelle, Raymond 1930, '31
Kolarac, George 1954, '55, '56
Kolmo, Bill 1956
Kolodne, Walter 1943
Koprowski, Marion 1973, '74
Krahling, Chick 1964, '65
Krajcovic, Jess 1929, '30, '31
Kramer, Marvin 1949, '50
Kramer, Paul 1953
Krouse, Bill 1939, '40
Krouse, Raymond 1947, '48, '49, '50

Kubany, Glenn 1968, '69
Kuchta, Joe 1948, '49, '50
Kurz, Jim 1946

"L"

Ladygo, Peter 1950, '51
Landolt, Dean 1968
Laneve, Ron 1957, '58
Lange, Robert 1973, '74
Lanigan, Pat 1924, '25
Larkin, Edward 1971
La Rue, James 1947, '48, '49
Latham, Ector 1922, '23
Lattimer, Charles 1951, '52, '53
Laughery, Bob 1952
Lavine, Stanford 1948, '49
Lavrusky, Jim 1965, '66, '67
Lawrence, George 1938, '39
Lawrence, James 1968
Lawson, J.W. 1892
Layman, Bob 1956, '57, '58
Lazaro, Bill 1958, '59
Lazzarino, Joe 1954, '55
Leatherman, John 1926
LeGore, Walter 1904
Lewis, Dickie 1956, '57, '58
Lewis, Gomer 1924
Lewis, Grenville 1894, '96
Lewis, Ron 1962, '63
Liebold, Leland 1952
Lillibridge, John 1896, '97
Lily, Hank 1963
Lindsay, Paul 1951
Linkous, Fred 1925, '26, '27
Lishack, Michael 1971
Lloyd, Edward 1938, '39
Lombard, Henry 1928, '29
Loomis, Lynn 1912, '13
Lovett, Bill 1966, '67, '68
Luckey, George 1923, '24
Lumsden, Milton 1939, '40
Lunn, Cameron (Tubby) 1906, '07
Lutz, James 1943

"M"

MacBride, Bob 1969, '70
MacDonald, Alexander (Ike) 1916, '17, '19, '20
MacDonald, John 1932
Mace, Ron 1962
Mackall, Thomas 1904, '05, '06, '07
Mackert, Roy 1919, '20
Madigan, George 1928, '29
Mahnic, Robert 1969, '70
Main, Wilbur 1956, '57
Makar, James 1943
Maletzky, Bill 1951, '52
Mallonee, Lloyd 1942
Manges, Mark 1974
Marciniak, Walt 1964, '65
Markoe, Dave 1964
Marshall, Larry 1969, '70, '71
Martell, James 1970, '71, '72
Martin, Andy 1963, '64
Martin, Bill 1957, '58
Martin, Charles 1963, '64
Martine, Roy 1950, '51
Massey, Paul 1946
Massey, Tom 1898
Massie, Leonard 1969, '70, '71
Matthews, J. Marsh 1900, '01, '02
Mattia, Peter 1968, '69, '70
May, Charlie 1929, '31
Mayer, George 1904
Mayhew, John 1932
Mayo, Edmund 1903
McCarthy, John 1936, '37
McCarthy, Joseph 1944, '45
McCarthy, Patrick 1943, '46
McCaw, Stewart 1934
McDonald, John 1927, '28, '29
McFadden, Earl 1943
McHugh, Thomas 1947, '48, '49, '50
McLaughlin, Tom 1935
McLuckie, Tom 1952, '53, '54
McManus, Edward 1970, '71
McNeil, Paul 1940
McNutt, Alonzo 1905
McQuade, Jack 1921, '22, '23
McQuade, Thomas 1949
McQueen, Lorie 1964, '65
McQuown, Wymand 1964, '65, '66
McVicker, John 1955
Meade, Jim 1936, '37
Meister, Bill 1968, '69, '71
Melcher, Dick 1963, '65
Melcher, Mick 1963, '64, '65
Merritt, Roland 1968, '69
Mess, R.W. 1913, '14
Michael, R.M. 1916
Mier, Jack 1941, '42
Mike-Mayer, Steve 1972, '73, '74
Miller, Charlie 1929
Miller, Chris 1973, '74
Miller, Gary 1963
Miller, Tom 1969, '70, '71
Miloszewski, John 1966
Minion, Ed 1933, '34, '35
Mitchell, Hanson 1896
Mitchell, John 1931, '32
Mitchell, Parker 1892, '93
Mitchell, Walter 1900, '01, '02, '03
Modzelewski, Dick 1950, '51, '52
Modzelewski, Edward 1949, '50, '51
Molster, James 1947
Molster, Charley 1918
Mona, Joe 1959, '61, '62
Mondorff, Pershing 1937, '39
Mont, Tom 1941, '42, '46
Montgomery, Tom 1913
Moore, Eric 1970
Moore, John 1919, '20, '21, '22
Moran, J. Patrick 1944
Morgan, Bob 1951, '52, '53
Morhinweg, Fred 1917
Morris, Scott 1943
Morris, William (Country) 1912, '13
Morrison, Clark 1921

Mortensen, Carl 1966
Morter, LaRoy 1945, '46
Morton, John 1939, '40 '41
Moss, Joseph 1949, '50, '51
Mudd, Khostka 1909, '10, '11
Mueller, John 1940
Mueller, Leo 1938, '39, '40
Mullikin, Clarence 1894
Murphy, Bill 1972, '73
Murphy, Joe 1939, '40
Myers, Dutch 1918, '19
Myrtle, Chip 1964, '65, '66
Myslinski, Tom 1965, '66, '67

"N"

Nairn, Roland 1950
Nalewak, Ron 1964, '65
Nardo, Anthony 1942
Nardo, Dave 1962, '63
Nash, John 1973, '74
Navarro, Frank 1950, '51, '52
Naylor, Ralph 1900, '01, '02
Nelligan, Bert 1896
Nelson, Richard 1932, '33, '34
Nesbit, Andy 1918, '19, '20, '21, '22
Nestor, Paul 1951, '52
Neville, Al 1971, '72, '73
Nickla, Ed 1958
Nolan, Dick 1952, '53
Norris, John 1930, '31
Novak, Dick 1959, '60, '61
Nusz, Dave 1953, '54, '55

"O"

Oberlin, Lyman 1914, '15, '16
Ochap, Gene 1974
O'Connor, Ed 1952
O'Donnell, Dick 1954
Oertly, Fred 1893
O'Hara, Dennis 1968, '69, '71
Oifebeson, Whitney 1915
Olecki, Bruce 1967, '69
Osborn, Downey 1923, '24
Osler, Jerry 1962
Owen, Norman 1943

"P"

Pagannucci, Romeo 1919, '20, '21
Page, Calvin, 1901
Palahunik, George 1952, '53, '54
Pancza, Joe 1967
Parker, Alvin 1924, '25
Parsons, Jim 1952, '53, '54, '55
Parsons, John 1926, '27
Pastrana, Al 1965, '66, '68
Pearson, Ron 1966, '67, '68
Pease, Al 1929, '30, '31
Pellegrini, Bob 1953, '54, '55
Pennington, Victor 1914
Perlo, Phil 1955, '57
Peters, Francis 1898, '99, 1900
Petronaci, John 1971
Petruzzo, Joseph 1950, '51
Petry, Phil 1964, '65
Pettit, Bill 1964
Phillips, Al 1946, '47, '48
Pietrowski, Joseph 1945
Piker, Robert 1945
Pinck, Guy 1904
Piper, Dan 1960, '61, '62
Pirronello, William 1943
Pitzer, John 1930
Plasnig, Dutch 1921
Plevin, Tom 1966, '67, '68
Pobiak, Ed 1948, '49, '50
Poling, William 1945, '46
Pollock, George (Rosy) 1921, '22, '23
Polyanski, Stan 1955
Poniatowski, Hank 1959, '60, '61
Poppelman, Ray 1930, '31, '32
Posey, Gilbert 1909, '10, '11
Posey, Walter 1913, '14, '15, '16, '17
Pouleur, A.L. 1902, '03
Prough, Pearse 1892, '93
Psira, Ken 1960
Pue, Dick 1892, '93
Pugh, Charlie 1927
Pugh, Ed 1921, '22, '23, '24
Purvis, Bart 1971, '72, '73

"Q"

Queen, C.J. 1896

"R"

Raba, Robert 1973, '74
Radice, Julie 1928, '29
Rae, Tom 1960, '61, '62
Raedy, Mike 1918, '19
Ratliff, Don 1970, '71, '72
Reilly, Charles 1969, '70, '71
Reilly, Jack 1960
Reitz, Mike 1972
Ribnitzki, Fred 1929
Rich, M.N. 1915, '16
Ridgely, Charles 1897
Rigby, Elmer 1940, '41, '42
Riggleman, Mickey 1972, '73
Riggs, M. Talbot 1919
Roberts, Augie 1927, '28, '29
Roberts, George 1928
Roberts, Guy 1969, '70, '71
Robertson, Gilbert 1899
Rock, Walter 1960, '61, '62
Rock, Wilbur 1943, '44
Rog, Ed 1962
Rogers, Stan 1972, '73, '74
Rollins, W.T. 1892, '93, '94
Romano, Frank 1972, '73, '74
Rooney, Thomas 1930
Rosenthal, Malcolm 1944
Roth, Earl 1947, '48, '49
Roulette, Robert 1948, '49
Rowden, Jake 1947, '48, '49, '50
Roy, Ken 1973, '74
Ruff, Seymour 1912, '13, '14

Ruffner, Robert 1905, '06, '07
Rusevlyan, Bob 1956, '57, '58
Russell, Frank 1972, '73, '74
Ryan, Charley 1943

"S"

Sachs, George 1933, '34, '35
Salley, Ernie 1974
Sandusky, Mike 1954, '55, '56
Sankovich, Tom 1959, '60, '61
Santa, Jim 1972, '73, '74
Santacroce, Leonard 1970
Santy, Tony 1965, '66, '67
Sappington, Earl 1899
Saunders, Oswald 1908, '09
Scarbath, Dick 1958
Scarbath, Jack 1950, '51, '52
Schaefer, Rich 1963, '64
Schick, Tom 1973, '74
Schmaltz, Richard 1974
Schnebley, Robert 1942
Schneider, Leroy 1943
Schoenherr, Charley 1943
Schrecongost, John 1945
Schroy, Ken 1972, '73, '74
Schultz, Ferdinand 1945
Schultz, John 1973, '74
Schwartz, Vic 1957, '58, '59
Schwarz, Edward 1945, '46, '47, '48
Schwarz, Kurt 1957, '58, '59
Scioscia, Karney 1949, '50, '51
Scott, Ken 1971, '72, '73
Scott, Vincent 1958 '59, '60
Scotti, Ben 1956, '57, '58
Scotti, Tony 1958
Seibert, Vernon 1946, '47, '48, '49
Selep, Tom 1954, '56
Semler, Eddie 1920, '21, '22
Settino, Joe 1931
Seymore, Art 1970, '71, '72
Shaffer, Dick 1939, '40
Shaffer, Ron 1957, '58, '59
Shamberger, D.F. 1898
Shank, H.A. 1915
Shank, Scott 1969, '70, '71
Sharpless, Rod 1973, '74
Shaughnessy, Emmett 1946
Shelton, Carl 1970, '71
Shemonski, Bob 1949, '50, '51
Sherman, Franklin 1896
Sherman, Henry 1893
Shihda, George 1973, '74
Shiner, Dick 1961, '62, '63
Shipley, Burt 1908, '09, '10, '11, '12, '13
Shipley, James 1897, '98
Shipley, Richard 1952, '53, '54
Shoals, Roger 1960, '61, '62
Shockey, Don 1940
Shugars, Jeff 1969, '70, '71
Silvester, Edward 1909
Silvester, Lindsay 1908, '09
Simler, George 1946, '47
Simoldoni, Joe 1965, '66
Simpson, John 1932, '33, '34
Simpson, Mike 1962
Skarda, Jim 1955, '56
Skinner, W.W. 1892
Skotnicki, Frank 1937, '38, '39
Slaninka, Richard 1968, '69, '70
Smith, Blair 1935, '36, '37
Smith, Bob 1939, '40
Smith, Bob 1972, '73, '74
Smith, Eager 1899
Smith, Jamie 1916
Smith, Ken 1960, '61, '62
Smith, Les 1944, '45
Smith, Wesley 1902, '04
Sniscak, Bernie 1946
Snyder, Gerald 1926, '27, '28
Snyder, Leo 1917, '18, '20
Snyder, Robert 1933
Sonntag, Ralph 1967, '68, '69
Soporowski, Raymond 1969, '70, '71
Sothoron, Norwood 1932, '34
Speer, Talbot 1915
Springer, Bruce 1965
Stabler, Sydney 1909
Stala, Dom 1952
Stalfort, Carl 1933, '34, '35
Stalnaker, Wally 1967, '68, '69
Stankus, Ray 1951, '52
Stefl, Tom 1955, '56, '57
Steiner, Ted 1969, '70, '71
Stem, George 1964, '65
Steppe, Bill 1957, '58
Stern, George 1963
Stevens, Jimmy 1917
Stevens, Myron 1925, '26
Stickel, Lou 1965, '66, '67
Stoll, Wilbur 1901, '02, '03, '04
Stonebraker, Jack 1934, '35
Stuart, Adam 1946
Stubbs, J.S. 1916, '17, '18
Stubljar, Mike 1967, '68, '69
Stull, James 1967, '69
Suchy, Bob 1955, '56
Sukeena, Dick 1961
Sullivan, Bob 1963, '64, '65
Sullivan, Jerry 1917, '18, '19,'20
Supplee, Bill 1923, '24, '25
Surgent, Mike 1935, '36, '37
Symons, Thomas 1898, '99

"T"

Tamburello, Frank 1954, '55
Tarbutton, Clyde 1914, '15, '16
Targarona, Jack 1949, '50
Tate, Darnell 1970
Tauszky, Carroll 1907
Tenney, Edward 1925, '26
Terry, Richard 1943
Teslovitch, Michael 1943
Thomas, Al 1968, '69, '70
Thomas, Lewis (Knocky) 1925, '26, '27
Tiesi, James 1970, '71
Tine, Chuck 1965, '66, '67
Toler, Dick 1945

Tonetti, Paul 1955, '56, '57
Torain, Ernie 1965, '66, '68
Trachy, John 1964, '65, '66
Trax, G.P. 1910, '11
Troha, John 1947, '48, '49, '50
Troll, Robert 1943, '44
Troxell, Walter 1925
Trust, Don 1960
Tucker, Hubert 1942
Tucker, Joe 1947, '48, '49
Tucker, Robert 1970, '71, '72
Tullai, Fred 1955
Turner, Bill 1955, '56, '57
Turner, J.M. 1901
Turyn, Vic 1945, '46, '47, '48
Tuschak, Richard 1943
Tweedy, James 1970, '71, '72

"U"

Ulam, Pat, 1972, '73, '74
Ulman, Bernie 1939, '40, '41
Underwood, Eddie 1900

"V"

Van Heusen, Billy 1965, '66, '67
Van Reenan, Don 1960
Van Sickler, Gary 1968, '69
Vellano, Paul 1971, '72, '73
Veradi, Gene 1957, '58, '59
Vereb, Ed 1953, '54, '55
Vesce, John 1973, '74
Vince, Larry 1966, '68
Vincent, Reginald 1940, '41, '42
Vincent, Rufus 1932
Visaggio, Dave 1972, '73, '74
Vucin, Milan 1964, '65, '66

"W"

Waganheim, Phil 1973, '74
Walker, Bill 1953, '54, '55
Walker, Clarence 1894
Walker, Frank 1900
Waller, Ron 1952, '53, '54
Walter, John 1920
Walters, Harry 1973, '74
Walton, Robert 1936, '37
Ward, Bob 1948, '49, '50, '51
Ward, Frank 1908, '09
Ward, Kevin 1972, '73
Warfield, Jack 1939
Warfield, Joshua 1900, '01
Waters, Jean 1954, '55, '56
Waters, John 1924, '25
Watkins, Ben 1896
Watkins, James 1970, '71
Watts, Harry 1901, '02, '03
Webb, Thomas 1932, '33
Webster, Fletcher 1903
Weiciecowski, John 1953
Weidener, Fred 1939
Weidensaul, Lou 1951, '52
Weidinger, Charlie 1936, '37, '38
Weimer, Clay 1892, '93
Weiss, Don 1972, '73
Welsh, George 1899
Wentworth, George 1903
Werner, Hubert 1942, '47, '48
Wethington, Ray 1970, '71, '72
Wharton, Al 1954, '55, '56
Wharton, Jim 1939, '41
Wharton, Thomas 1893, '94
Whelchel, David 1925
White, Charles 1911
White, Donald 1962
White, F.M. 1908
White, Floyd 1970, '71
White, Henry 1912
White, Randy 1972, '73, '74
White, Walter 1973, '74
White, Wellstood 1904
Widmyer, Earl 1932, '33, '34
Wikander, Gary 1961
Williamowsky, William 1943
Williams, Avy 1915, '16
Williams, E.P. 1910, '11, '12, '13
Willis, Vic 1934, '35, '36
Wilson, Len 1912
Wilson, Roger 1905, '06, '07
Wilson, Tim 1974
Wingate, Elmer 1947, '48, '49, '50
Winslow, J.L. 1903
Wolfe, Percy 1943
Wolfe, William 1935, '36, '37
Wondrack, Arthur 1926, '27, '28
Wood, William 1930, '32
Woods, Al 1930, '31, '32
Woodward, A.N. 1910
Wooters, William 1892, '93, '94
Worthington, Arthur 1892
Wright, Jack 1941, '42, '46
Wyres, James 1970, '71

"Y"

Yarnell, Dennis 1971
Yeager, Charles (Buddy) 1933, '34, '35
York, Bob 1964, '65, '66
Young, Walter 1921, '22, '23
Younge, Joe 1972, '74

"Z"

Zachary, Pete 1973, '74
Zannoni, Steve 1972, '73, '74
Zernhelt, John 1974
Zetts, Michael 1943
Zulick, Charlie 1936
Zulick, Earl 1925, '26, '27